IMAGES
of America

AROUND NORTH YARMOUTH

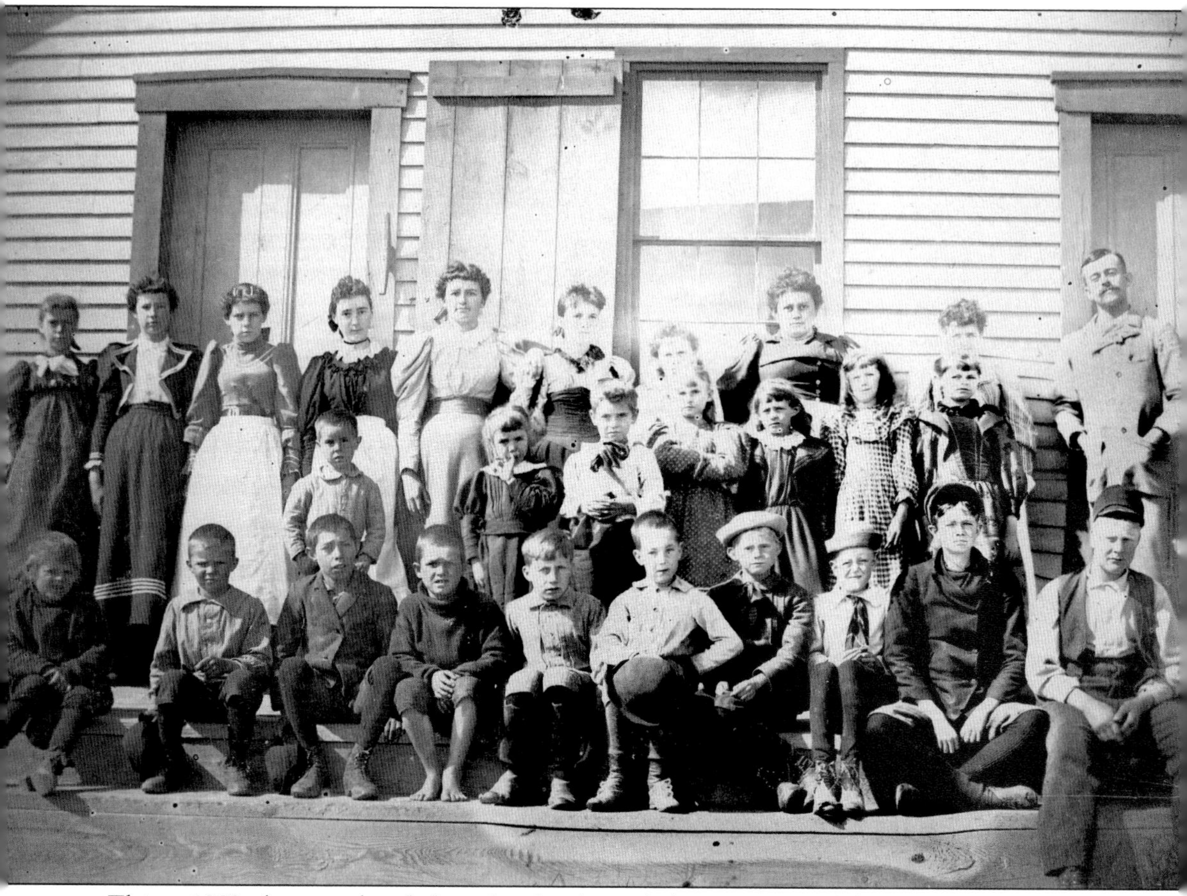

This *c.* 1882 photograph is believed to be the only known view of the original District No. 4 schoolhouse, Ryder's Hill on New Gloucester Road. In the front row is Ralph Jewett (fifth from left) and Charles Allen (far right). In the back row is Alice Perley (third from left) and the school teacher (far right). In 1894, a town-wide school committee was adopted and replaced separate government for each school. William T. Dunn was supervisor and argued that this schoolhouse was dilapidated and a new location needed as this one was not suitable. The Hicks School at Mill Road replaced it in 1895. (Courtesy of Mark Heath.)

On the cover: Norman Reed and his wife, Marion, ran the Cedar Spring Dairy Farm from 1942 until 1977, selling their milk first to the North Yarmouth Dairy and later to Oakhurst Dairy. They produced high-fat-content milk by feeding their Guernsey cows corn or hay silage made with the forage harvester shown in this 1950 image. Here Marion leads the horse-pulled wagon in collecting the chopped hay while Norman drives the chopper along the windrows. Norman's father, Elbridge Reed (1881–1957), captured this image. Photography was an interest he shared with his daughter-in-law Marion, who recorded many important scenes around town. (Courtesy of Marion Reed.)

IMAGES
of America

AROUND NORTH YARMOUTH

Lincoln J. Merrill Jr. and Holly K. Hurd

ARCADIA
PUBLISHING

ISBN 978-0-7385-4594-3

Published by Arcadia Publishing
Charleston, South Carolina

Printed in the United States of America

Library of Congress Catalog Card Number: 2006928824

For all general information contact Arcadia Publishing at:
Telephone 843-853-2070
Fax 843-853-0044
E-mail sales@arcadiapublishing.com
For customer service and orders:
Toll-Free 1-888-313-2665

Visit us on the Internet at www.arcadiapublishing.com

To those who shared their photographs and stories
and to our families who shared their time.

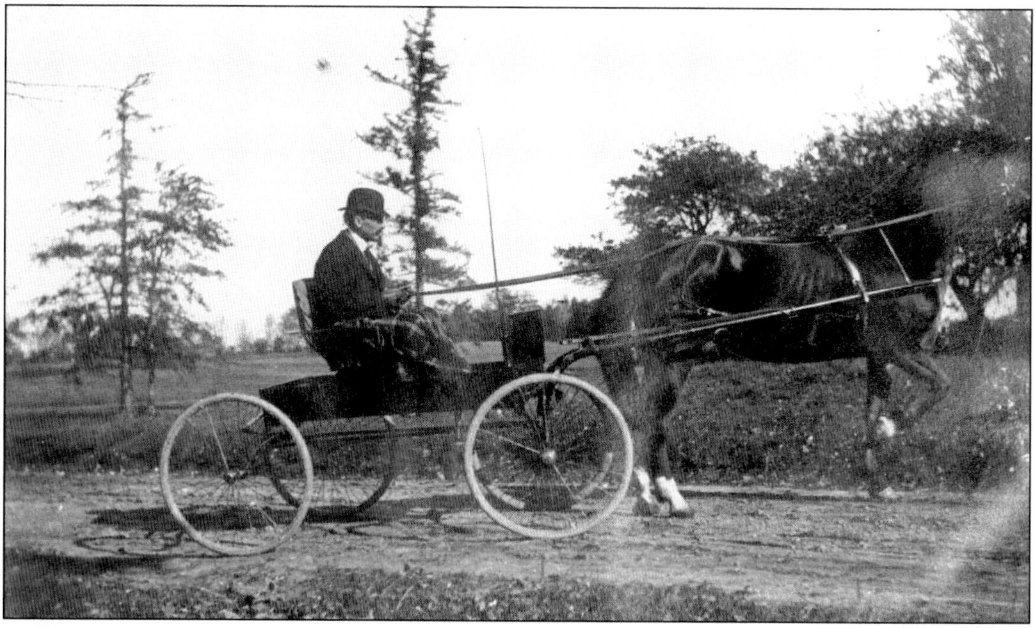

William Trickey Dunn drives a Bailey Buggy at Dunn's Corner about 1902. The wheels of the buggy are inflatable bicycle tires with wire spokes. Will's brothers Charles and Ansel, sharing an interest in harness racing, bred and raised racehorses that competed at local fairs including the New Gloucester Fair. The newspapers frequently mentioned offers that the Dunns received for their prize-winning horses.

CONTENTS

ACKNOWLEDGMENTS

Unless otherwise noted, the images in this book come from the collections of the North Yarmouth Historical Society (NYHS). Thanks to Pres. Katie Murphy, Ursula Baier, and other members of the NYHS who encouraged and supported us with open access to the society's photograph collection. Marilyn Hinkley and the Yarmouth Historical Society, Carolyn Small and the Cumberland Historical Society, North Haven Historical Society, and the Maine Historical Society have also offered help and contributed photographs.

We especially want to thank the following people and families of North Yarmouth who have shared their photographs and stories: Marion Reed (Crockett family); Ginger Collins (Sawyer family); the Dunn, Hathaway, Barter, Allen, Knight, Smith, Leighton, Anderson, Baston, Jewett, Small, Hilton, Hamilton, Pullen, Atkins, McIntire, Hayward, Tompson, Hayes, Parker, Grover, Fountain, Lawrence, York, Chadbourne, Goff, Semmes, Nelson, Gallant, Bowie, Doughty, Richards, Sweetser, and Skillin families; Barbara Fox; Phyllis Smith; Mark Heath; and Irene Lavoie.

Also thanks to those who allowed the North Yarmouth Historical Society to record their life stories and memories in written and recorded format. They have passed on, but they continue to live through the permanent records that we draw on today.

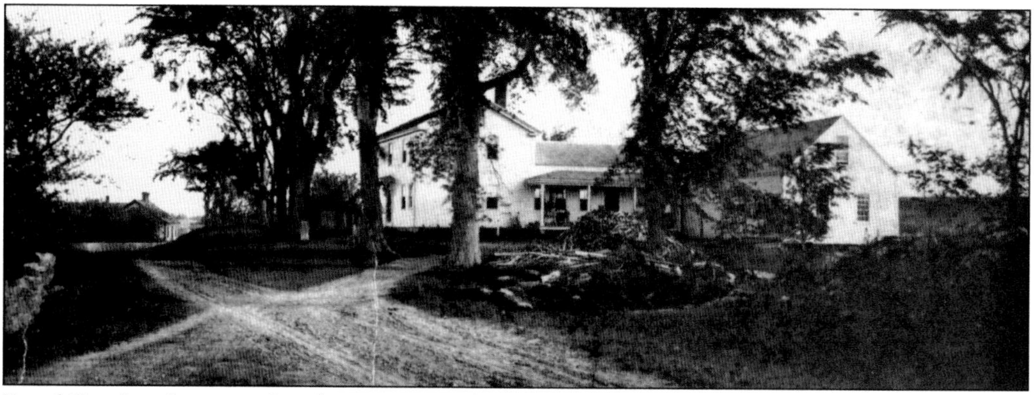

Royal Road is the town line between North Yarmouth and Pownal. This c. 1900 photograph shows the North Yarmouth home of ship carpenter Major Lombard, at 346 Royal Road, on the left and the home of Daniel Lovell of Pownal on the right. Lombard was the father of Edwin M. Lombard, the local monument maker at Crockett's Corner. His house was built around 1826 and is believed to be the oldest on the road. Al Bernard, who died in 1980, ran a bakery here for many years. (Courtesy of Mary Dunn.)

INTRODUCTION

The story of North Yarmouth is one that cannot be told in photographs alone; it needs the memories of our native residents to bring it to life. While photographs capture static scenes of our past, the stories fill in the details. Passed down from generation to generation, they recall the real events that built our values and shaped our identity as a rural Maine town. The memories formed through war and peace, destruction and rebuilding, failed businesses and new endeavors, births and deaths, and simple community activities are those that have been shared with our children. We hope this book does justice through both its photographs and words.

Our history is an emotional one whose undercurrent is captured on the town seal, "The Town Where Others Began." This reference recalls the original 1680 North Yarmouth plantation, which encompassed the lands from Cumberland to Harpswell including Mere Point in Brunswick. The town was one of the oldest and had one of the largest populations in the province of Maine. Settlers divided the land into lots and built along the immediate coast, particularly in the area around the Royal River. The river is named for William Royall, the owner of a 1635 land grant in the area called Wescustogo.

Early settlers faced ongoing war with the native tribes. King Philip's War in 1675, further attacks in the 1720s, and the French and Indian War in 1755 resulted in widespread destruction as settlers were killed or driven off and their homes burned. However, they were resilient and continued to return until eventually an active farming community emerged from the forest. Peace prevailed in time, and the town began to prosper.

Large families were common, but not all descendants could make a living from the original homesteads. In the late 1700s, they began to move away from the shore and to the interior, where they built new homes and cleared land for farms. The first families who came at that time constructed their houses along new county roads or in wilderness with potential for a future road. As settlement spread, far-flung residents found it difficult to attend the church supported by their taxes. Their business often required a full day of travel by boat, wagon, horse, or on foot to a town hall located as many as 10 miles away. Secession plans sprang up throughout the town, and North Yarmouth watched as new towns were formed and it grew constantly smaller. In spite of opposition, Harpswell set off in 1758, followed by Freeport and Pownal in 1789, and Cumberland in 1821. The final and deepest cut came in 1849, when after failing in earlier efforts at secession, political and business interests in Yarmouth village overcame the objections of outlying farmers and the town was split. This close-knit community was divided; the coastal community became Yarmouth, while the interior farmland retained the original name.

The loss of Yarmouth was a big blow, as business ties were very strong between the village and the interior. Trees cut for lumber near Walnut Hill were used to build ships in the village. Farms produced crops that were sold in the village, and village merchants sold goods to the rural farmers. Access to ship transportation in Yarmouth was essential, as trains had not yet come to the interior. The traditional institutions that the residents enjoyed such as the town hall, Masonic lodge, North Yarmouth Academy, the Baptist church and its burying ground, the militia, the town band, the fire company, and the Abolitionist Society now existed within the boundaries of the town that split away. The secession of Yarmouth left residents without a core from which to build their town. Even so, a shred of local pride was left in the now landlocked community. The Maine legislature approved the separation, but ensured the surviving town access to the sea and legal possession of the earliest records dating back to the 1600s, including an original copy of the Declaration of Independence.

These small victories did little to help with establishing a new identity when a disagreement arose over where to build the new town hall. The villages of Walnut Hill and East North Yarmouth both vied for the building, and a compromise was reached in 1853 to locate it in the geographical center of town. No village had been developed there, so all residents were equally distant from the town hall, quieting the issue that had led to the earlier secessions. The outbreak of the Civil War saw 120 of North Yarmouth's 600 eligible men enroll in the service, and home front efforts were focused on keeping life going while the men were away. By the time the war ended in 1865, the town had seen little development. However, residents held onto their sense of pride and worked to promote their community as they dealt with a precipitous decline in population that continued until World War II.

To boost a sense of community, residents started the Improved Order of Good Templars, Wescustogo Grange, Women's Christian Temperance Union, Boy Scouts, Camp Fire Girls, Community Club, and a baseball team. Also instituted were a lending library, a creamery and summer hotel, mineral springs where water was bottled, and many small businesses. This effort worked to instill pride in a town dismissed by its neighbors and often suffering the indignity of being mistaken for the northern part of Yarmouth. Even in recent years, the telephone directory did not outline the town on its own map. In spite of this, the photographs in this book show that North Yarmouth has its own unique identity, shaped by events of the past.

While the difficulty of travel on rough roads led to the downsizing of our town, it also created a self-contained community that met the needs of residents. The invention of the automobile in the 20th century and improved road conditions in the last few decades have allowed residents to satisfy their social and economic needs in surrounding communities. This has resulted in a loss of many local services in the last half-century, which has changed the feeling of community experienced in former years.

Today North Yarmouth is a town in transition with a renewed focus on establishing a distinct sense of community that residents can share with pride. Our new village green with a bandstand and summer concerts, our many parks, open spaces, and walking trails, new churches, an active historical society, Skyline Farm and Carriage Museum, the Congregational church's strawberry festival, chicken pie suppers and Friday lunches, new sidewalks, May town meetings, and Fun Day all contribute to this effort.

The families who loaned their cherished images for publication feel a deep sense of pride in this town and the role they played in making North Yarmouth a warm and caring community. They hope that the telling of early times will encourage others to help make North Yarmouth an even more vibrant place in the future.

Only two previously published works detail the history of North Yarmouth since its separation from Yarmouth in 1849. Therefore, this book with formerly private photographs and stories will vastly expand the general knowledge of our proud history and give other researchers a base of information upon which to build. In the process of sorting through images and researching historical facts, we discovered errors in other publications. We have corrected them in our captions, but expect that others will later discover that we have made our own mistakes. Just as we are grateful to those who first printed our history so that we knew what to research, we hope you will overlook our errors and record the facts correctly for the next generation.

One

VILLAGES WE SETTLED

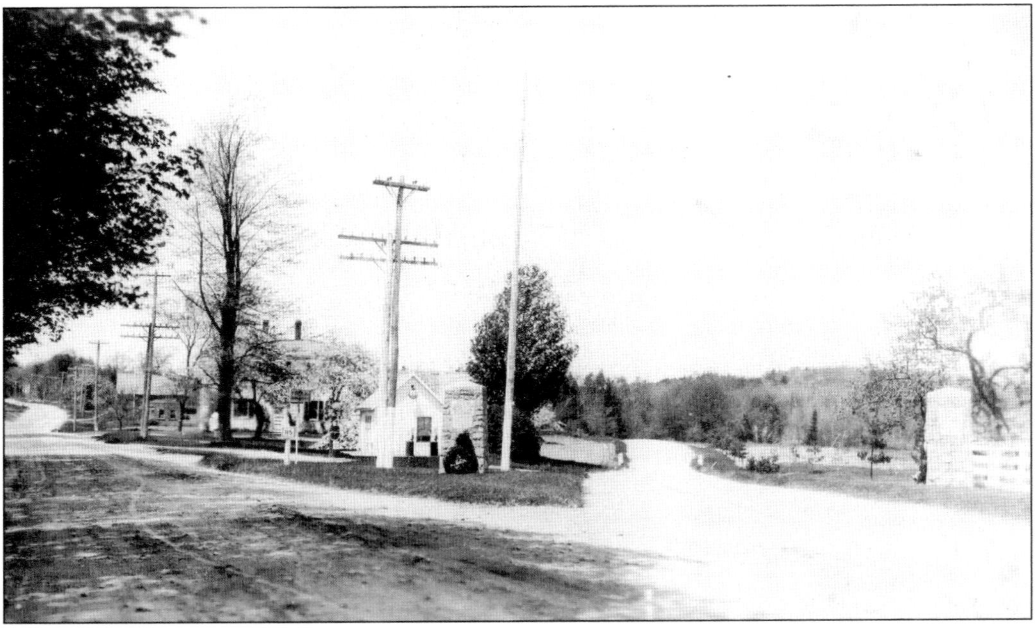

This *c.* 1925 view shows Walnut Hill Village at Routes 115 (left) and 9. The town's original inhabitants settled along Walnut Hill Road in the late 1700s, but the village of East North Yarmouth developed soon after Route 9 was laid out as a stagecoach route around 1800 and became the connector between the town's two villages (four miles apart). When the old Stage Road was dedicated as Memorial Highway to honor the town's war veterans in 1922, identical stone monuments were set in both villages, here and where Memorial Highway meets North Road. The triangular intersection of crossroads is a remnant of early travel by carriages, which were unable to turn as sharply as modern automobiles. Memorial Highway was recently rerouted to the left of the memorial markers to create a safer perpendicular crossing. The little house in the "heater" (triangle) was Jordan's ice-cream store. The *c.* 1815 house behind is still standing, although changed from the original by joiner Nathaniel Lufkin Jr., who ran a carpenter shop there during much of the 19th century. A blacksmith shop and cider mill stood behind this home in the late 1870s.

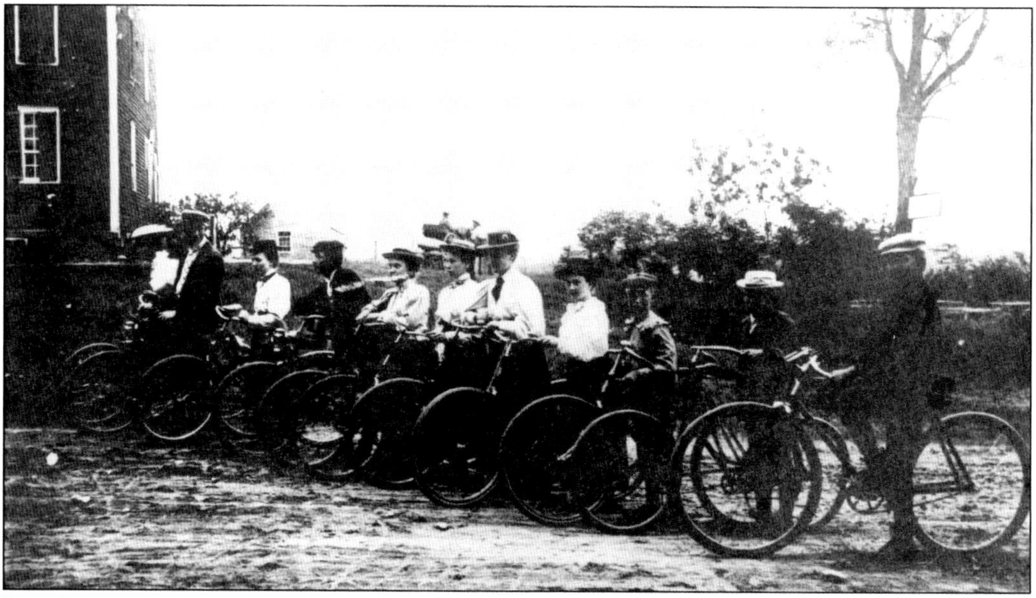

Bicycling was very popular at the beginning of the 20th century. A touring book published in 1895 describes a route through Walnut Hill to the "Wescustigo Spring," a popular picnic site on Wescustogo Hill. The cyclists are at American Express agent Frank Dolloff's house, formerly the Jeremiah Buxton Tavern, in Walnut Hill at the crossroads of Routes 9 and 115. Frank's daughter appears in this *c.* 1900 photograph.

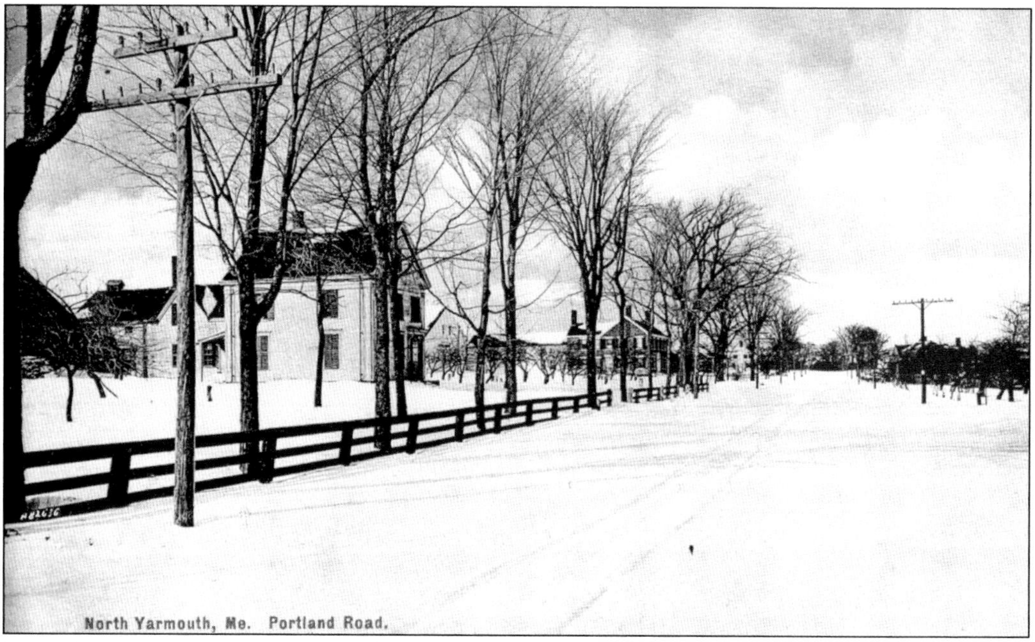

This 1910 postcard view of Route 9 looks toward the Dolloff house in Walnut Hill village. On the left are the 1871 homes of sea captains Samuel H. Sweetser and James Sawyer. Fences made with rough-cut granite posts like the one seen on the left were common and unique to the area. Store owner and postmaster Henry H. York published a series of winter scenes taken around North Yarmouth. These popular cards are still found in the collections of many local families.

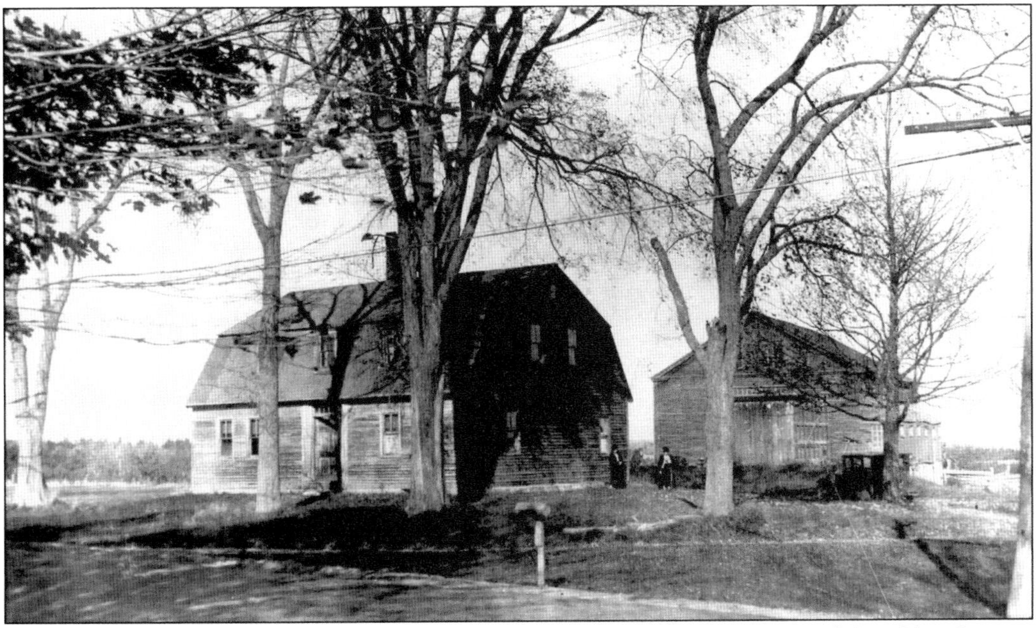

The Drinkwater Tavern, built at 415 Walnut Hill Road about 1770, is one of the oldest homes. (The ell of the house at 534 Walnut Hill Road is likely an older home that was moved from the top of Walnut Hill.) Originally located where the Congregational church vestry stood, the tavern was moved to its present location when Stage Road (Route 9) went through, around 1800. This directed traffic to the junction of Routes 9 and 115 and allowed the development of a small village there.

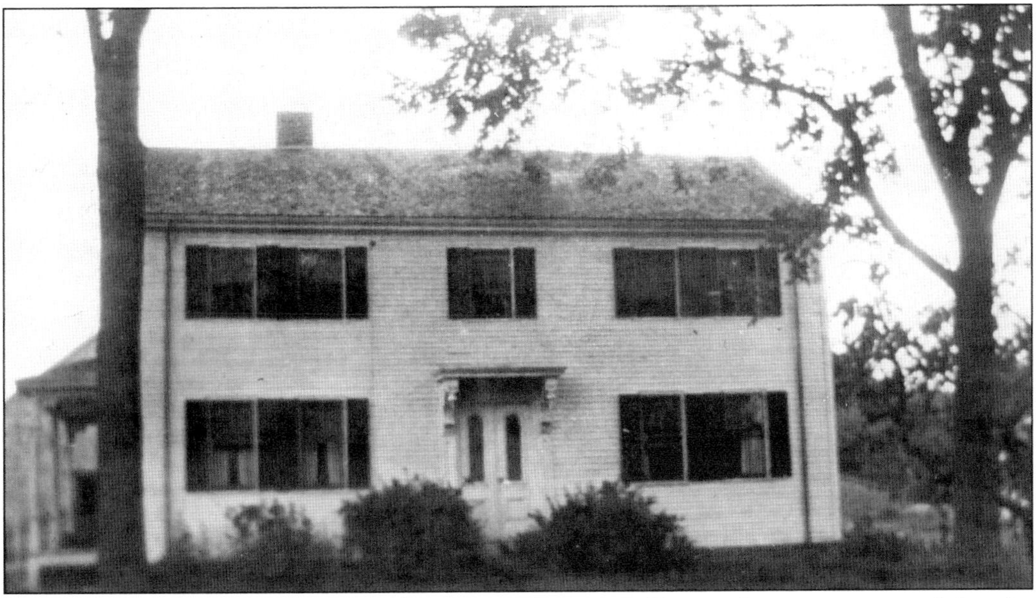

The Buxton Tavern Stand served as an early post office and tavern operated by the entrepreneurial Buxton family to accommodate stagecoach traffic. Jeremiah's red house lodged travelers while cattle drovers stayed at his son Edward's stand with its large stable. A second-floor ballroom in the ell was used for social events. The barn was destroyed by fire in 1942, but residents and area fire departments saved the house. (Courtesy of Kenny Allen.)

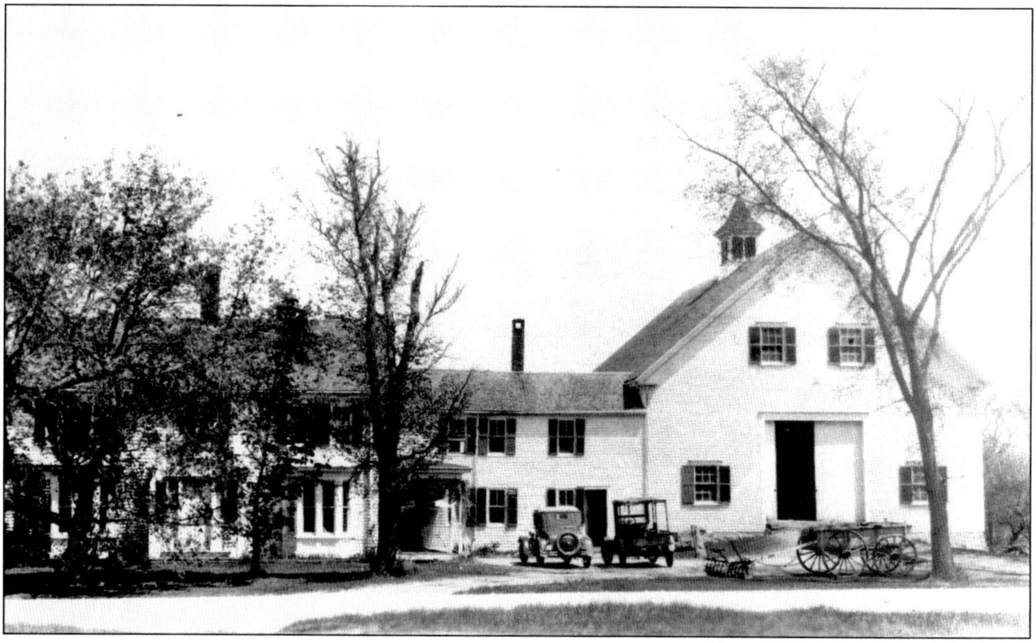

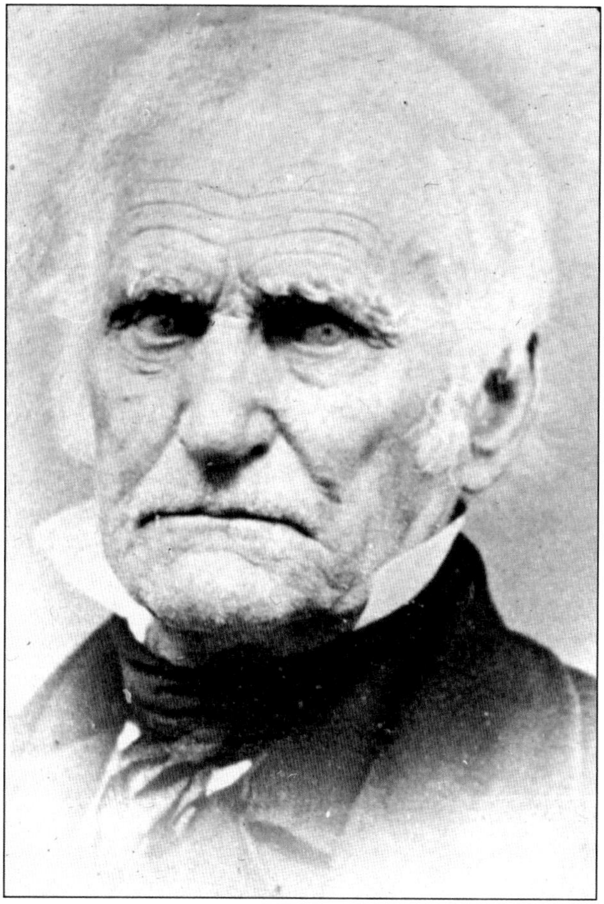

Joiner Col. Thomas Chase (left) built the William Buxton House at 403 Walnut Hill Road in 1798. Chase, a trader, drew the plans used to construct the Old Baptist Meeting House in Yarmouth in 1796 and the Pownal Congregational Church in 1811. This house was sold to the Blanchards, who ran it for many years as a tavern. In 1836, when the tavern's liquor license was denied, Jeremiah Buxton's son William bought this home adjacent to his father and heavily remodeled it into a private residence for his new wife, Jane Chadbourne. He took over his father's extensive business affairs and served in the Maine legislature for 13 years. William was town clerk and selectmen and a wealthy and influential citizen. (Courtesy of Kenny Allen.)

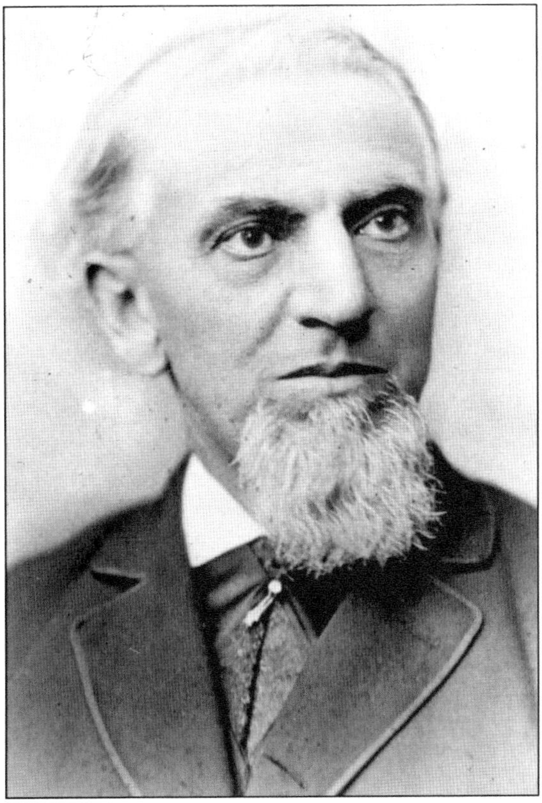

For over 150 years beginning in the 1830s, a general store occupied this site. A cooperative venture called the Union Store erected this building in 1853 based on a popular national model. In 1861, Isaac S. Stanwood (right) became proprietor and ran it until his death in 1892. The North Yarmouth Post Office was here when Stanwood served as the postmaster; there was a postal substation here in 1966 when Ernest Reardon operated the store and lunch counter. The shop carried clothing, shoes, food, grain, hardware, and later electrical appliances. James Dunn, the Collins brothers, Glidden and Glidden, L. F. Smith, and Gordon also ran this store. Ames Farm Center began its successful business in the 1970s in the left side of this building. The store is pictured below in a 1930s postcard. (Courtesy of Kenny Allen.)

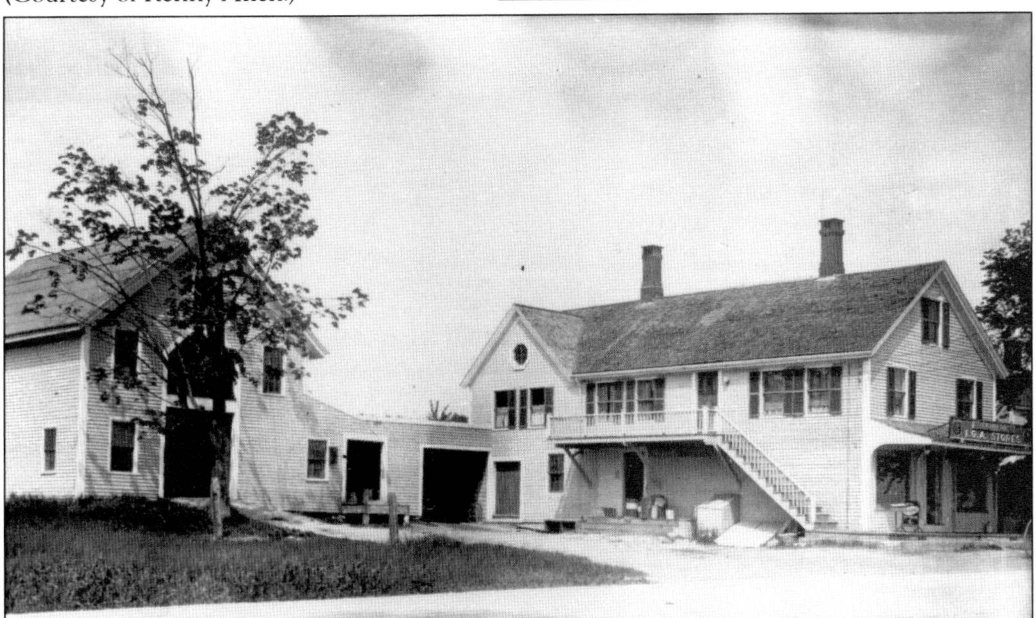

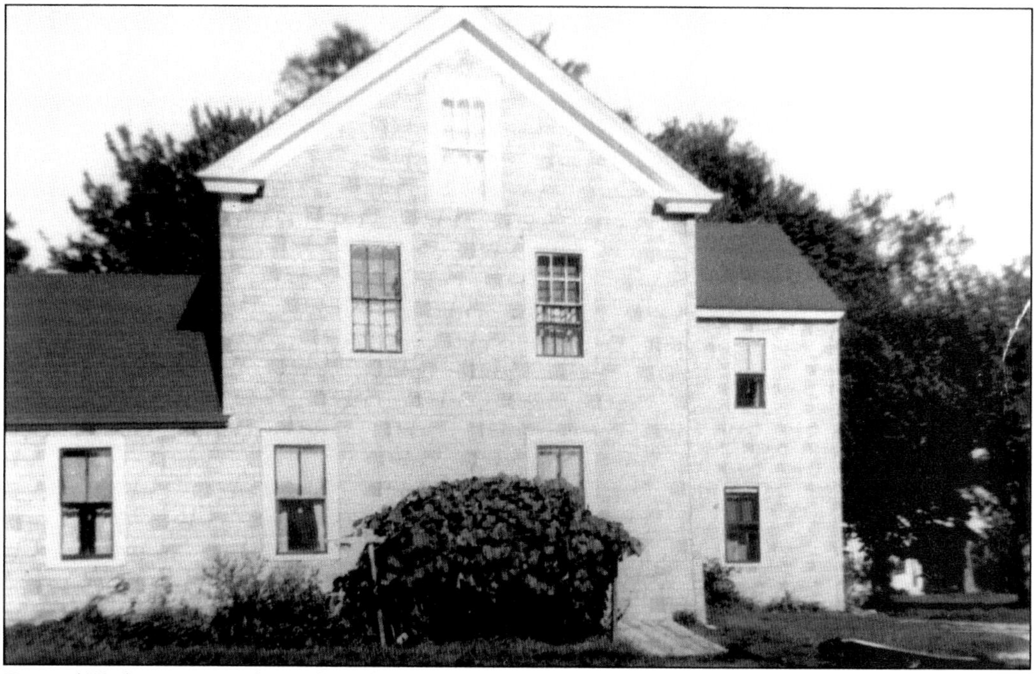

Samuel York was an early settler who built this house at 352 Walnut Hill Road in the late 1700s. Albert Devoe, a Portland contractor who salvaged scrap from World War II ships, extensively remodeled this building into a one-story home in 1953. He used his crane to lift the top off the house and make it into the detached garage. He assisted fellow Grangers in the construction of Wescustogo Grange Hall by lifting the wooden beams into place.

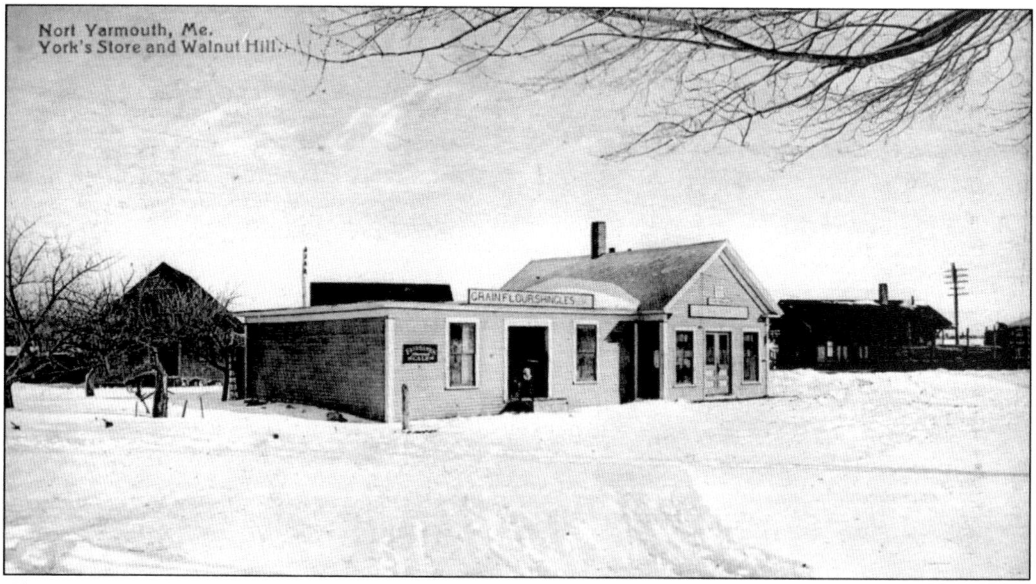

The H. H. York Store was built in 1901 at the Maine Central Railroad depot (far right) on Walnut Hill Road near Pea Lane. Henry York was a railroad employee who ran this general store and post office. The depot was busy through 1911, when the railroad line moved to its present location. York moved his store to the new depot and converted this building to a popular dance hall. The storage building on the left was the original Buxton Schoolhouse.

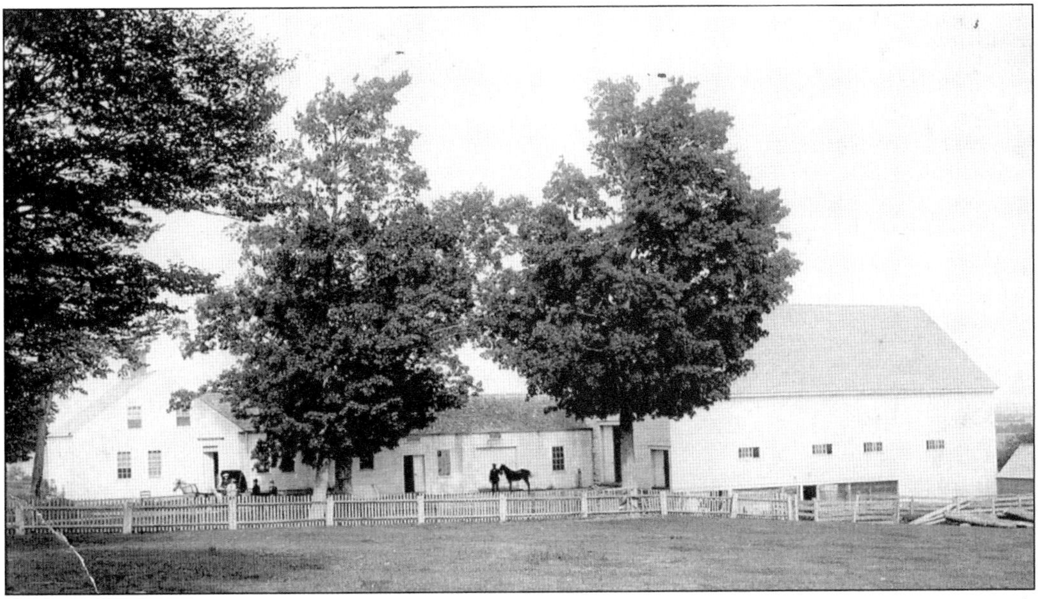

The Charles R. Loring home stands at 119 Memorial Highway, across from the North Yarmouth Memorial School. Loring, an active member of the Congregational church and the Cumberland Farmers Club, worked his oxen for other farmers. The barn at this home is considerably smaller today; it was shortened due to its poor shape. Maynard Scott used the barn and the Old Town House on Memorial Highway to build boats in the 1960s. (Courtesy of the Small family.)

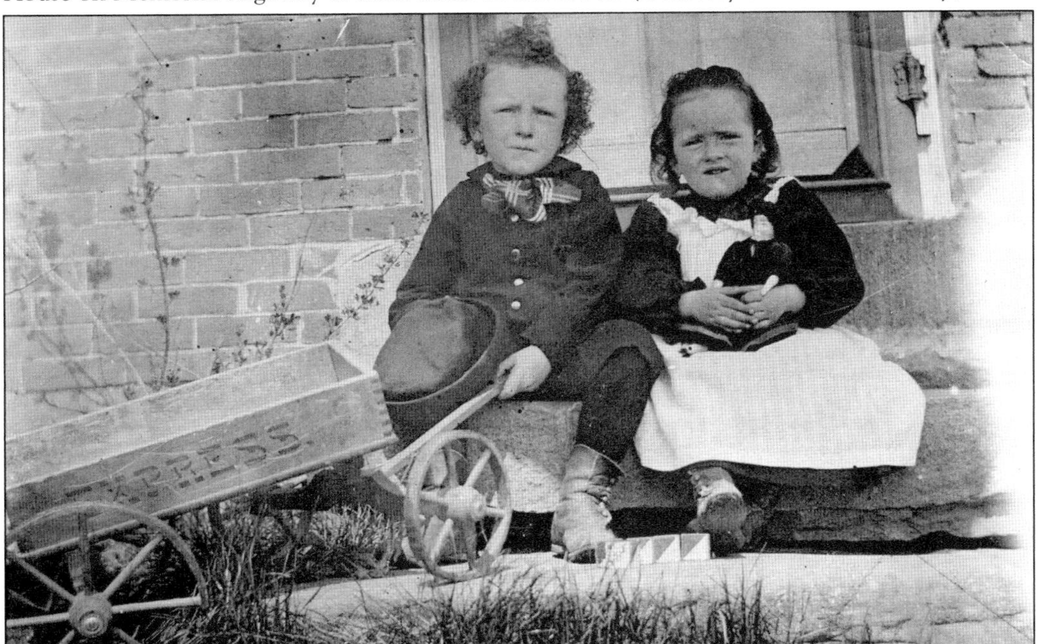

Herbert and Myra Davis, grandchildren of Capt. John Mountfort, are seated on the steps of their uncle Edward and aunt Emma Hayes' brick home at 160 Memorial Highway, across from Sweetser Road. The Hayes' daughter Eleanor later owned the property where her father was a market gardener, and some of the land became the Eleanor Hayes Town Forest in 1973. From the 1960s to the 1980s, this was a large poultry farm. (Courtesy of Dick Baston.)

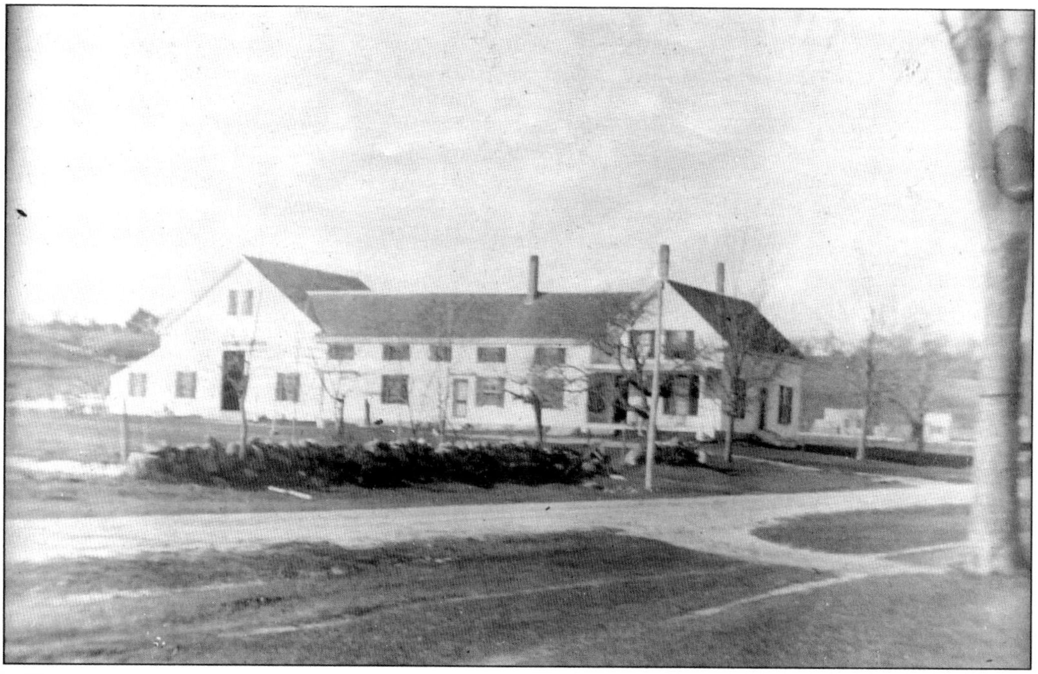

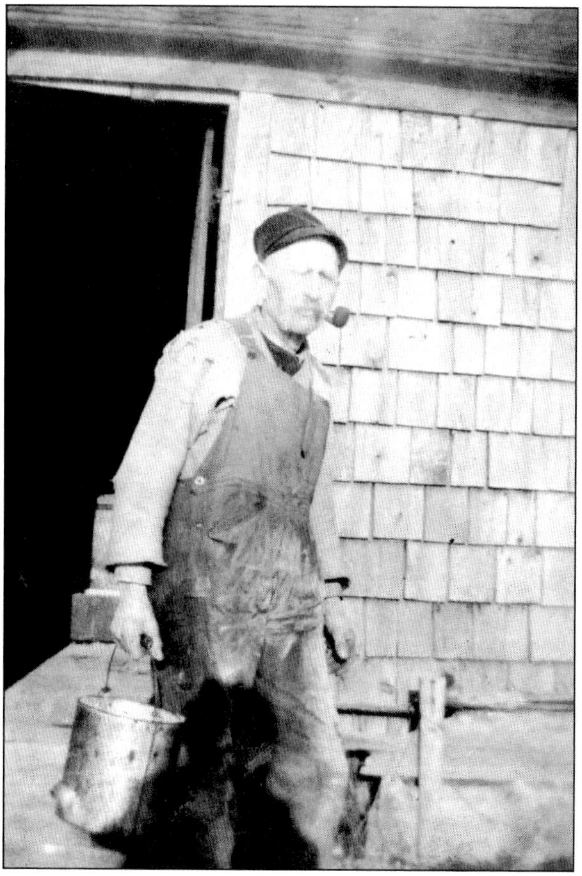

Capt. James F. Mountfort (1850–1931), shown below, was born in Gray but later moved to Mountfort Road. When steam-powered ships replaced the sailing ships he loved, he decided to settle into the life of a farmer. In 1891, Mountfort purchased the above house, at 546 Walnut Hill Road. He raised poultry and shipped eggs, increasing their production by feeding a mixture of fish heads and mashed potatoes. He ran portable sawmills on woodlots for Capt. James Sawyer. He also kept the machinery operating for the Walnut Hill Creamery. Married twice, his children included Elizabeth and Florence, who both married into the Baston family. His grandson Richard Mountfort Baston, a carpenter and retired North Yarmouth fire chief, now owns this house. Mountfort was buried in the Old Baptist Meetinghouse cemetery in Yarmouth. (Courtesy of Dick Baston.)

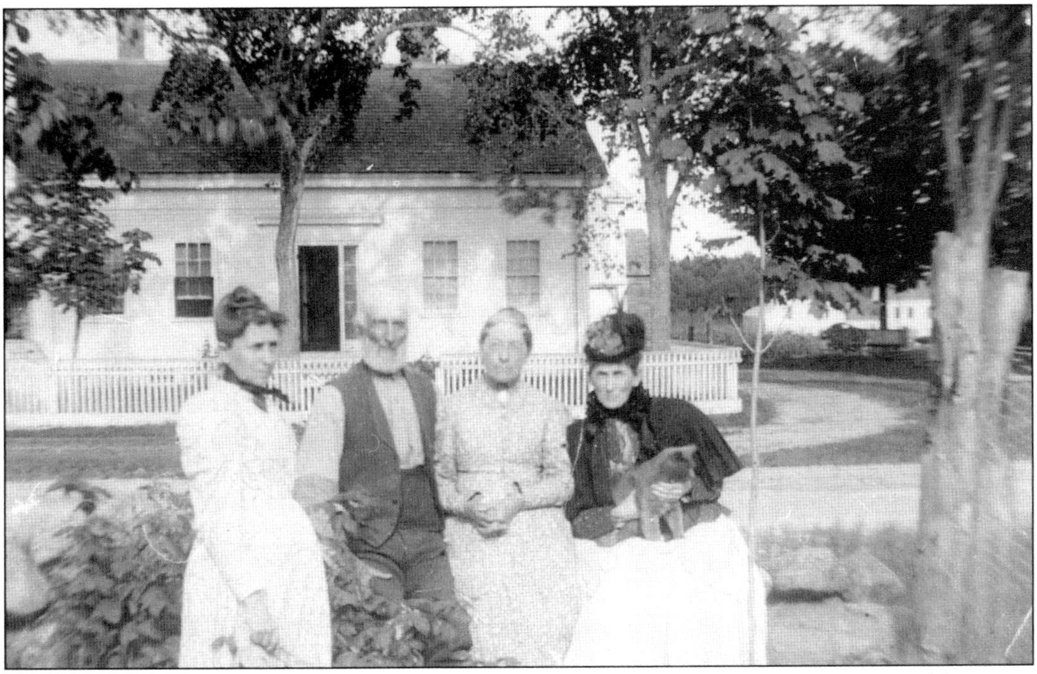

John and Mary Staples Barstow (center) stand in front of their 1847 Greek Revival home at 543 Walnut Hill Road near Parsonage Road around 1903. John worked as a farmer. They were charter members of Wescustogo Grange, where he served as the Grange chaplain. Mary was the sister of John Staples Jr., who ran the carriage shop business next door. The barn was taken down in the late 1930s. The Congregational church parsonage appears in the background.

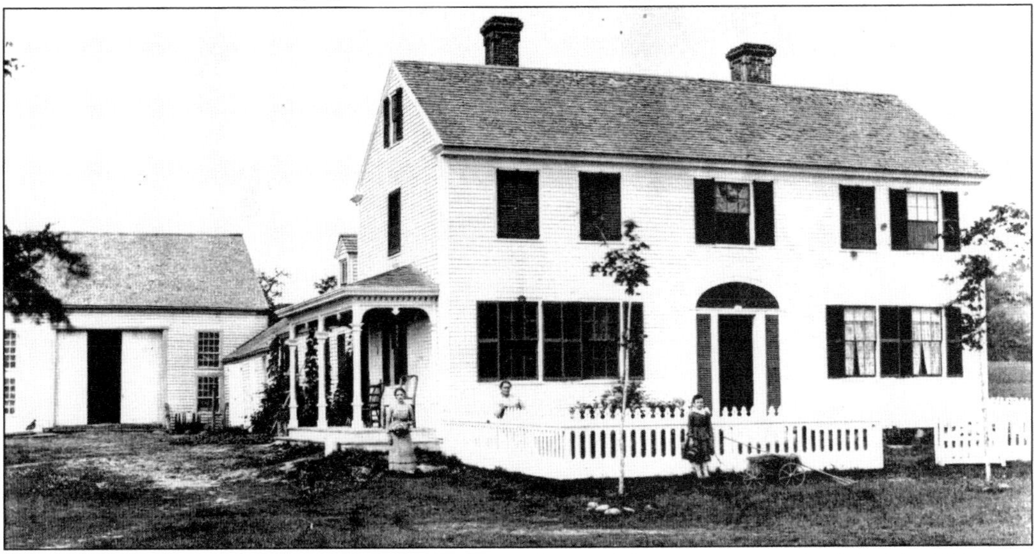

The Jonathan P. Rowe house, located across from Walnut Hill Cemetery, was built by David Parsons about 1800. Rowe was a deacon at the Congregational church. His wife, Nancy, is shown with their granddaughters Gertrude and Edith McIntire around 1900. Their father, Edwin McIntire, later owned the home and drove his cows across the street to a pasture. He dug graves in the cemetery and took his grandson Paul with him to help. Local lore says that the town's earliest schoolhouse, built around 1780, originally stood on this site. (Courtesy of Paul McIntire.)

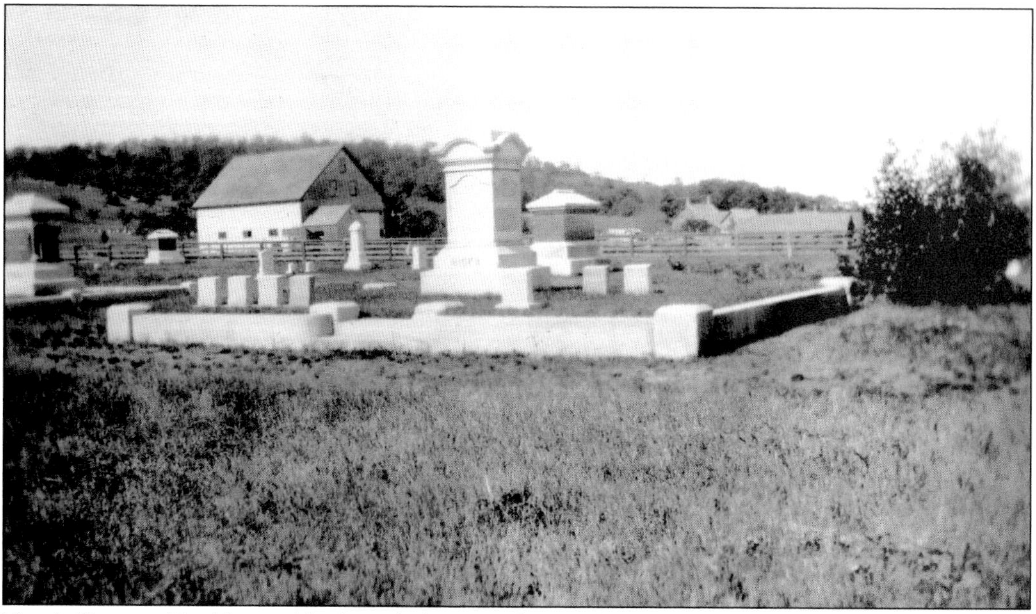

North Yarmouth's oldest public burial place, Walnut Hill Cemetery occupies land acquired from Jacob Hayes in 1801. The town has no known family graveyards. Records show that there are several pre-1800 burials on this site. Perhaps this is because the first schoolhouse was also used as a meetinghouse, and residents may have been buried nearby. This *c.* 1915 view shows several buildings that are gone and Walnut Hill in the background. (Courtesy of Mark Heath.)

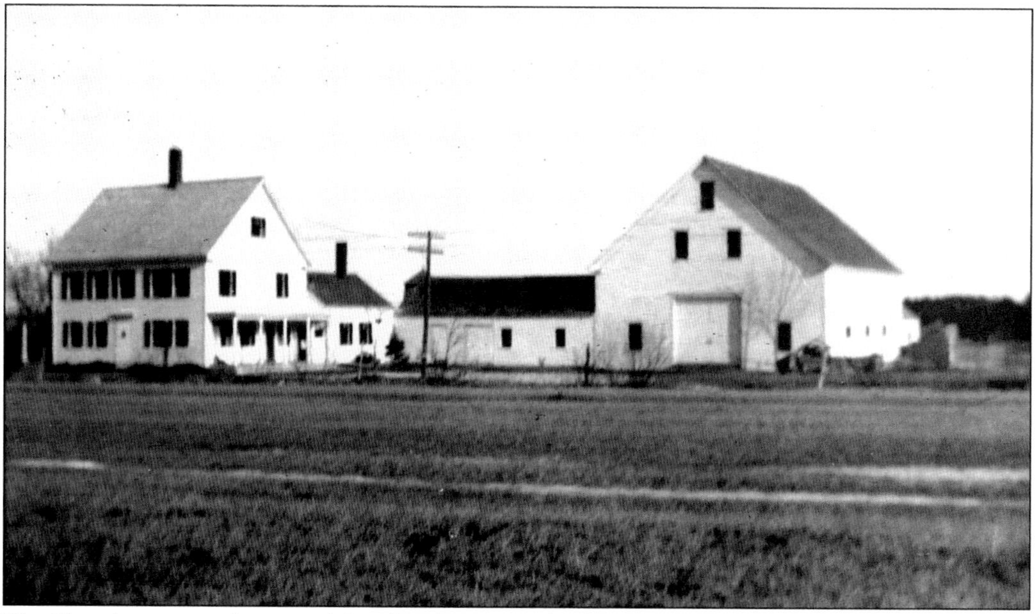

The Hamiltons owned many of the older homes at the foot of Walnut Hill, and their descendants still live in town today. Edward R. Hamilton occupied this home at 525 Walnut Hill Road in the early 1800s. About 1967, Maynard Robinson opened a gravel pit for his excavation business by purchasing the property from Arthur Dunn, who ran a floral business here. Robinson used the motto "We Move the Earth" on his trucks. The house disappeared about 1980 and the town now owns the pit.

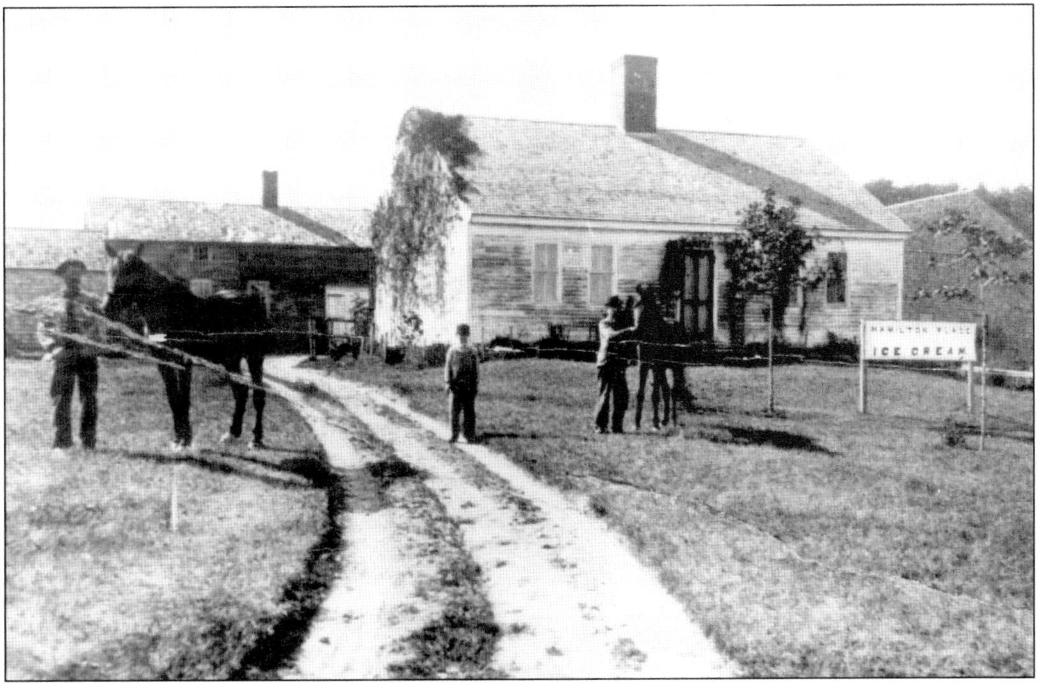

John Hamilton Jr. of Chebeague built this house at 598 Walnut Hill Road in the late 1700s. He settled here permanently during the Revolutionary War when the British attacked Portland. Hamiltons probably had an earlier home, as son William is recorded as the first person born on Walnut Hill in 1762. In 1894, this house became the town's first community library, known as the Hamilton Place Library. Other libraries for organization members included ones operated by the Congregational church (1820s), the Templars (1873–1883), and the Grange (1970s). (Courtesy of Barbara Fox.)

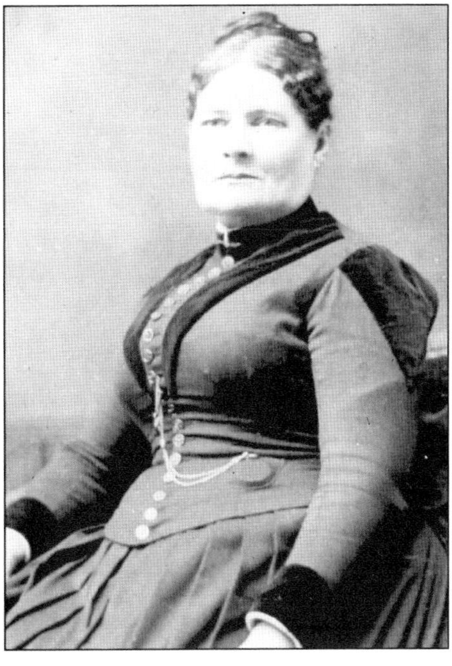

Lura A. Hamilton (1842–1932) served as the Hamilton Place librarian, purchasing books from Boston. She was the wife of Horatio, a great-grandson of John Hamilton, who is shown above (left) with sons Ernest (middle) and Herbert. The library boasted 1,800 volumes, a reading group, and its own stamp to mark borrowed books. By 1909, the Hamiltons had begun selling ice cream that they made using their cow milk. After 40 years, the library closed when Lura died in 1932. (Courtesy of Kenny Allen.)

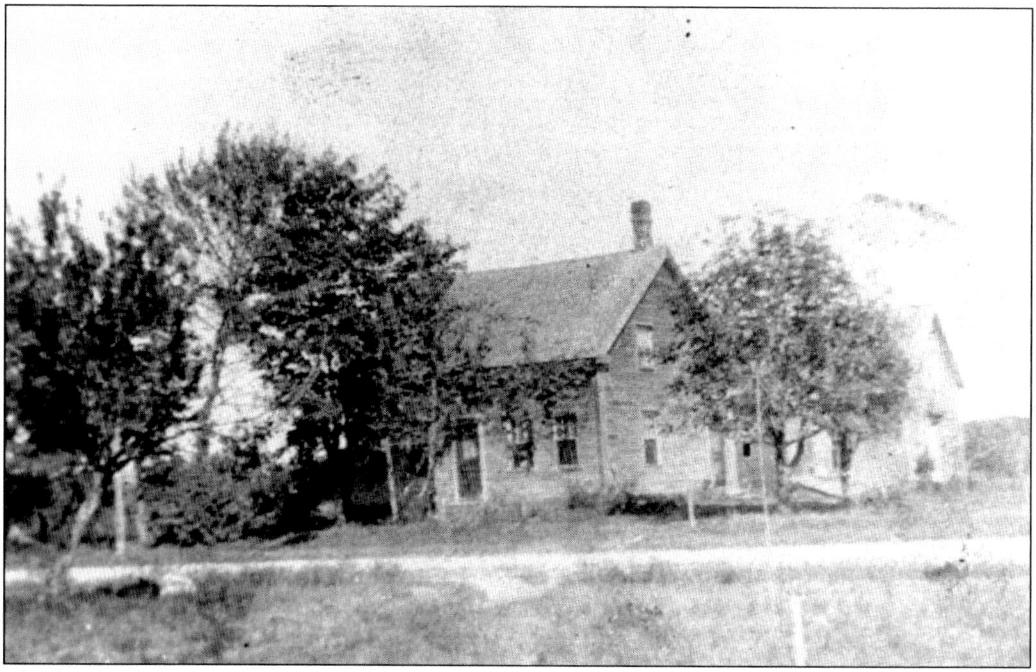

The home of Vyra Hamilton Tompson at 164 Hill Road was originally owned by John Hamilton. A modest residence on a small lot, it was not the typical large connected farmhouse of the period, nor was the one next door, owned by his brother John Hamilton. This is because they both worked with their father, Edward, on his adjacent farm (seen on page 18) and thus did not need their own big barns.

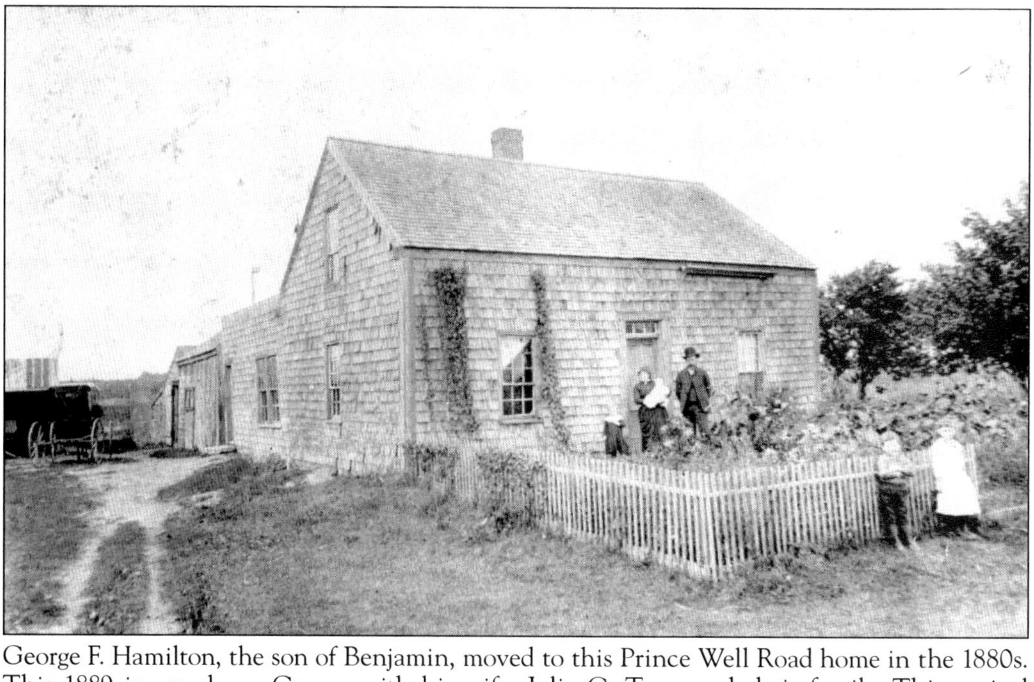

George F. Hamilton, the son of Benjamin, moved to this Prince Well Road home in the 1880s. This 1889 image shows George with his wife, Julia C. True, and their family. This typical connected farmhouse, razed in 1975, included an ell, a backhouse, and a barn.

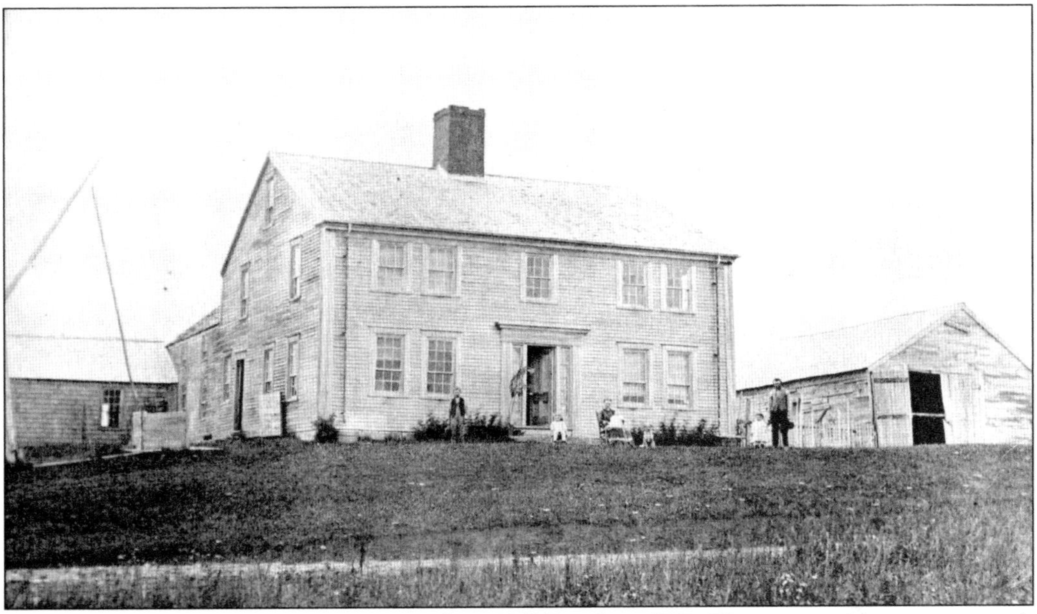

Eleazer Ring built this home at 108 Walnut Hill Road in 1772. This original barn was struck by lightning during a July 1898 thunderstorm and burned, but the Sewall Baston family, shown here in 1881, saved the house by throwing well water on the roof. Teenaged Mabel inadvertently spared the family's dairy herd when she disobeyed her absent father. She left the cows in the field thinking them more comfortable on that humid day and so prevented their fiery deaths. (Courtesy of Lee and Ursula Baier.)

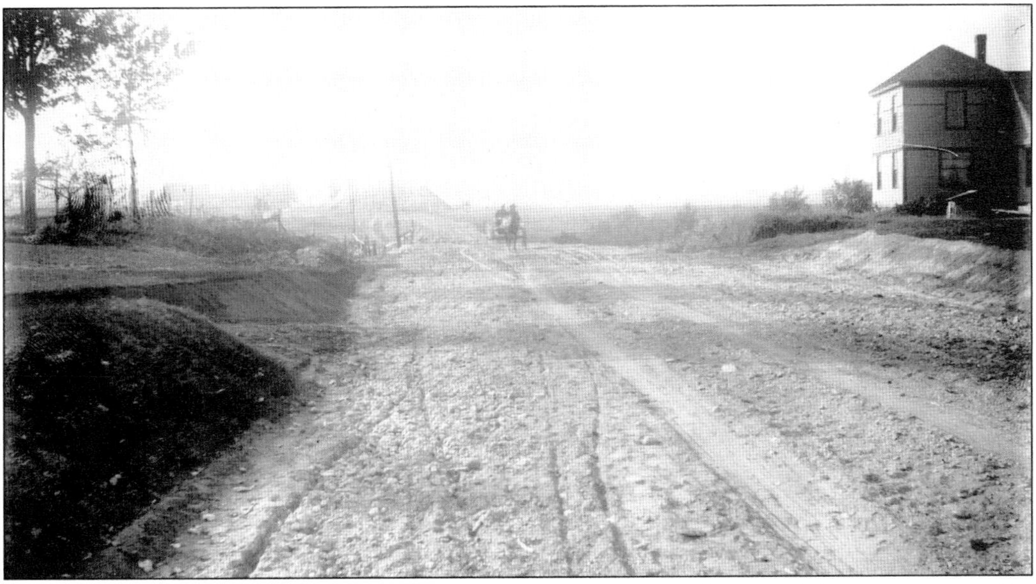

In this 1911 view of Route 115 from Yarmouth, both wagon and automobile tracks are visible, along with the construction of the road overpass built when the Maine Central Railroad rerouted its line. Older residents recalled that the overpass for the Grand Trunk Railroad, just behind this view, was originally a road traveling under the railroad line. In the distance and just over the town line is the Joseph Barstow house, built in 1848. On the right is Beckwith's Farm Market in Yarmouth. (Collection of the Yarmouth Historical Society.)

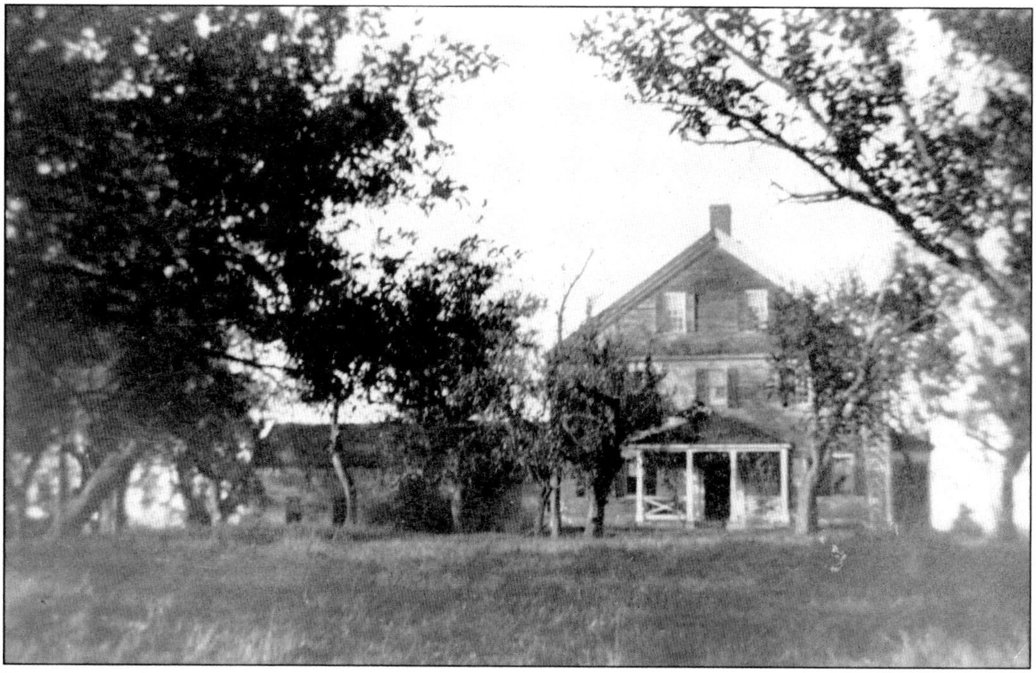

James Dunn bought this Dunn's Corner house in 1816 and ran a large farm there, cutting wood and pressing hay for others. The Atlantic and St. Lawrence Railroad passed through his land in 1849, so he built a general store next to the tracks. Sons William and Isaac constructed homes on either side of the tracks and continued to build the family business. James died in 1852 and his son James Jr. inherited the farm.

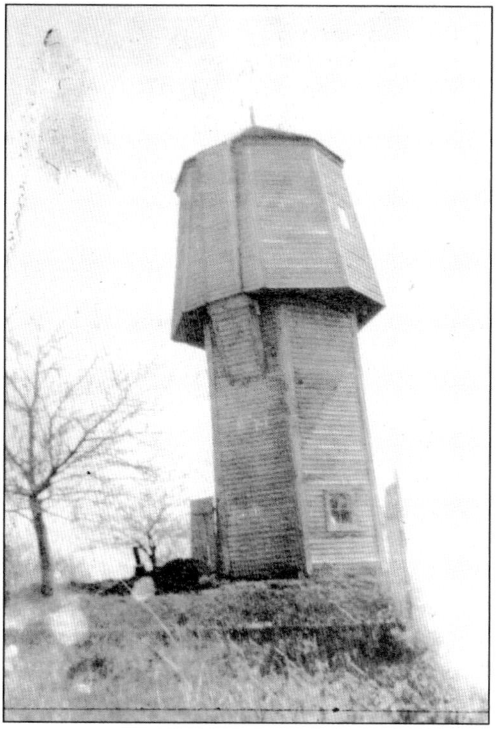

A windmill pumped water from Royal River to this unusual wooden water tower, located along the railroad tracks and shown about 1920. Pipes carried it to the Dunn family homes and store. Dug wells in the area supplied drinking water, while this river water was used for livestock. (Courtesy of the Hathaway family.)

This c. 1875 family portrait depicts Capt. Charles Lee Loring of Crockett's Corner and his grandchildren, from left to right, Lucy Skillin Dunn, Ansel Loring Dunn, and William Trickey Dunn. Charles adopted their mother, Marie Colley, when her own mother passed away. Lucy died young, but her brothers (including Charles, not pictured) went on to important positions in the community and successful businesses of their own. William moved to California and became a banker.

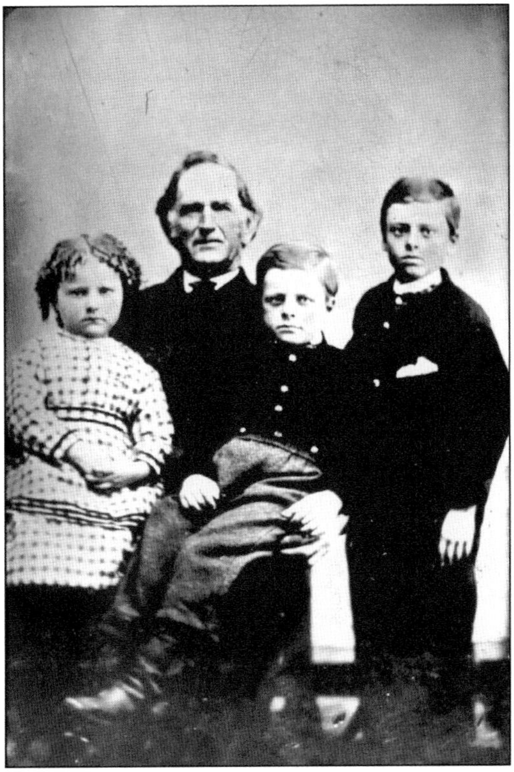

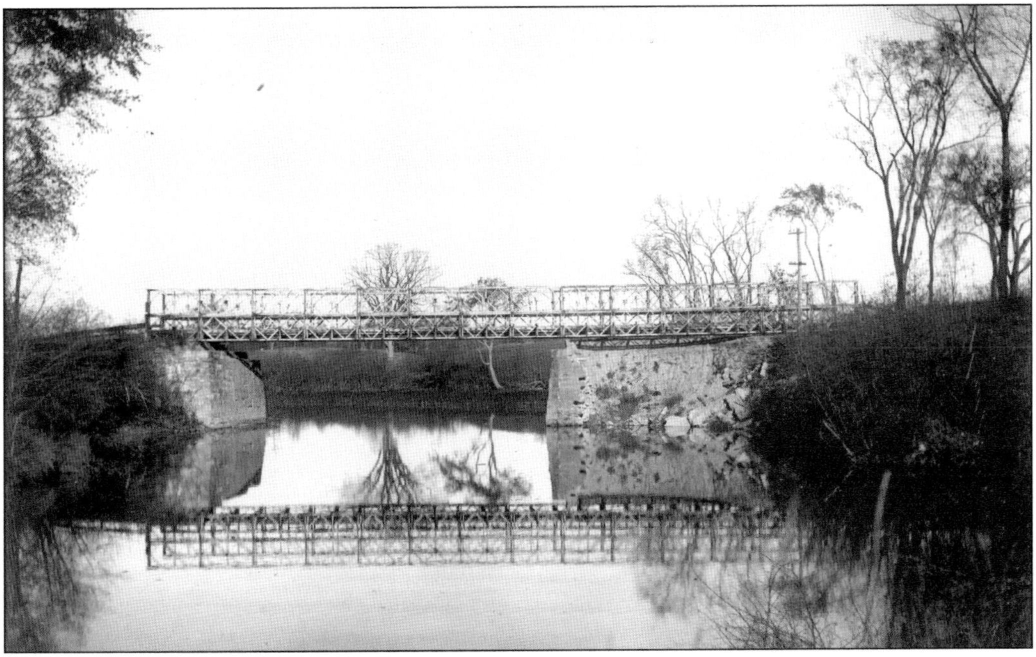

Frequent flooding at a big bend in the river was fixed by digging a channel under the current bridge on Memorial Highway. This temporary iron bridge was placed over the Royal River during the construction in 1955. Baston Park, dedicated in 2004, is located on the island that remained after the river course was changed. It is seen here on the left edge of the photograph.

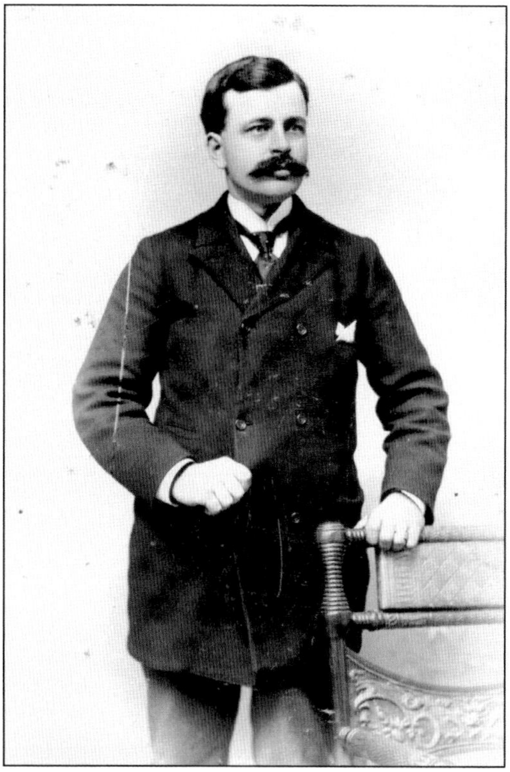

Ansel L. Dunn (1866–1942) graduated from Kents Hill School and acquired Dunn's Store. Disliking the grocery business, he went to work for the New England Telephone Company, selling service throughout Maine. He also ran the Wescustogo Hotel and bottled Wescustogo Spring water. A state legislator and selectman, Dunn participated in designating Memorial Highway. He was married twice, though had no children. He raised cattle and racehorses.

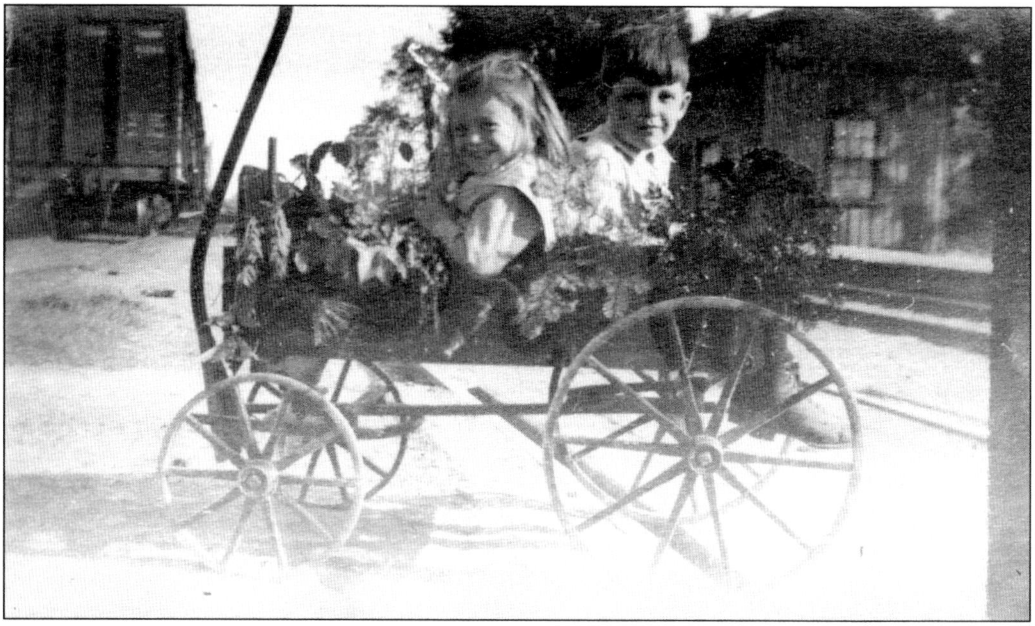

Dorothy Dunn and her brother Charles Dunn Jr., children of Charles L. (1873–1949) and Lucinda L. Dunn (1878–1951), pose at Dunn's Depot in front of the freight building, which says "North Yarmouth," around 1915. The Dunn family owned this land when the Atlantic and St. Lawrence Railroad came through in 1849 and quickly opened a store and post office to take advantage of the train traffic. (Courtesy of Ginger Collins.)

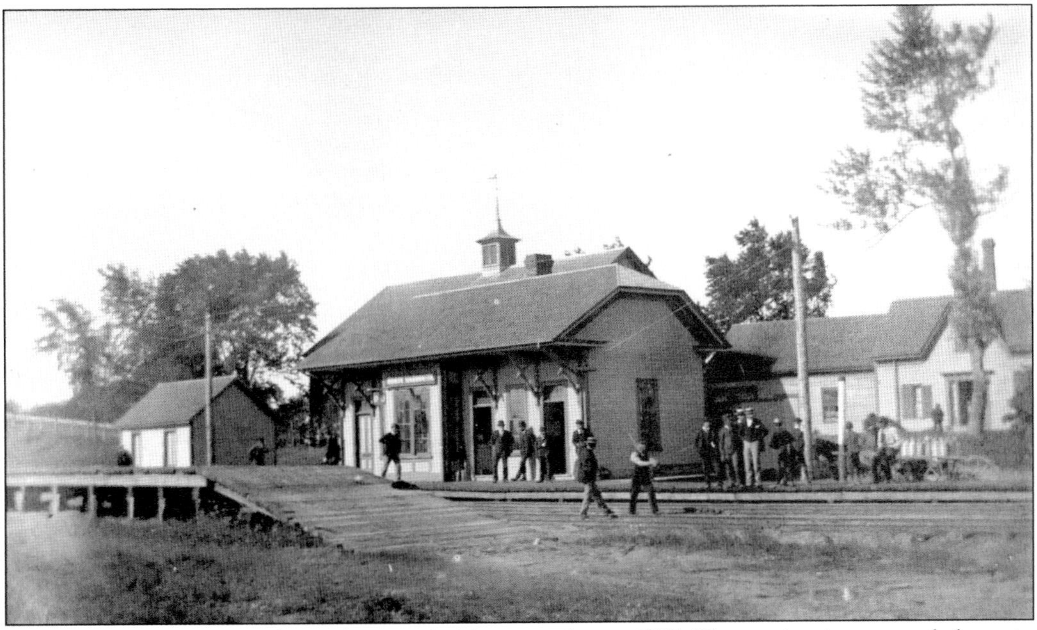

Dunn's Depot was a very busy place, with 16 stops a day in 1855. The station is captured above in the only known photograph, taken on July 4, 1892, from in front of Dunn's Store. Ansel Dunn's house appears in the background. Notice the farmers who have brought their milk in cans to ship to the city market. Passengers await the next train. Below is Dunn's Store (left), which sold everything from clothes to hardware and food. The East North Yarmouth Post Office was inside the store. The storage building (middle) was torn down in the 1990s. The gristmill, which later became a grain store owned by Charles Heywood, is on the right. Railroad cars pulled onto the side rail in front of the buildings and grain and freight was unloaded on the platform. A blacksmith shop behind these structures did a brisk business shoeing horses. The station house was torn down in October 1941. (Above, courtesy of Lincoln Merrill Jr.; below, courtesy of Ginger Collins.)

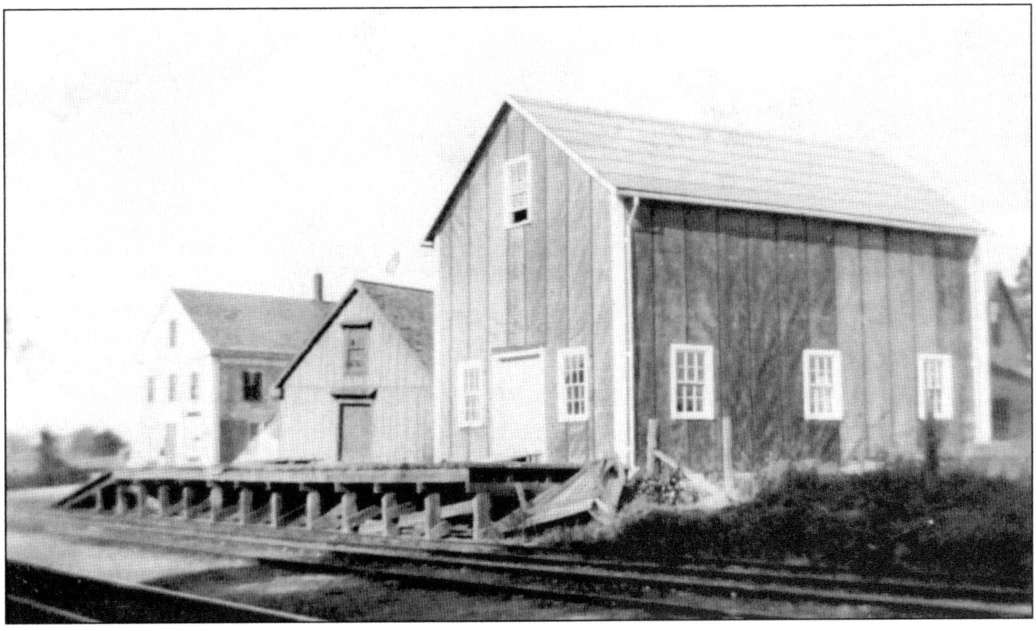

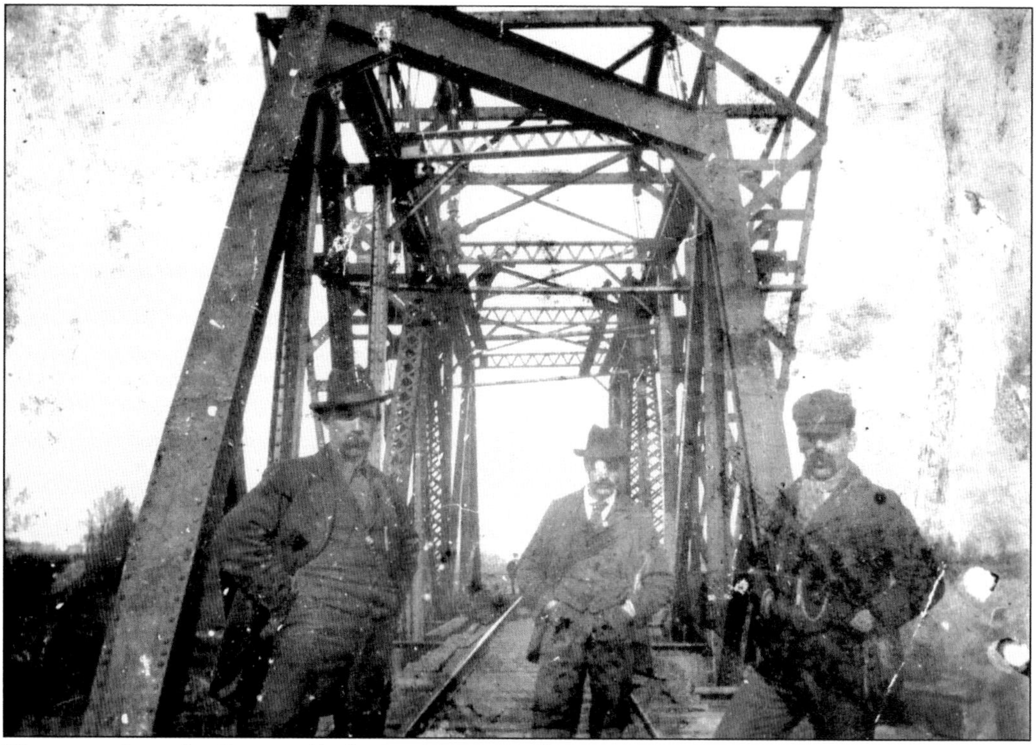

The crew from the Detroit Bridge and Iron Works Company builds the well-known railroad bridge over the Royal River in 1900. Visible from North Road, it is the only iron railroad bridge in North Yarmouth and the only place the tracks cross the main river. The men in front appear to be engineers. Notice the men working up on the steel.

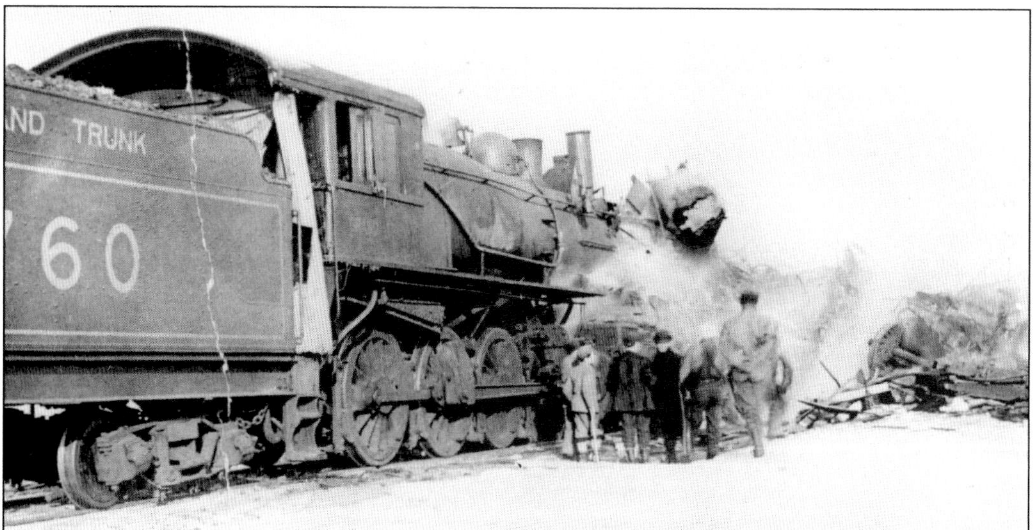

An early morning head-on crash at Dunn's Depot in February 1912 between two trains woke local farmer George Sawyer. He saw that the collision had caused the wooden freight cars to burn. Neighbors shoveled snow onto the wreck to try and save a man trapped beneath the cars. When it was apparent the fire could not be halted, Dr. Barker crawled under the car and used chloroform to prevent a painful death. (Courtesy of Lincoln Merrill Jr.)

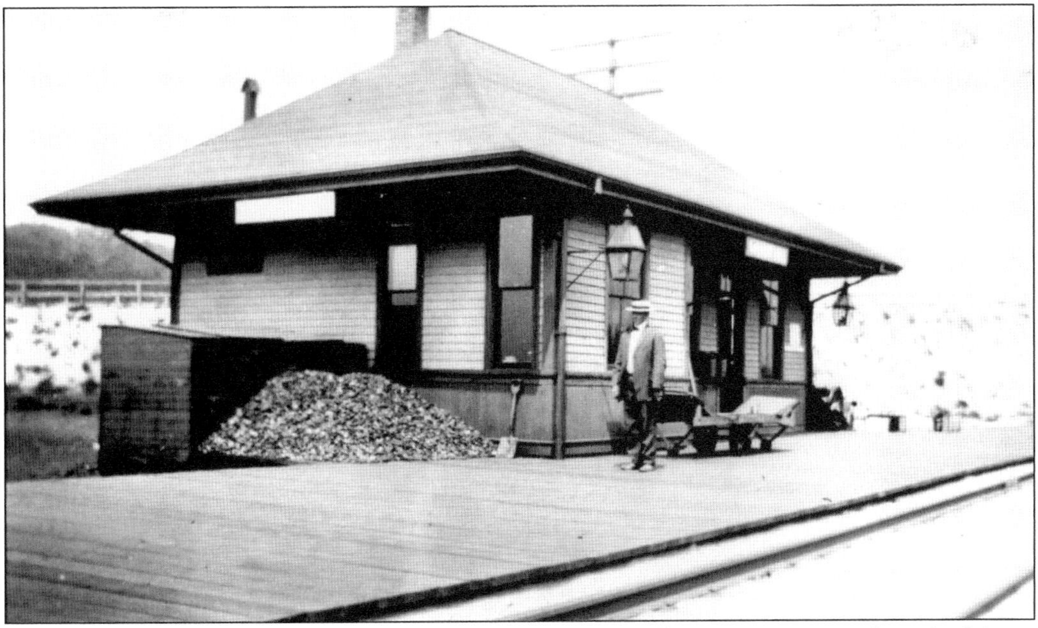

John Barrowes of Portland constructed the new Walnut Hill station in 1911, when the Maine Central Railroad rerouted its track away from Walnut Hill village. This station was not very active due to its distance from the village and proximity to Dunn's Depot. The popularity of the automobile ultimately led to its demise. Notice the coal used to heat the station. Memorial Highway and the overpass appear in the background.

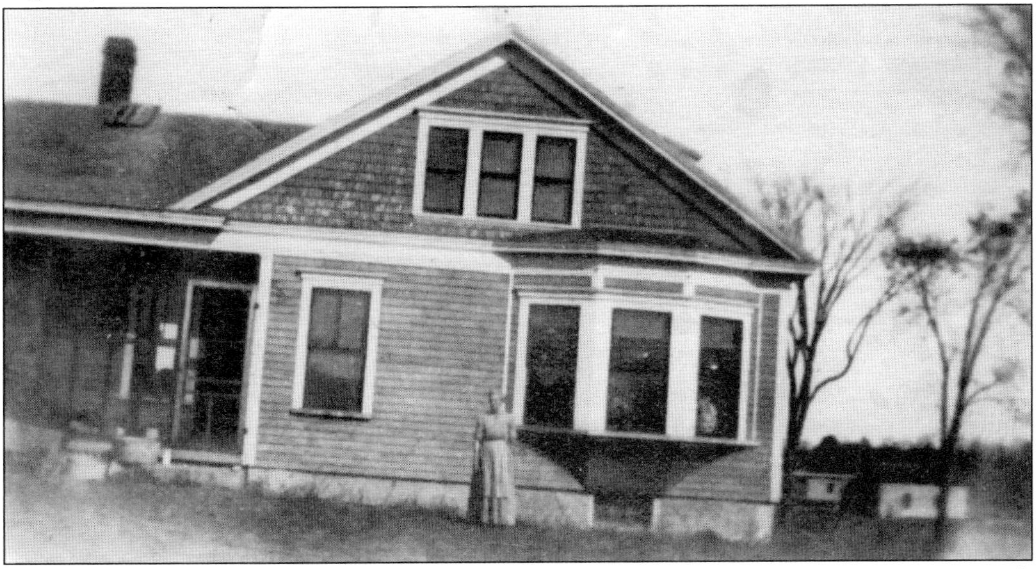

The Clifford and Hazel Anderson home, at 384 Memorial Highway, was built in 1914 with materials salvaged from dismantling the Wescustogo Hotel. The structure in the distance just to the right of the house is the railroad freight building. The depot shown above and Henry York's new store built around 1913 are to the left behind the house. The structure to the right of the freight building is unknown, but was probably associated with the railroad depot. York ran the post office from the store for a short time, but eventually the shop failed along with the station. (Courtesy of the Anderson family.)

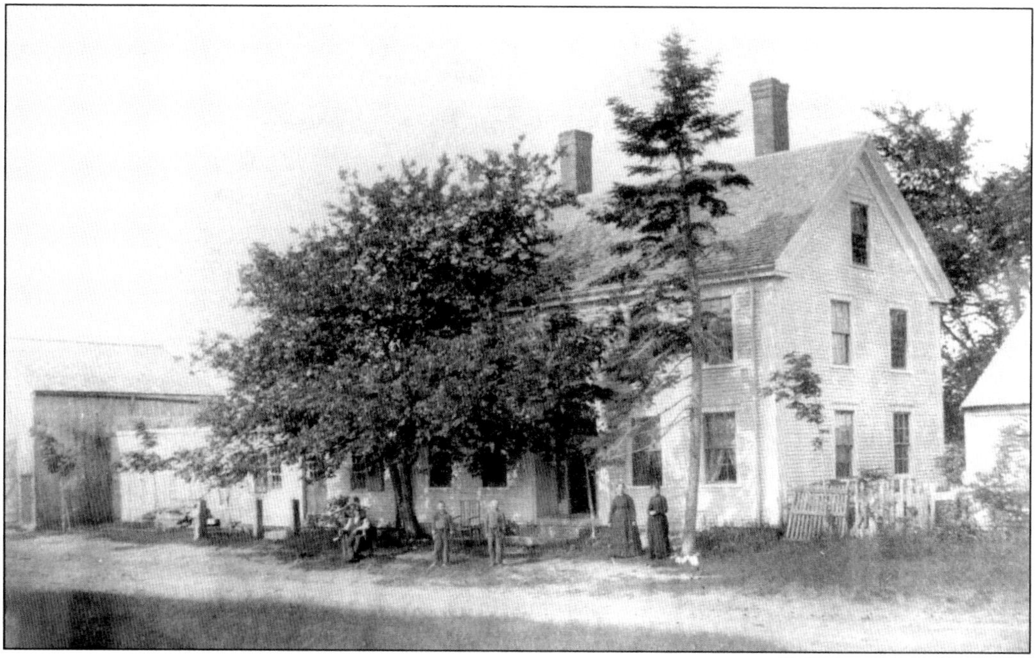

Ebenezer Lord owned the house at 8 West Pownal Road in the early 1800s and ran a general store across the street. Enoch Crockett purchased the store and then the home in 1834. Crockett's Corner was the center of commerce in East North Yarmouth until about 1850. Enoch's wife Harriet Mann Crockett (right of doorway) poses with daughter Amanda Tuttle and her twin sons, Ervin and Ernest, in this 1870s image by the house, which remained in the family until the 1980s. The man in the chair might be Solomon Crockett, Enoch's son who lived in the building on the right.

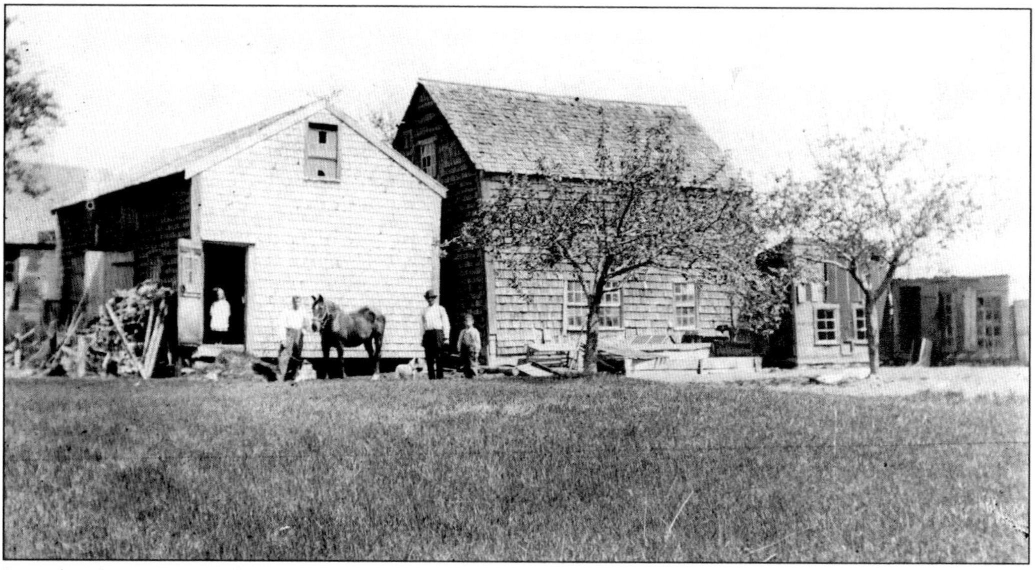

Joseph Cleaves, a cordwainer (shoemaker), purchased the Charles Humphrey house, at 25 West Pownal Road, in 1838. In the busy Crockett's Corner area, Cleaves ran his shop and also obtained a peddler license. He served as justice of the peace. This set of buildings is shown around 1910, when owned by Bertwell Yates and Mabel Doyle Yates.

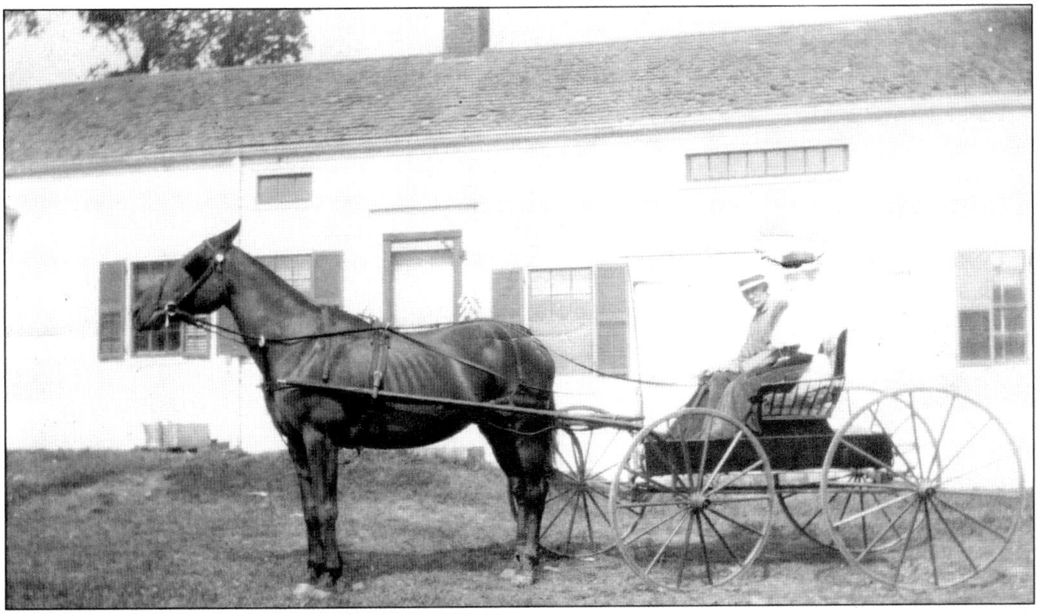

Built about 1815 for Henry Whitney at 155 West Pownal Road, this house was owned by Frank H. and Alice F. Marston photographed here around 1915. Frank was a farmer who died in 1916. After World War II, the power company wanted to run electricity along this road, but all residents had to sign up. Alice refused to do so. (Courtesy of Noyes Lawrence.)

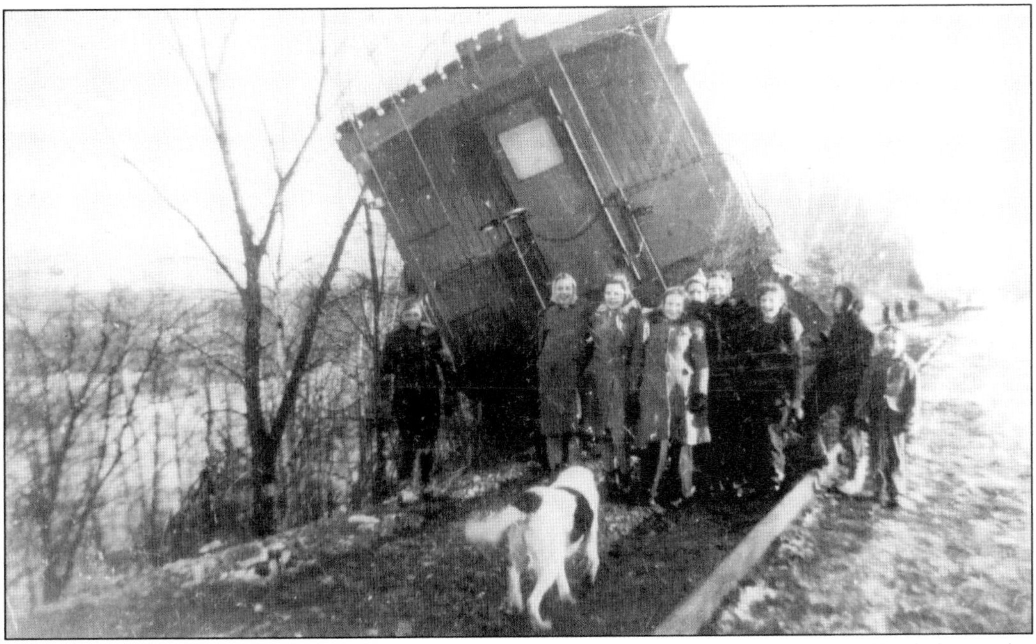

Seventh- and eighth-grade schoolchildren attending the Old Town House walked down the Grand Trunk tracks to see this railcar accident in 1944. The mishap occurred behind the Bearce house on North Road. The children collected the wheat that had spilled out from this overturned grain car as a souvenir. Pictured here, from left to right, are Elwood Bearce, Roberta Jewett, Grace Edwards, Eva Allen, unknown, Nellie Barter, Ann Pierce, Ernest Allen, Philo Bearce, and Philo's dog Rover. (Courtesy of Nellie Kendrick.)

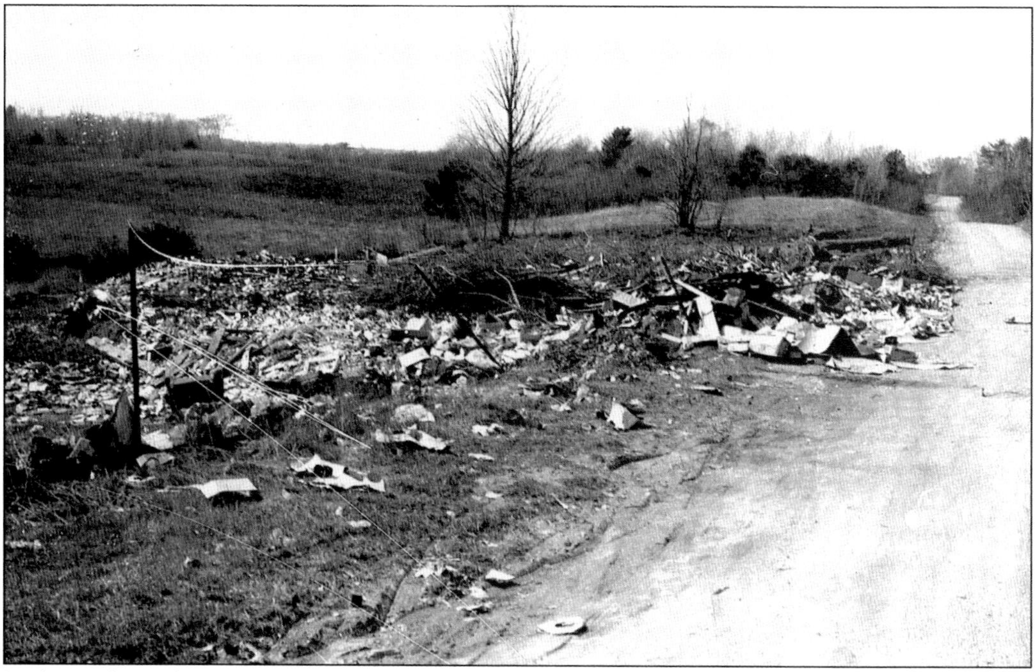

Early residents disposed of trash in gullies behind their homes and even in the river. Garbage was also thrown over the bank of the gravel pit on Doughty Road around 1930. The first of two town dumps opened in 1963 on a one-acre lot at 488 Mountfort Road purchased from Herbert Lawrence. As seen in this photograph, trash was thrown just off the road and blew throughout the neighborhood. After this dump closed in 1968, a new one was located on West Pownal Road. (Courtesy of Phyllis Smith.)

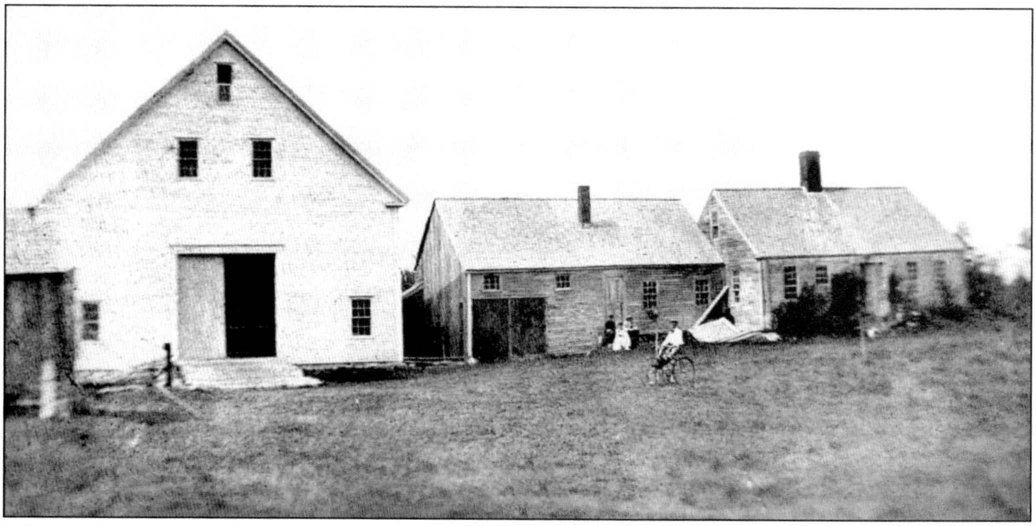

Edward Small built this home at 344 Mountfort Road around 1806, and it was the only one on the road for several decades. An early painting shows a different English-style barn. The house, owned by the Titcomb family for about 150 years, has been remodeled and the barn is gone. In the early 1900s, Fred Titcomb kept sheep and cows here, but walked the dairy herd to his Yarmouth home each fall. This 1880s photograph shows Fred on a tricycle with his sisters Georgia and Sarah and mother, Phanelia. (Courtesy of Dick Knight.)

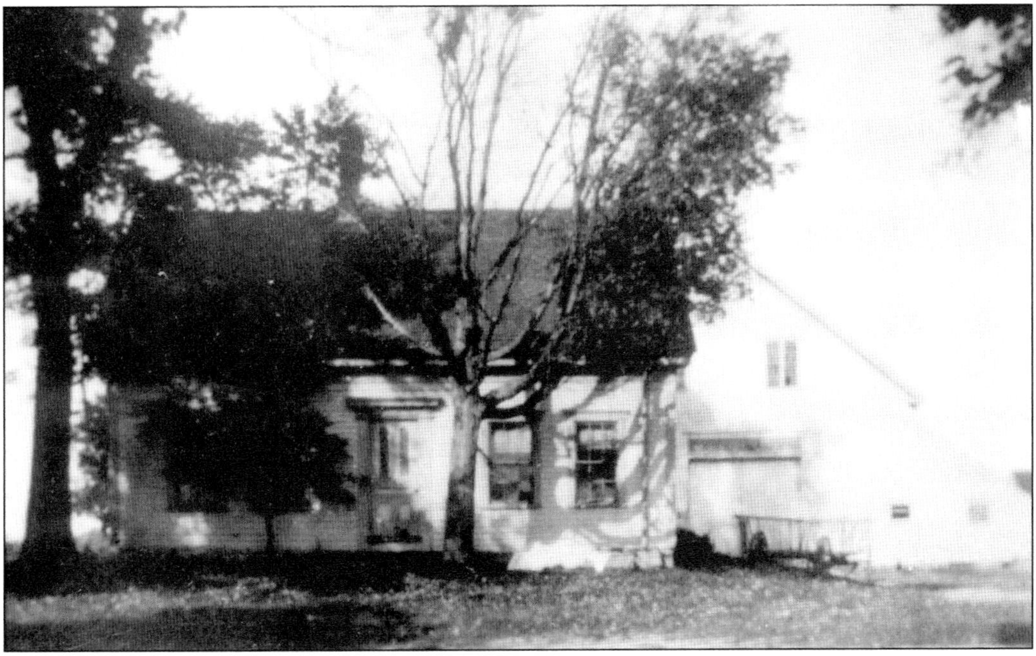

The John Merchant home, at 1573 North Road, was part of a large dairy farm. A spring on the land across the street fed water through a pipe to a cistern in the cellar. John's son William Merchant, who inherited the property in 1919, was a farmer and a clarinet player in local dance bands. The home was razed in 1942, and the current residence was built on the old foundation.

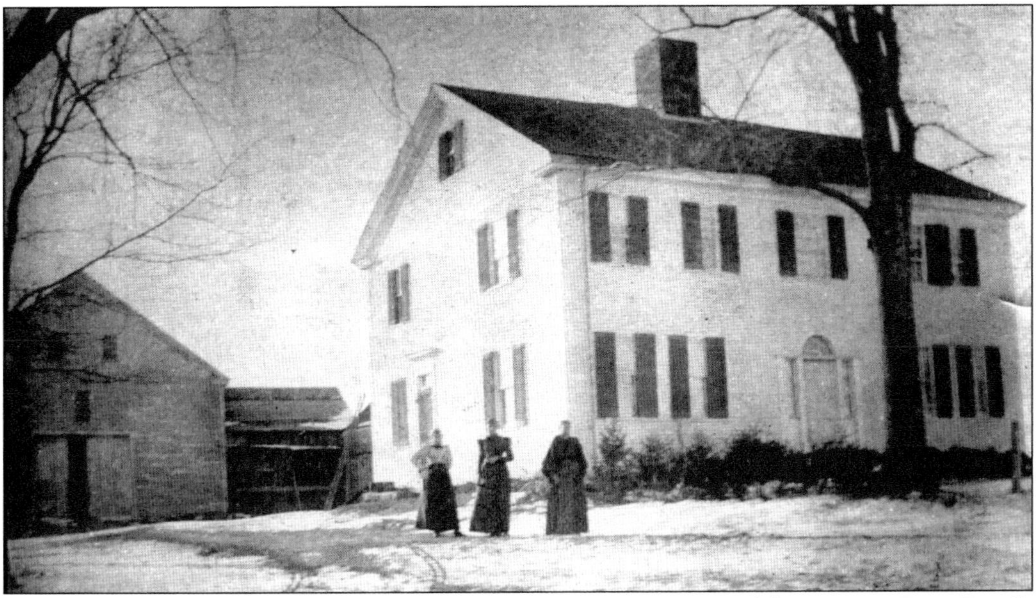

In 1813, Jabez Cushman built this home at 344 New Gloucester Road (near Town Farm Road), where he ran what may have been the town's first post office in the early 1830s. The Noah and Hannah Jewett family, shown in this *c.* 1900 photograph, moved here from Cornish in 1868. Noah was a farmer whose family developed a new apple variety around 1842 known as the Jewett Red. His son Ralph had a large family, but spoke out against funding for schools at town meetings. The house burned in 1960.

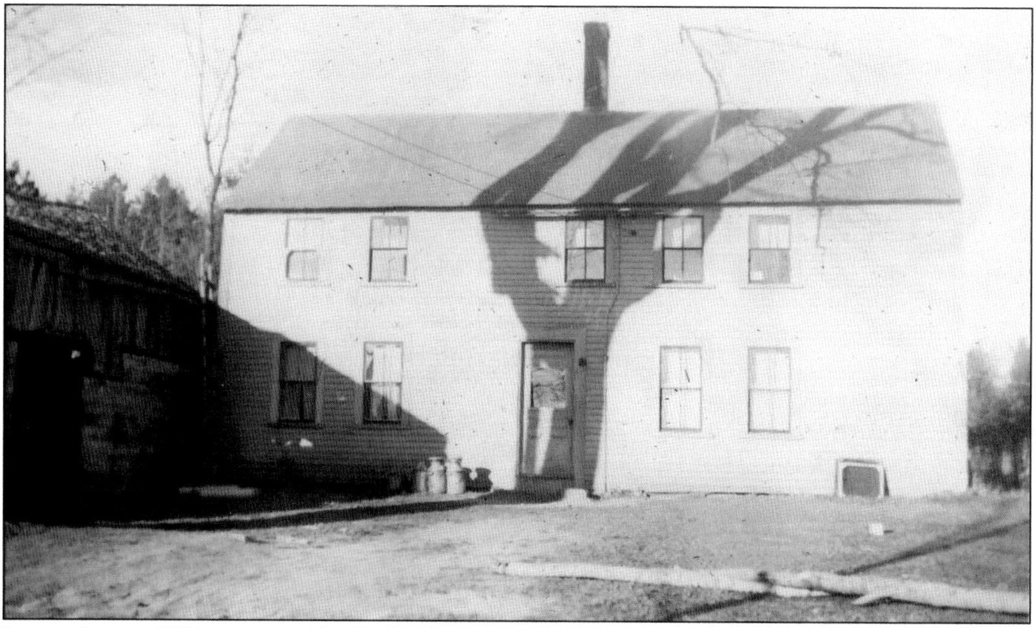

Located near 47 Town Farm Road, this house was built after 1857 and disappeared after 1970. It was owned for many years by George Ryder, a farmer whose brother Wesley ran a dairy farm on Route 231 near the Gray line. The two shared Wesley's property in later years. Ralph Jewett's son Euan worked for George, and bought the house for $700 before he was killed in World War II. (Courtesy of the Jewett family.)

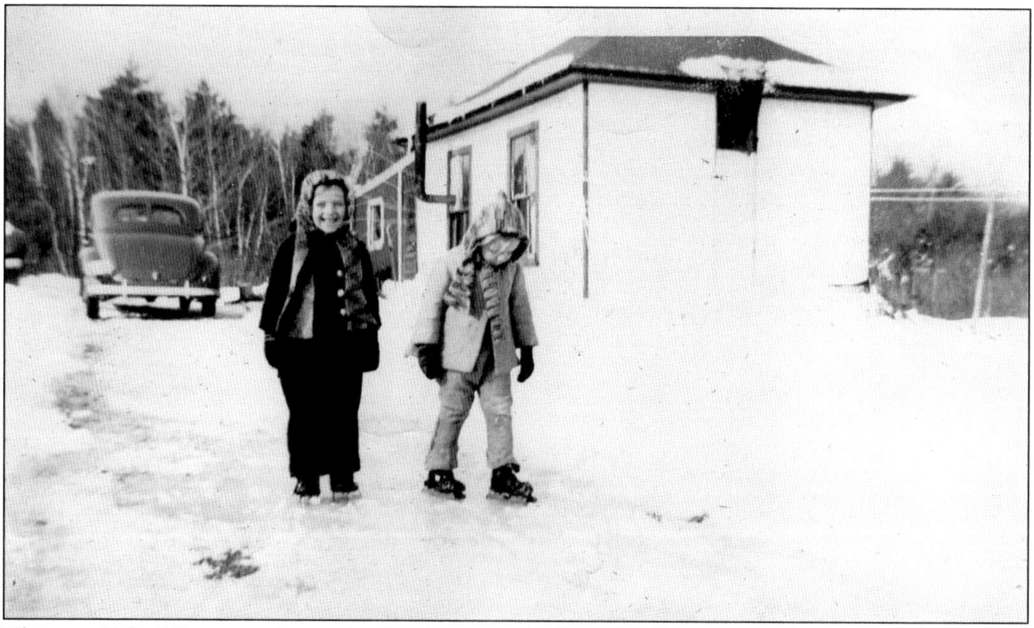

This small building was formerly the baggage shed at the West Pownal depot of the Grand Trunk Railroad. In 1943, Osborne Jewett bought it for $1 and moved it to the present site of Gallant's Auto Sales, at 712 New Gloucester Road, to serve as his family's temporary "camp home" while he built a new house. Jewett's daughters Brenda (left) and Valarie are pictured here. (Courtesy of the Jewett family.)

Two

BUSINESSES WE OWNED

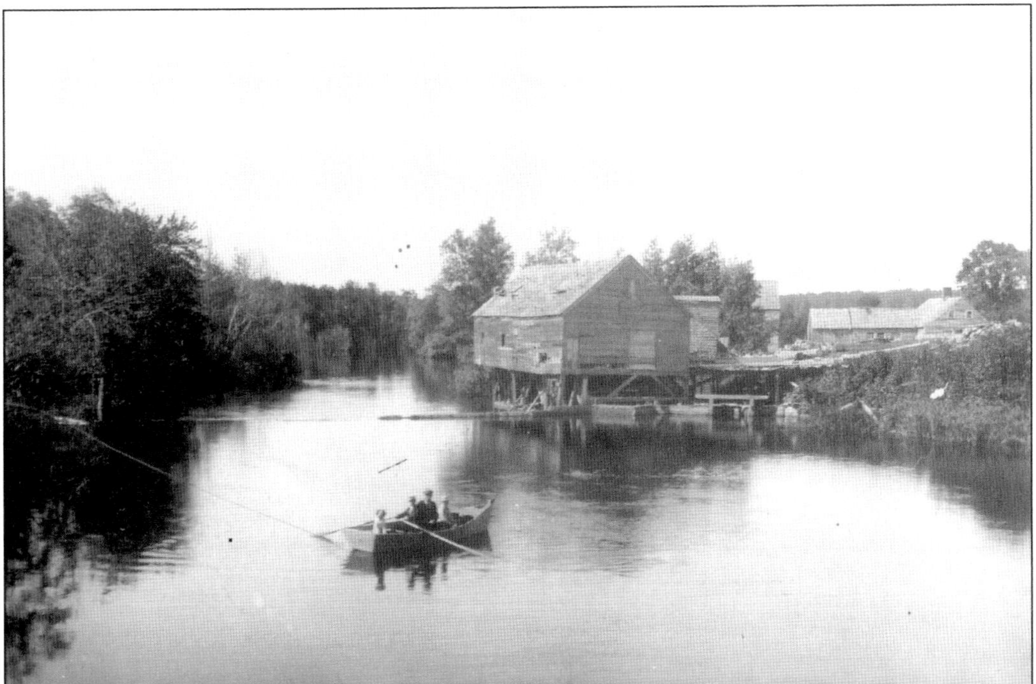

This 1892 view of the Hayes Mill (first Porter, later Perley) on the Royal River off Mill Road is the earliest known photograph of a mill in North Yarmouth. The house on the right belonged to Sylvanus Porter, who ran the mill for many years after his father, Barbour, helped build it in 1850. This tranquil scene of a father and his children rowing across the millpond with the quiet sawmill on the west bank may have been taken in July, when mills were closed down so that farmers could hay their fields. The millpond was created by a wooden dam, which was eventually replaced by a concrete one (removed in the 1960s). A gristmill, likely powered by the same dam, was located on the east side of the river in 1892. Many townspeople recall swimming and fishing for eels in this millpond. The original Porter Mill was begun around the time of the closing of the town's first mill, Marston's Mill on Chandler Brook, which ground grain and cut wood from the 1790s until the 1850s. (Courtesy of Lincoln Merrill Jr.)

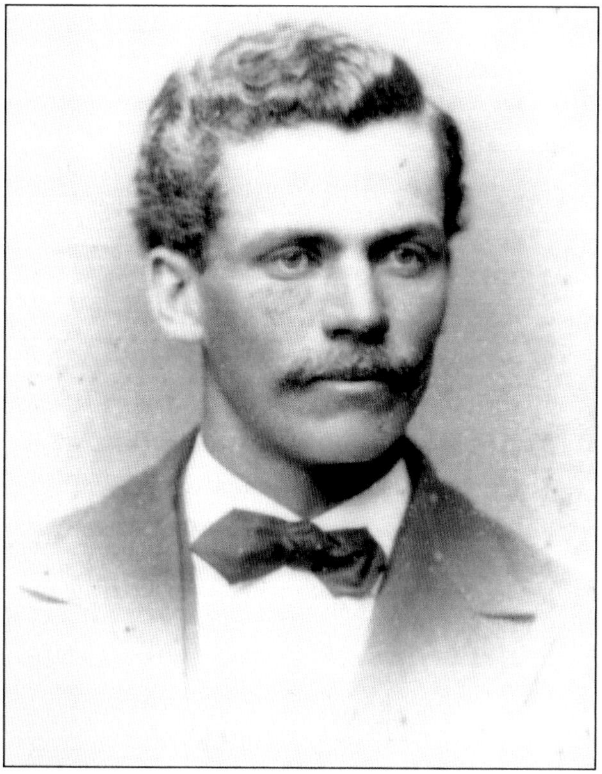

Isaac E. Hayes purchased the Hayes Mill in 1885 and raised his family in the home his father built at 395 New Gloucester Road above the Royal River. His sawmill was noted for its long saw carriage, which could cut boards up to 30 feet in length. Hayes Mill boards were used to build the Wescustogo Hotel, Dunn School, and York's store, and its slabs fueled the kilns of the nearby Liberty and Gagnon brickyards. Local farmers used sawdust from the mill for animal bedding and insulating icehouses.

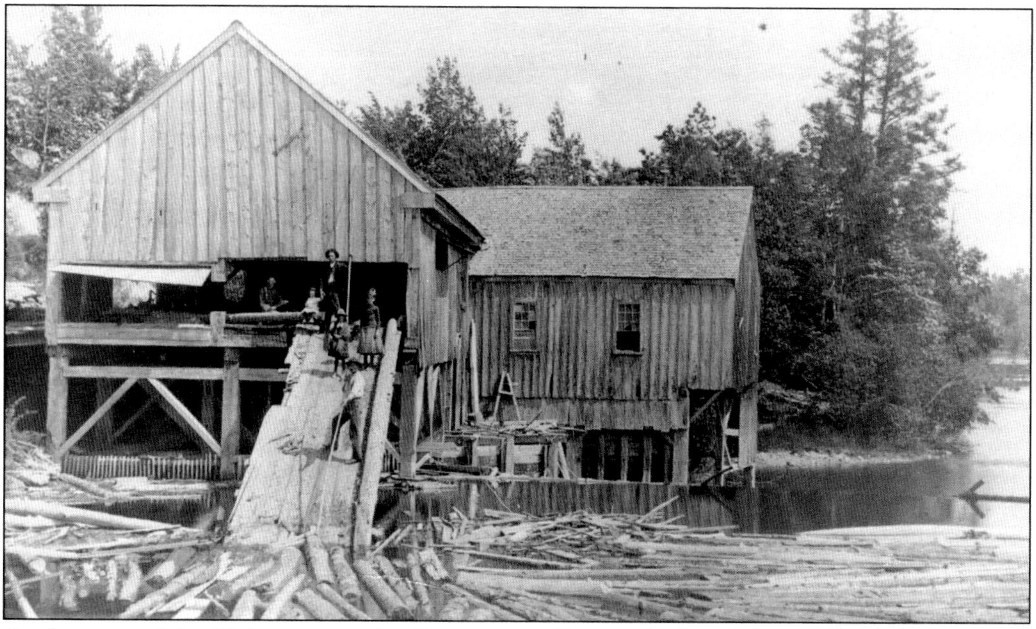

At the start of the 20th century, the Hayes sawmill was rebuilt on the east bank of the river. The new mill may have been constructed on the site of the old gristmill, which operated until 1901. This sawmill burned in 1908, but was rebuilt and operated by Isaac's son Maurice until closing permanently in 1946, after nearly a century of use. Isaac Hayes was a representative to the legislature and an active participant in town government.

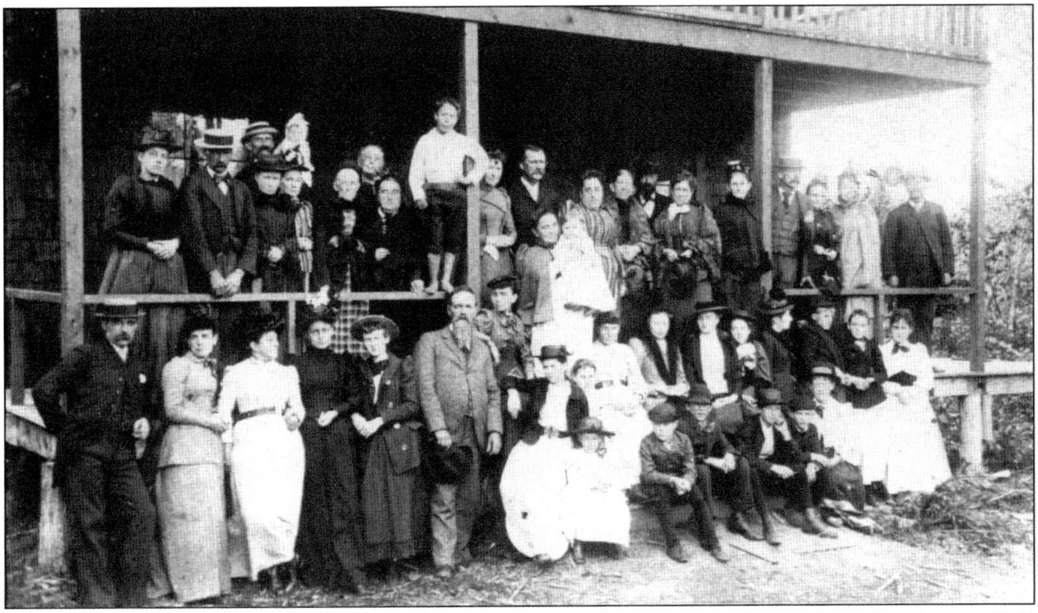

This *c.* 1900 image is the only known view of the Wescustogo Hotel, located on Wescustogo Hill (between Routes 9 and 231). It was a site for picnics and outings by local people and visitors. The building operated occasionally as a summer hotel beginning in 1891 and held dances until the rerouting of the Maine Central Railroad line in 1911 led to its demise. It was taken down in 1914, and the wood was used to build the Anderson house on Memorial Highway (seen on page 27).

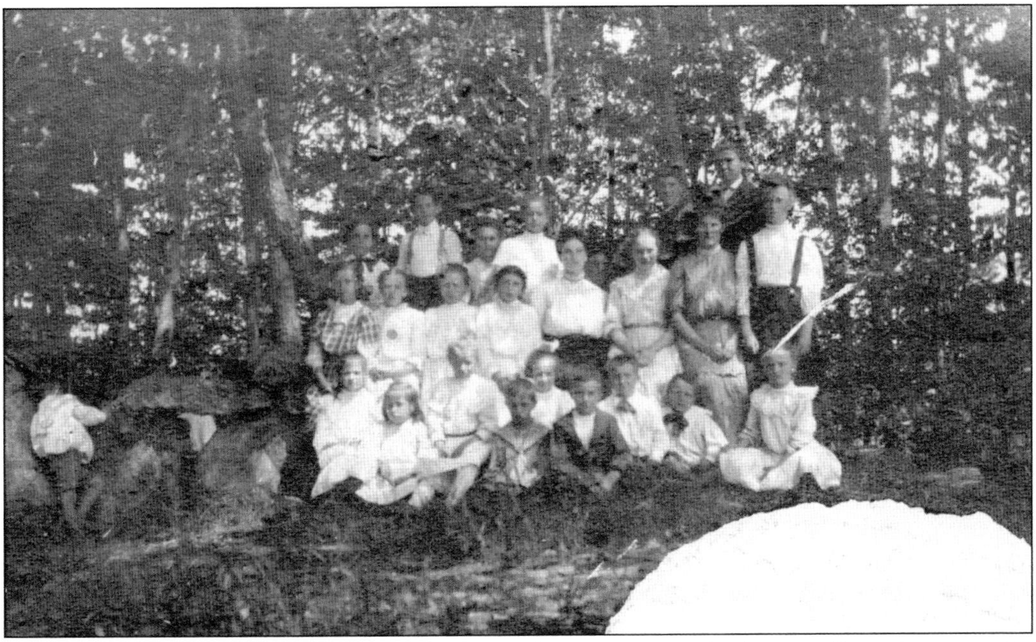

The Wescustogo Hotel advertised its pure mineral spring water, which was collected in a granite basin where it flowed out of the nearby ledge. The water was bottled and sold as a popular commodity around the beginning of the 20th century. Visitors accessed the hotel by rail or by the steamboat *Hoyt*, which traveled up the Royal River from Yarmouth. Here local schoolchildren enjoy an outing believed to be near the site of the spring. (Courtesy of Ginger Collins.)

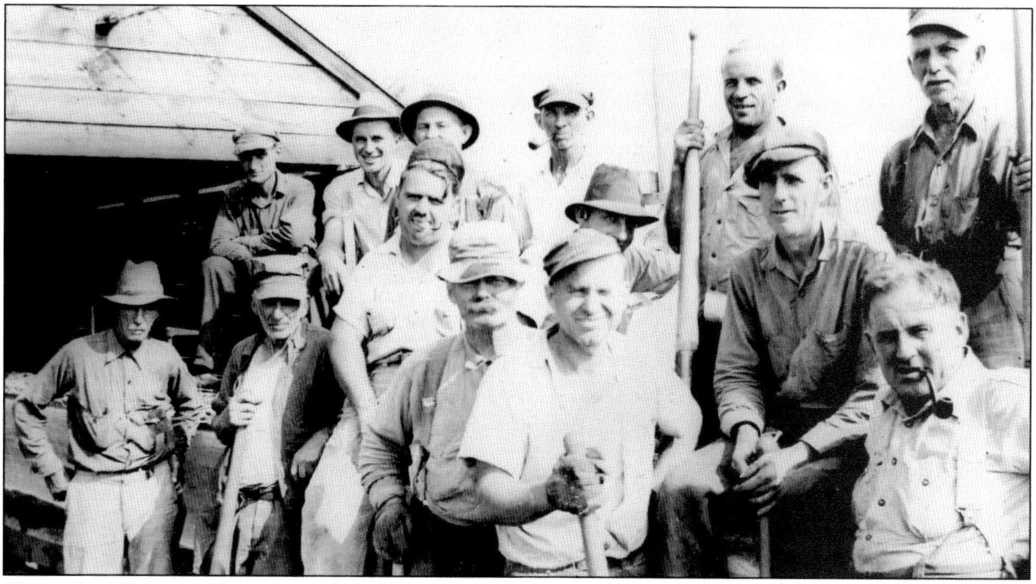

Philip Knight, seen above with his crew, operated a sawmill and lumberyard at Crockett's Corner, between Hallowell and West Pownal Roads, from the 1920s to 1953. Shown on August 24, 1942, from left to right are (first row) Jerry Connor, Allen Carter, John Gregor, Clarence Fickett, Earle Fickett, Clifford Anderson, Fred Upton, and Philip Knight; (second row) Arthur Atkins, Frank Knight, Lewis Rowe (the sawyer), George Bragdon, Henry St. Claire, and Wilbur Chadbourne. Knight was a large employer who cut lumber for building materials and sold building supplies. He also made boxes for farmers to ship their produce to market. In the photograph below, a truck from the Portland Barrel Company is loaded with these boxes in 1938. (Courtesy of Marion Reed.)

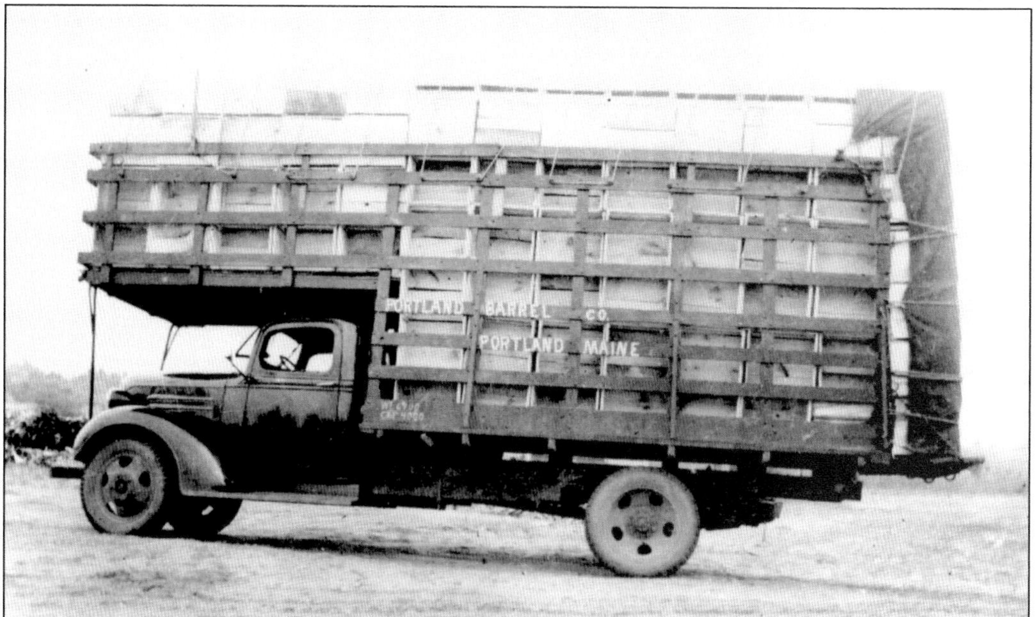

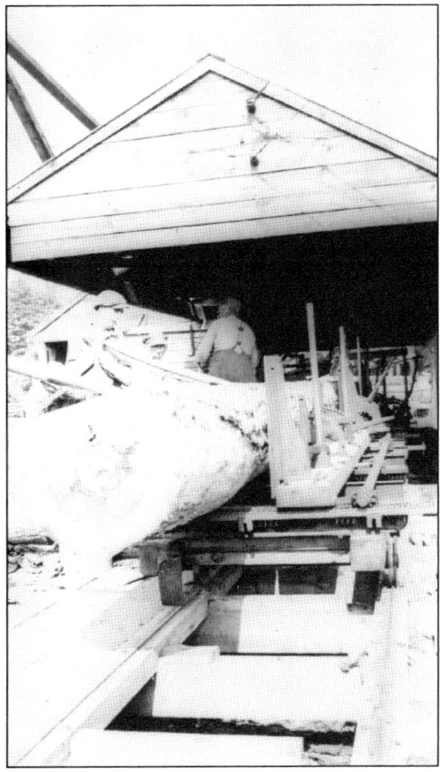

After the Japanese attack on Pearl Harbor, the Casco Bay Shipbuilding Company was commissioned to make five wooden barges, which could be built faster than steel-hulled vessels and could not be detected by magnetic mines. Local sawmill owner Philip Knight was hired to locate, cut, and plane the wood needed for these Red Oak barges, named for the wood that was their major component. The trees were cut all over southern Maine. At right, workers at Knight's Mill cut a 1,051-board-foot log into oak stem for the bow in August 1942. These large logs were processed into planks and sent to South Freeport, where the barges were built. Below, the first Red Oak is launched in 1943. (Right, courtesy of Marion Reed; below, courtesy of Ginger Collins.)

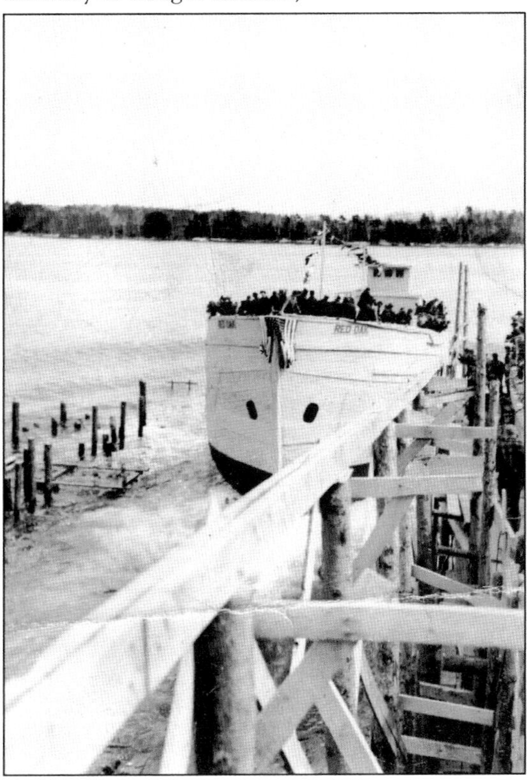

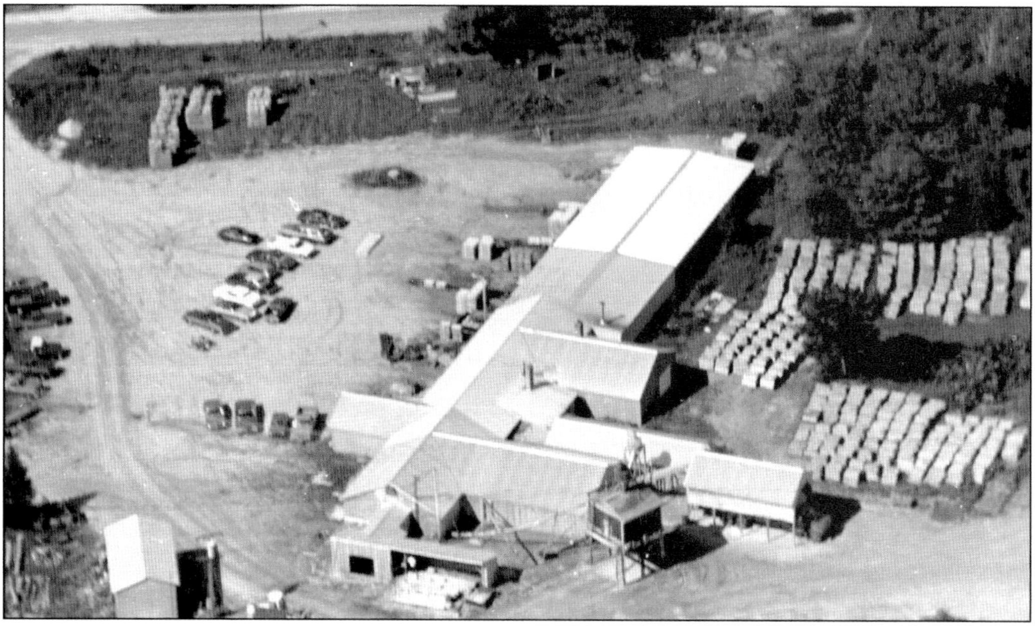

Clifford G. Anderson started a woodworking business making snowshoes and baseball bats from his home on Memorial Highway during the 1930s. The bats were made on a lathe by hand and were sold to high school and college teams. Snowshoes, selling for $5 to $8 a pair, were made with cowhide Anderson cleaned in the nearby Toddy Brook. By 1938, he had begun producing wooden lobster traps, which became his main commodity after World War II. In 1953, Anderson and his sons purchased Knight's Mill at Crockett's Corner and expanded their business to the site shown above. The facility employed about 35 people, while another 25 worked at home knitting the heads (netting) for the traps. Anderson and Sons produced about 50,000 traps per year, making it the largest manufacturer in the country. Clifford's sons Lewis (left) and Richard appear below with their wooden traps about 1953. (Courtesy of the Anderson family.)

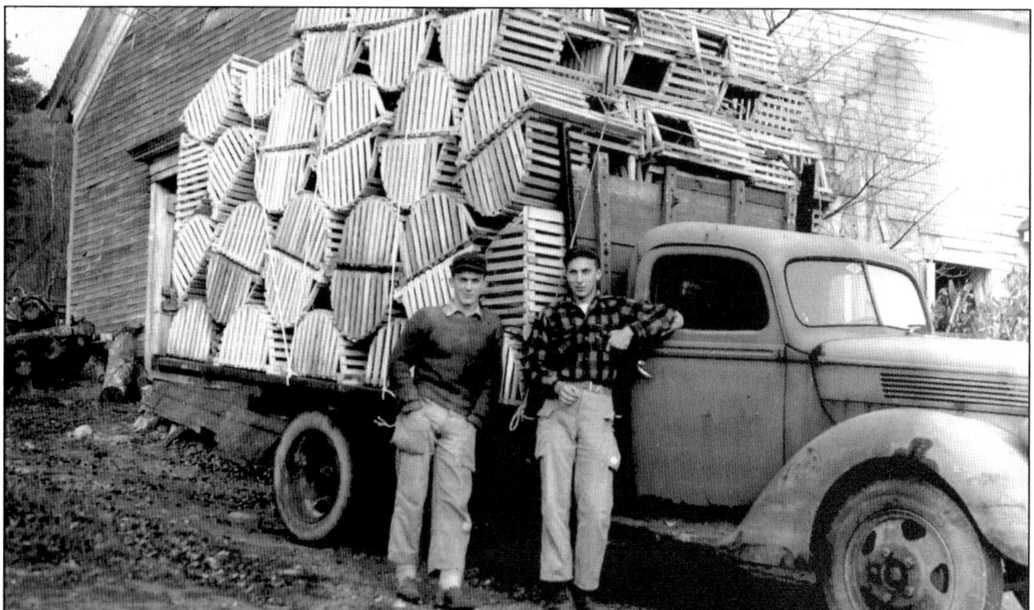

The Mill Road was an industrial center during most of the 20th century, as three major brickyards operated near where the Royal River crossed. The vast clay deposits in this area supplied the raw material for the bricks. French families such as the LaChances, the Blaises, the Libertys, and the Gagnons owned the yards. They hired workers from Quebec who had moved to Lewiston to make bricks from spring until the first fall frost. A separate crew traveled from yard to yard and burned the bricks in wood-fired kilns that ran 24 hours a day for 7 to 10 days per firing. In the image at right of the Blais yard, Edmund Blais sets newly molded bricks in the sun to dry before they are placed in the kiln. Seen below around 1965, the Fred S. Liberty brickyard was later known as the Royal River Brickyard. (Right, courtesy of Irene Lavoie.)

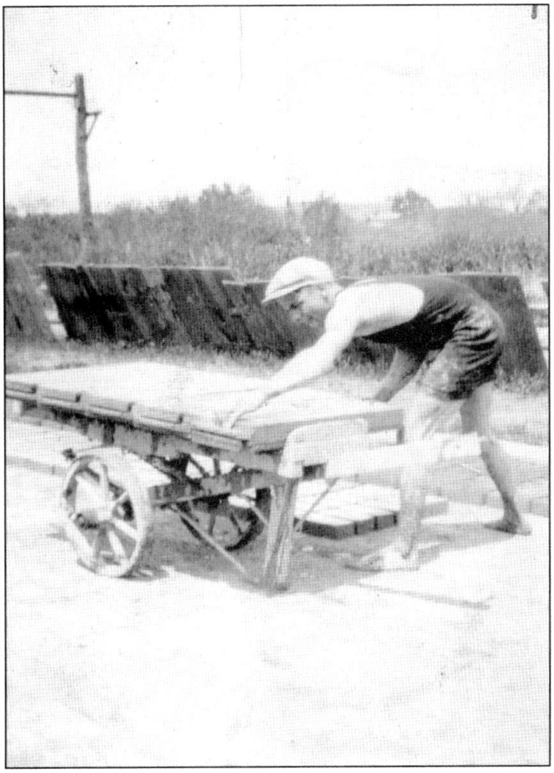

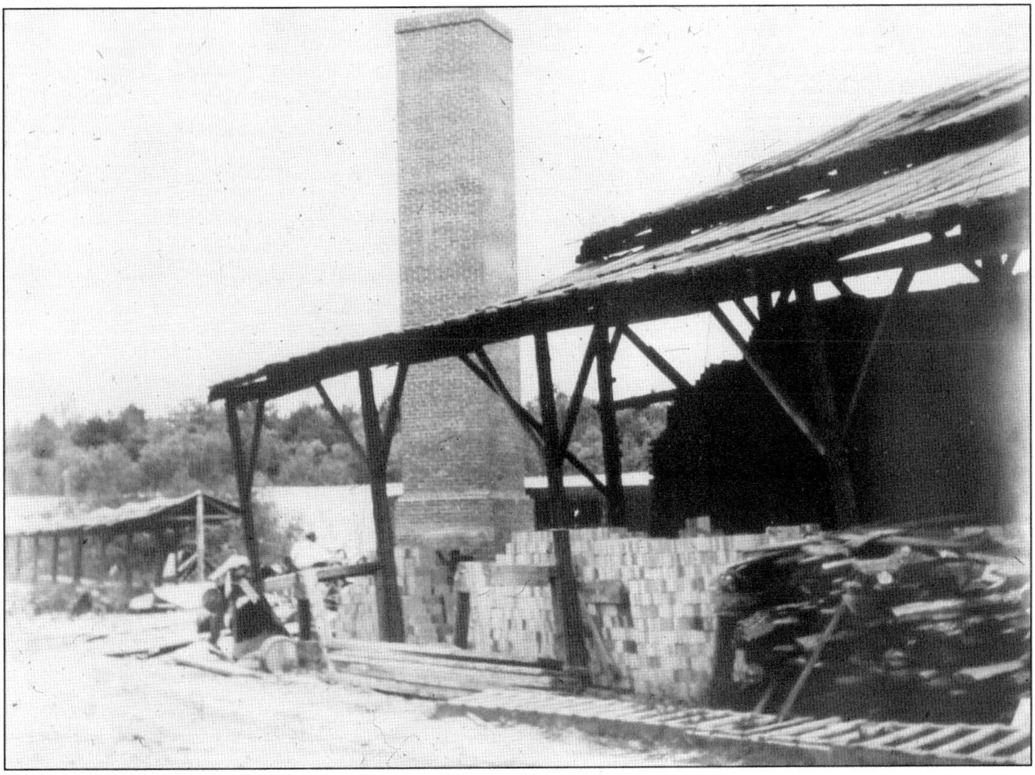

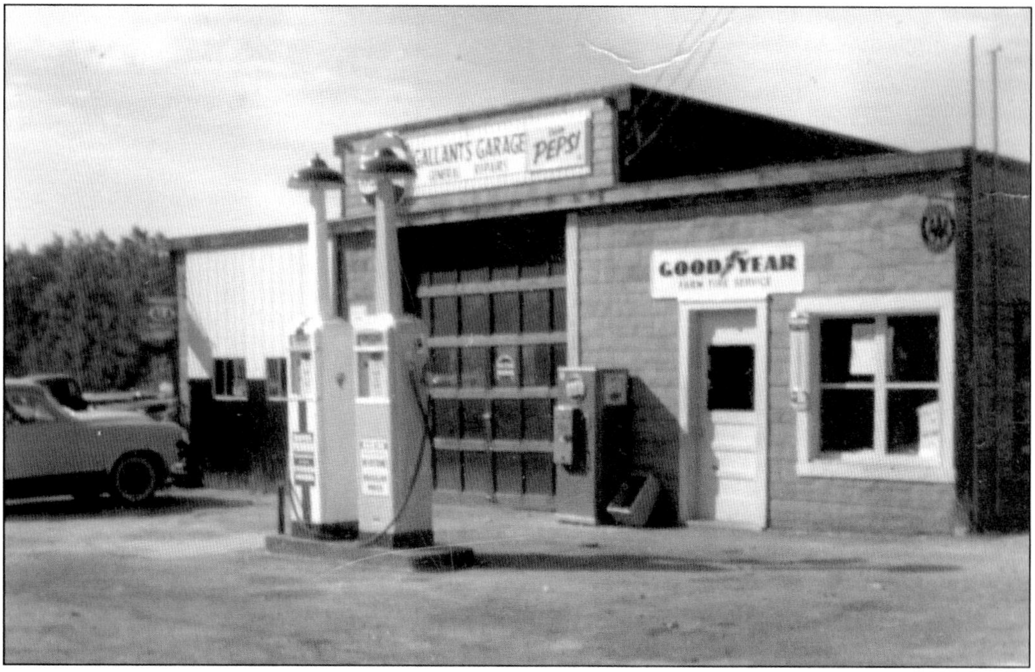

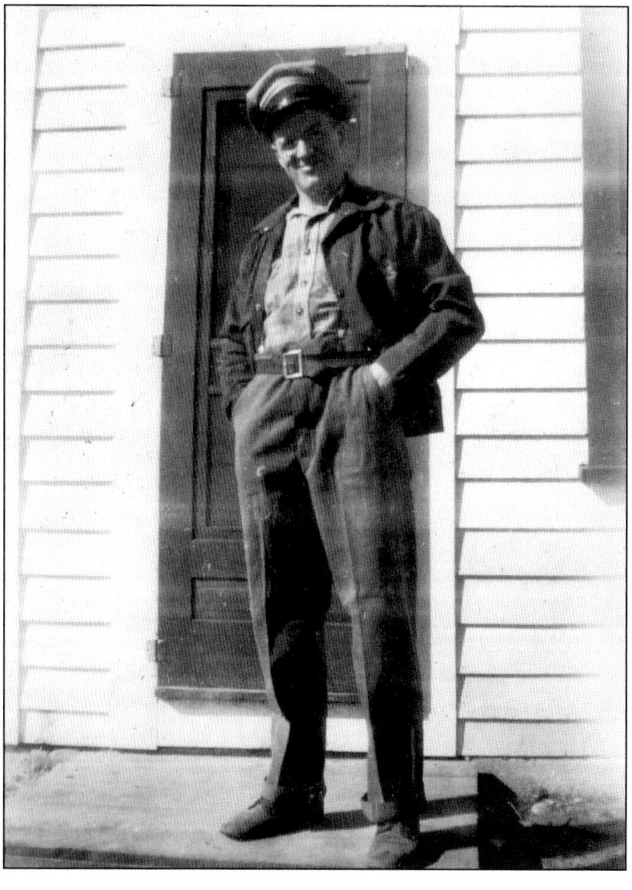

In the early 1940s, Osborne "Ossie" Jewett built the above garage at 712 New Gloucester Road, where he sold gasoline and repaired automobiles. It was just down the street from the home where he grew up with his large family and parents, Ralph and Laura. He later moved to Raymond to work in a summer camp and served as master of the Grange there. Purchased by Cliff Gallant, the garage operates today as an automobile salvage yard. Wearing service station attire, Ossie poses at left on the porch of his home next to the garage. (Above, courtesy of the Gallant family; left, courtesy of the Jewett family.)

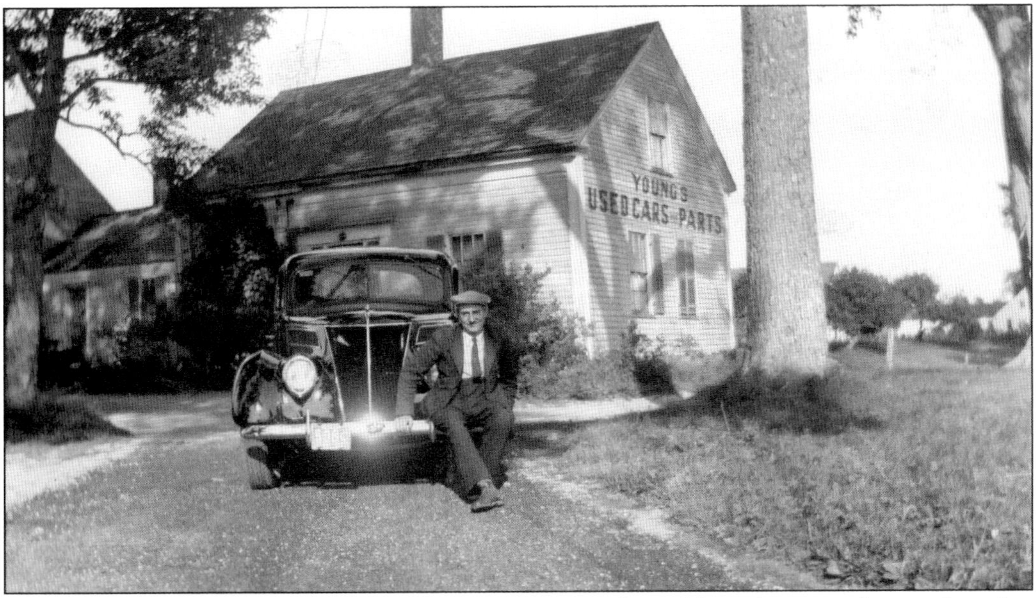

Orinn Young (1888–1962) was an early businessman who sold used cars and parts from his c. 1812 residence at 786 North Road, the first house after the Yarmouth town line. Here Young is seated on the bumper of his car about 1943.

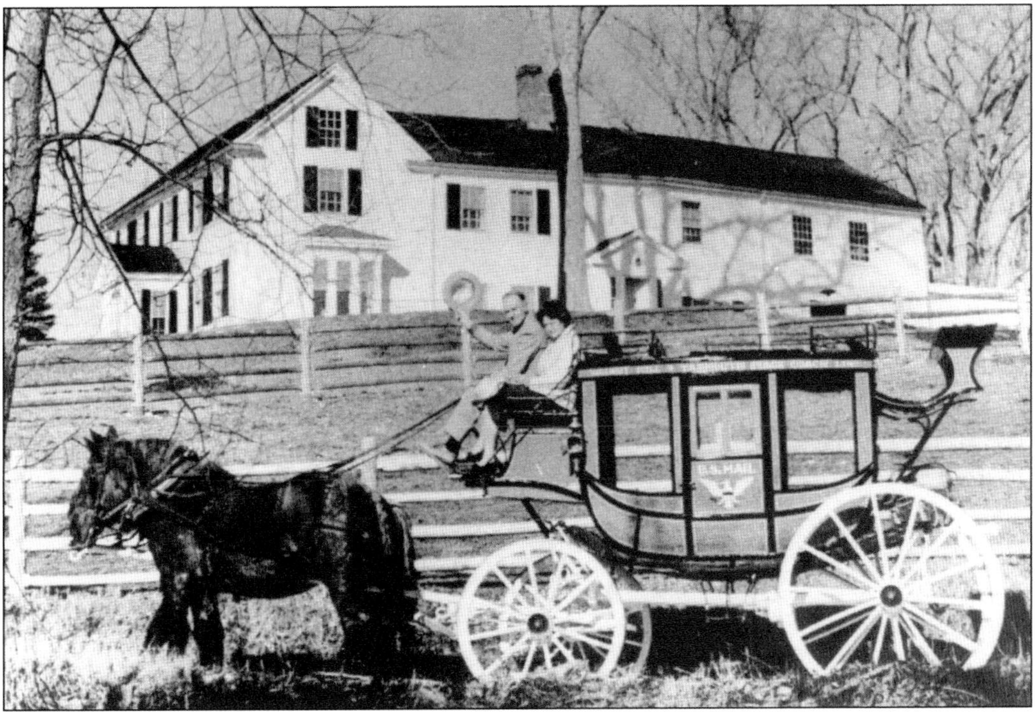

Col. Byron Skillin and his wife, Adele, pose on their 1878 Concord stage in front of their home at 10 Shenandoah Hill off Gray Road. In 1962, Skillin retired and opened Squire Skillins Country Inn at his family's Deerbrook Farm, which had a riding stable and carriage collection. This c. 1820 Federal home has been extensively remodeled. A mural depicting the stagecoach, once painted on the barn by Eugene Collins, served as a local landmark.

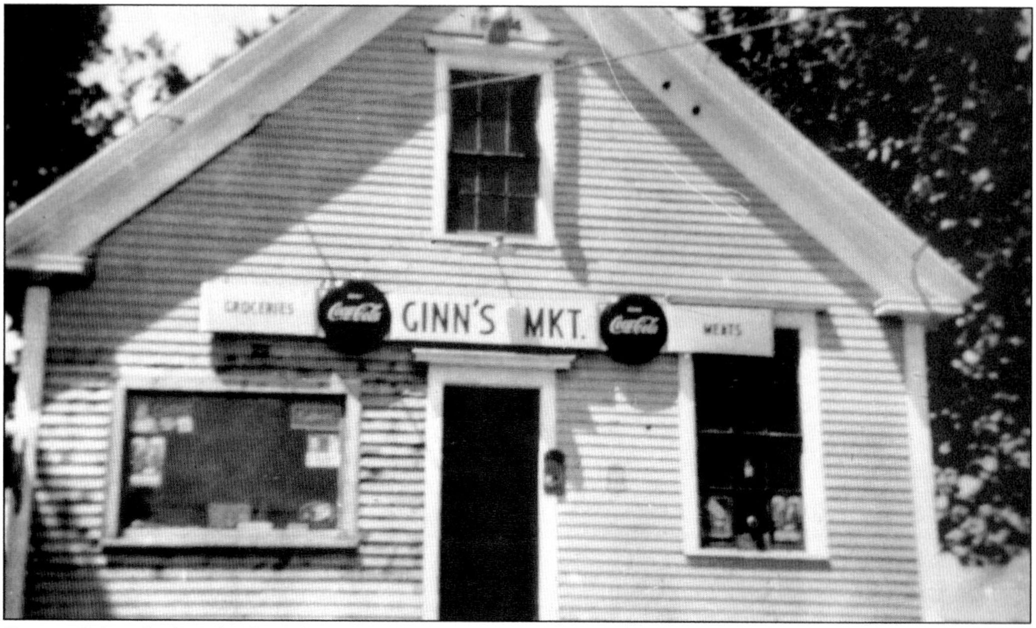

Dunn School closed after the new Memorial School opened in 1950. Don and Jennie Barter Ginn purchased the structure and remodeled it into a small store and a home for their new family. They sold groceries and even converted an old bus into a traveling grocery store. The bus ran a regular schedule and made stops at homes, allowing residents to buy their groceries by walking up and down the center aisle. It closed in 1953.

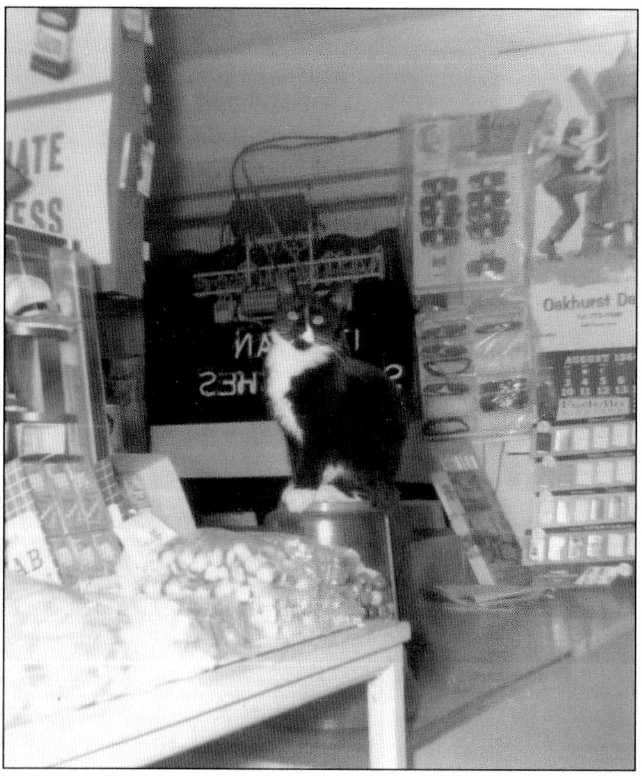

Arthur and Irene Blais Lavoie opened this convenience store at 401 Gray Road near Mill Road in the 1960s. For about eight years, the couple served sandwiches and pizza to workers from the brickyards and Pineland Center. Irene installed an intercom to hear break-ins. One night after a loud crash, Arthur ran to the store with his gun to find the cat had knocked over the gumball machine. (Courtesy of Irene Lavoie.)

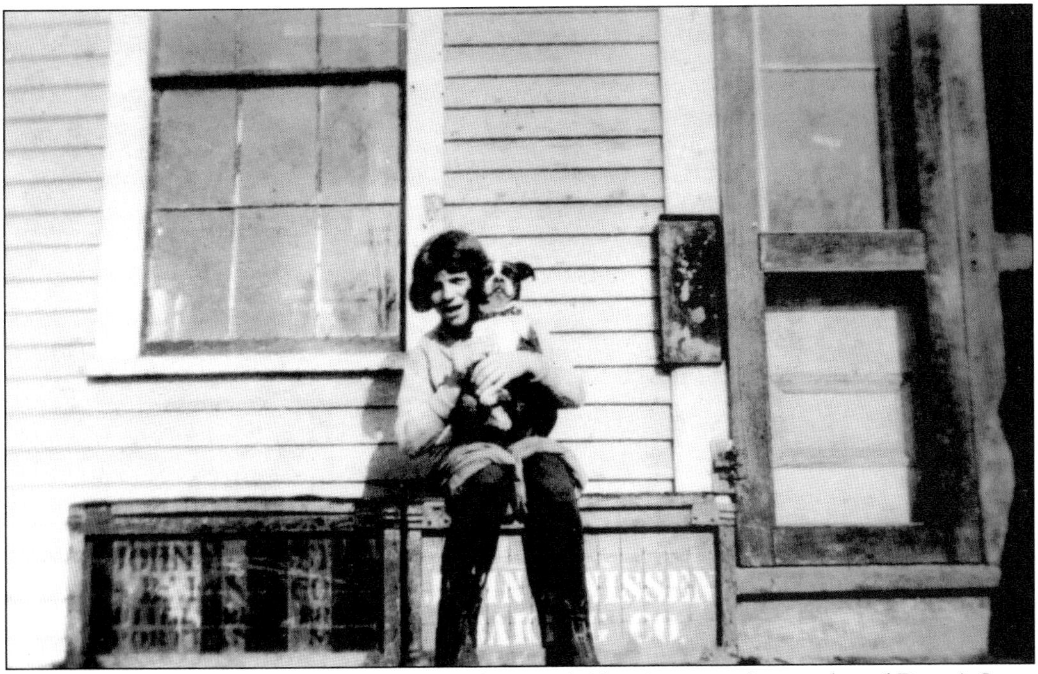

Margery M. Loring was the daughter of Frank W. and Alice Loring, who purchased Dunn's Store in 1901 and ran it for 40 years as an active general store and post office. Here she poses on a John J. Nissen bread box in front of the store about 1930. Margery married Herbert Blackstone of Pownal and, when her mother died, she became the youngest postmistress in Maine. (Courtesy of Ginger Collins.)

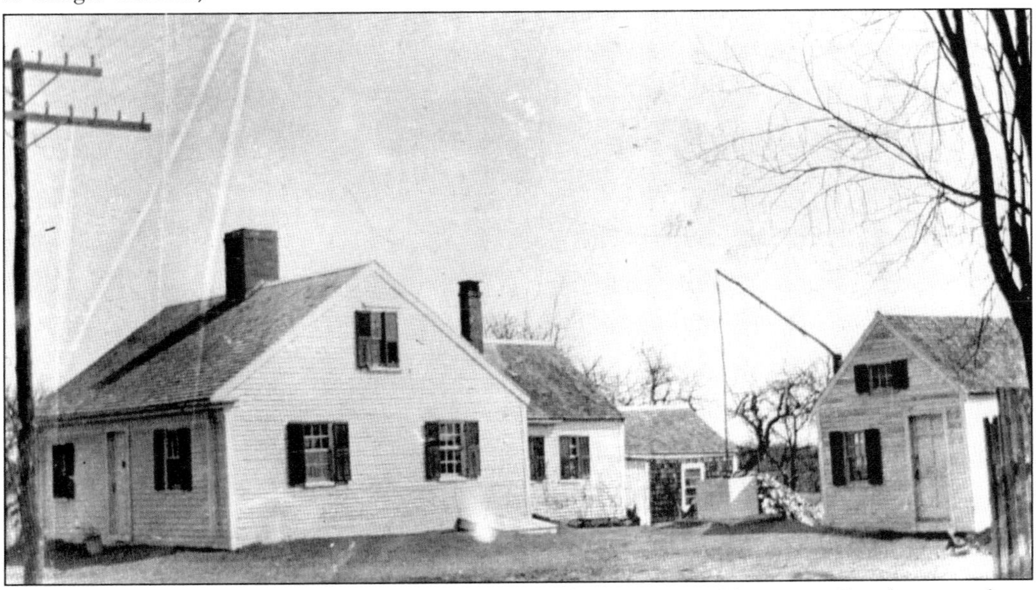

The William Lufkin house, pictured in 1908, stood at 13 New Gloucester Road, across from the Congregational church. Active in the Wescustogo Grange, the Lufkins ran the cooperative Grange store at their home from 1874 until William died in 1900. The store bought goods such as grain, plaster, and ashes by the carload for the members, who met in the vestry across the street. The well-sweep was used to bring water up from the dug well.

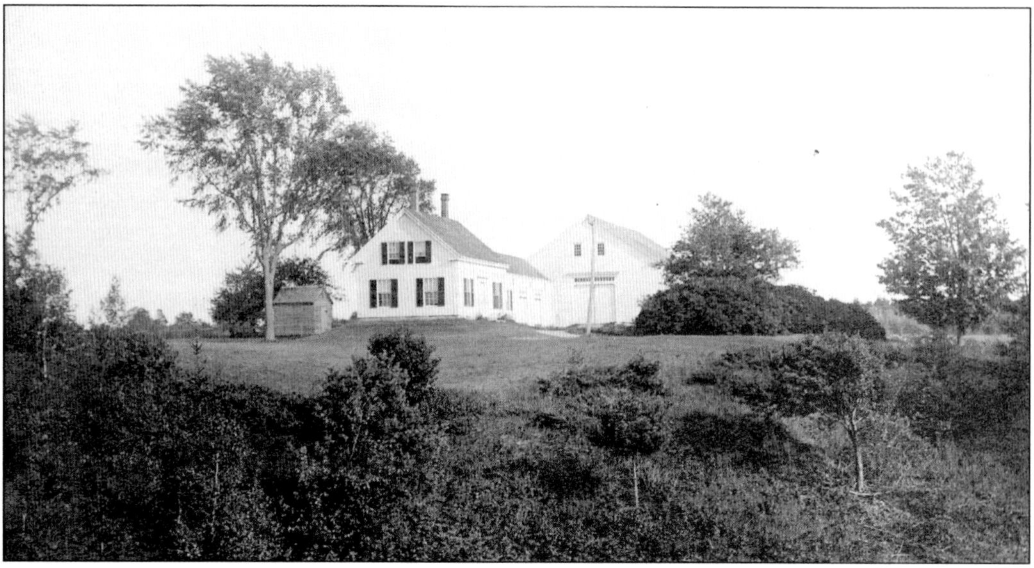

Skyline Farm is the home of a carriage museum on The Lane located behind this Greek Revival residence. It was built in 1857 on land originally owned by early settler Thomas Loring. A nonprofit organization was formed in 1999 to preserve the farm. The group purchased it the next year and opened the museum, which presently includes about 100 antique carriages and sleighs. In 2006, the museum held its first exhibit in the newly renovated riding arena.

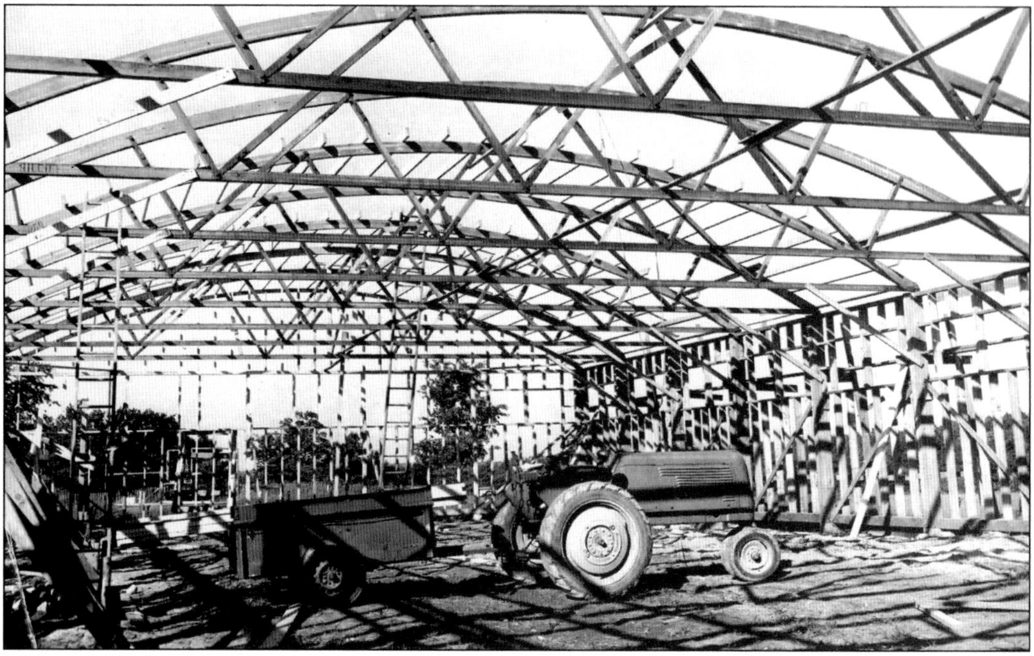

Abbie Dolloff, whose family once owned Skyline Farm, and her husband, Carleton Semmes, bought the property in 1944 and provided its current name. Semmes was active in the town, serving as a selectman and school bus driver. This 1959 photograph shows the construction of what is believed to be the oldest surviving indoor riding arena in the state, built by Semmes for his stable and trail riding business. Many local residents learned to ride at Skyline Farm, and Semmes became 4-H leader for the Crop and Canter Club. (Courtesy of Sally Pierce.)

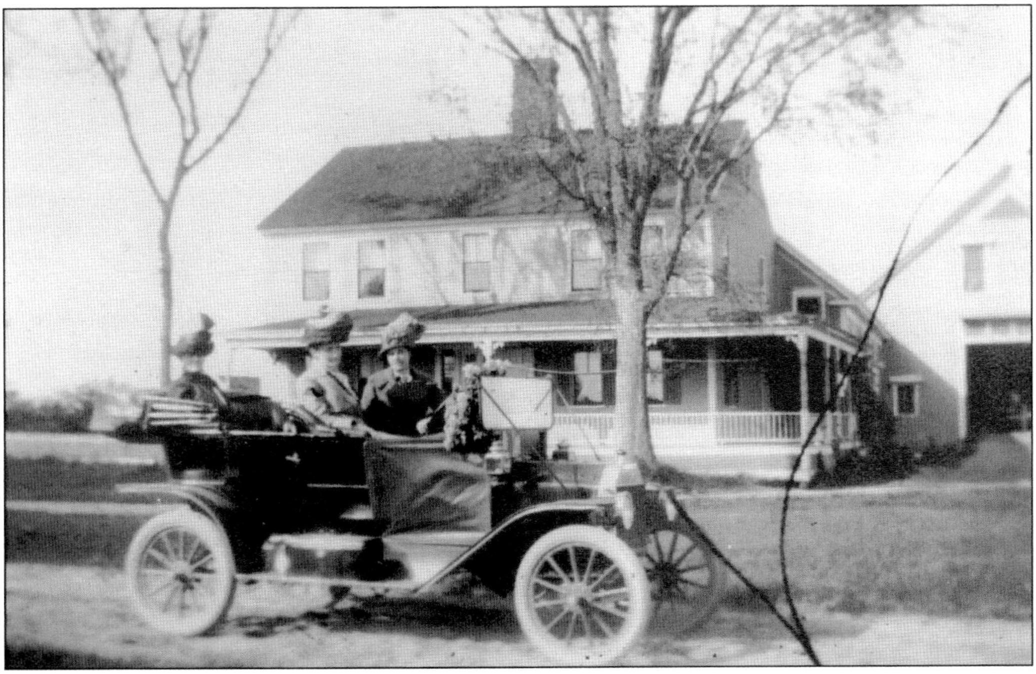

George E. and Fannie North Baston lived in the above home, built around 1857 for Samuel Baker, at Baston and Sweetser Roads. From the 1890s until the 1920s, they bottled and marketed mineral water from the Kohinoor Spring behind the farm. Selling for 15¢ a gallon, state assayer F. C. Robinson labeled it as good as Poland Spring water. The Bastons kept a journal that recorded remarks made by satisfied consumers and used them as testimonials. The spring closed when abutting landowner Yarmouth Water District pumped the water level low enough to dry it up. The porch shown in the above image no longer exists, and the barn was converted to house poultry. Right, Father George H. Baston appears in 1919 in front of his adjacent c. 1830 Federal-style home. Isabella Hayes, sitting in the front passenger seat of the car, is the great-great-granddaughter of Samuel Baker. (Above, courtesy of Mark Heath; right, courtesy of the Small family.)

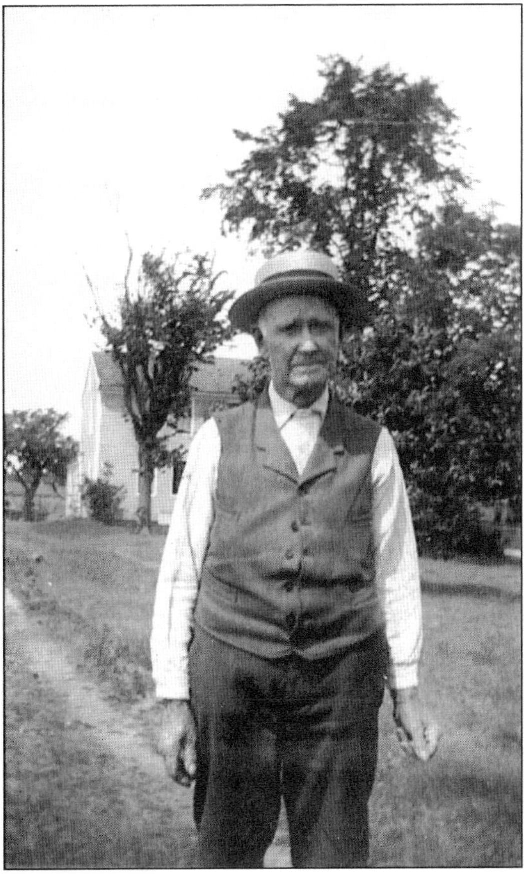

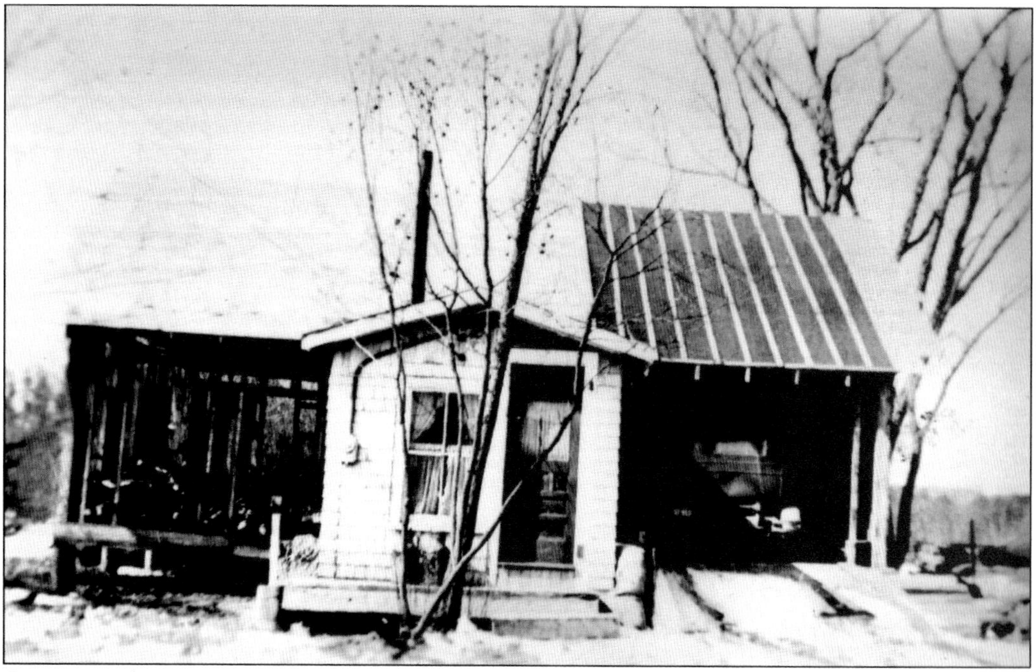

Constructed as a small camp in the 1930s by Fred Litchfield, the above building served as an ice-cream store run by Charles Dunn's daughters Ruth and Lucy on the side lawn of their home at Dunn's Corner. Their summer business consisted of selling ice cream, candy, and soda. One young customer even rode out from Yarmouth on a horse to get her treats. The store was eventually moved around the corner to Hallowell Road, where Richard and Minnie Long were building a house. The Longs lived here during a long construction period that was delayed by World War II. When their residence was completed, Long opened a business in his home called Long's Chinchilla Ranch, shown below in 1953. Cages full of the furry creatures inhabited his garage. Chinchilla fur was a rage at that time and he hoped to cash in.

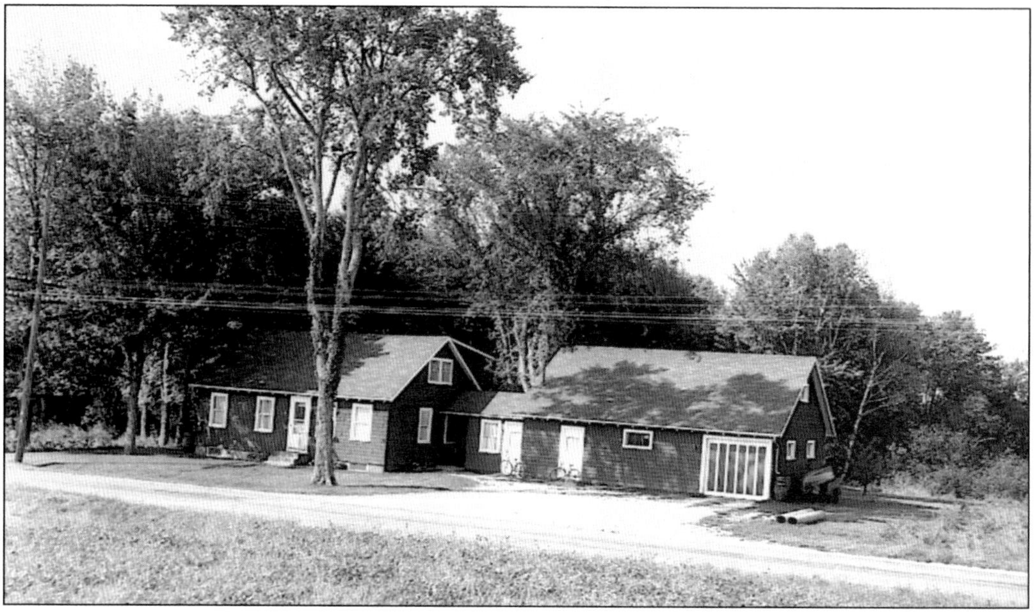

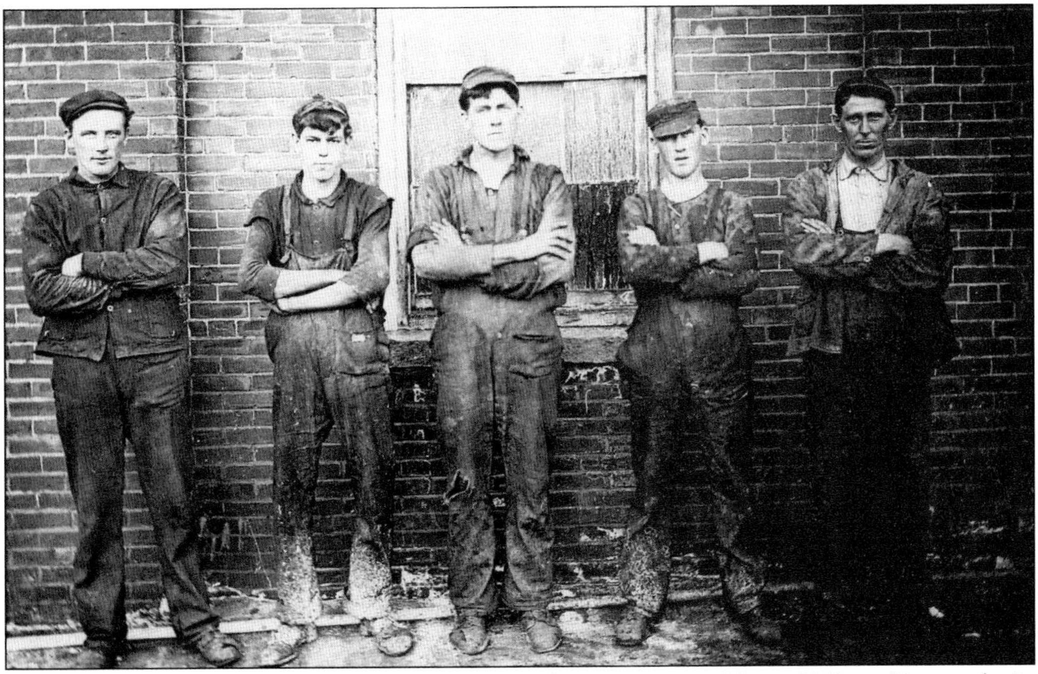

The Royal River supported many manufacturing businesses near Upper Falls in Yarmouth. In 1874, the Forest Paper Company, later a division of S. D. Warren in Westbrook, opened a large soda pulp paper mill there. Running until 1923, the mill bought pulpwood from North Yarmouth farmers. It employed local men including, from left to right, Lewis, Howard, Gilbert, and Horace Hamilton and an unknown man, pictured outside the mill in their work clothes about 1900.

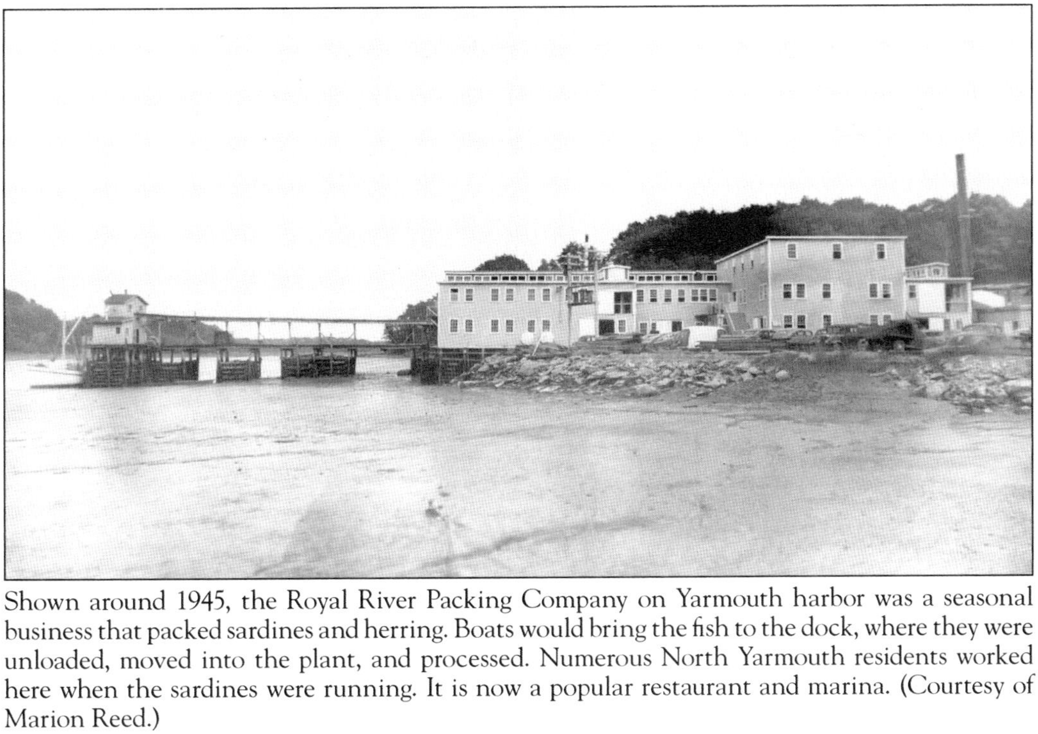

Shown around 1945, the Royal River Packing Company on Yarmouth harbor was a seasonal business that packed sardines and herring. Boats would bring the fish to the dock, where they were unloaded, moved into the plant, and processed. Numerous North Yarmouth residents worked here when the sardines were running. It is now a popular restaurant and marina. (Courtesy of Marion Reed.)

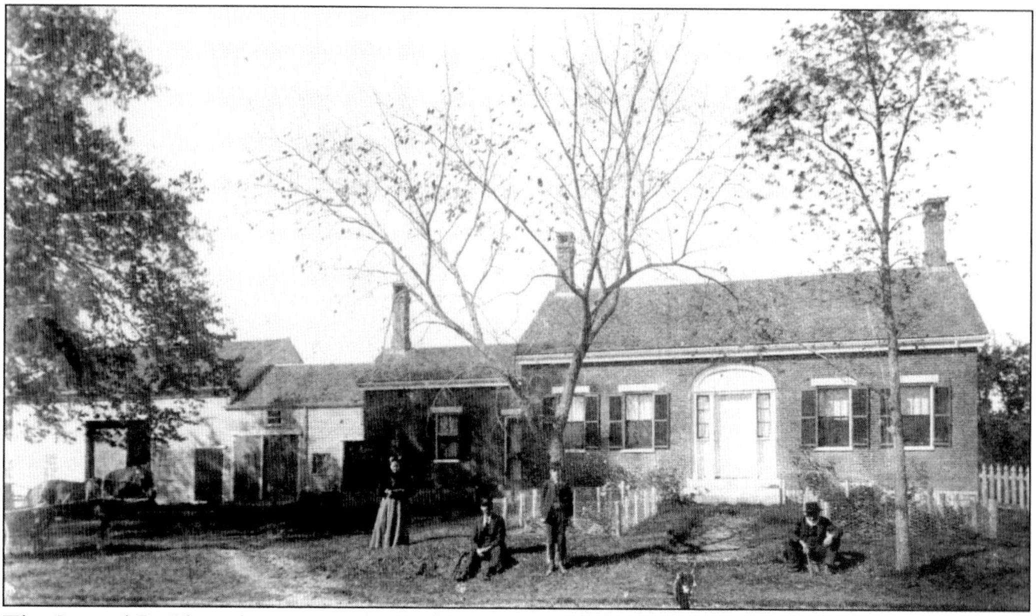

The Samuel B. Chase house, seen here about 1900, was constructed at 220 Cumberland Road in 1831. Chase was one of the town's earliest manufacturers of carriages and sleighs, and after his death in 1857, his sons carried on the business in Portland and elsewhere. An 1849 painting of this home shows the carriage-making shops to the right with ramps that allowed the vehicles to be wheeled to the second-floor paint shop. Chase also built ships in Walnut Hill that were then transported to the Yarmouth coast.

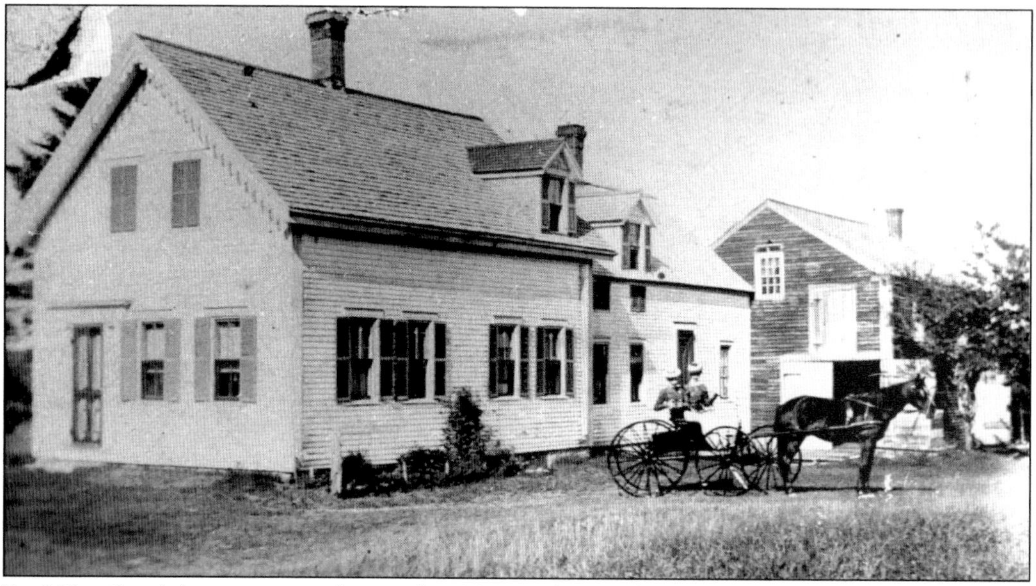

Fred Hamilton's home, pictured around 1900, was designed with distinctive period gingerbread trim and built at 643 Walnut Hill Road about 1840. Hamilton was a carriage painter who applied details to wagons and wheels. In 1905, he painted the market wagon of Frank Loring from Dunn's Depot, which is now in the Skyline Farm collection. Wagons were lifted by pulley into the barn's second floor, where Hamilton had a landscape mural painted on the wall. Two of his buildings are thought to have previously served as schoolhouses.

Shown in the 1930s, the building at 4 Parsonage Road has been used in the transportation industry since it was built, a century and a half ago. John Staples Jr. made carriages here beginning in 1867. In 1889, William True purchased it for his blacksmith shop. The building was sold in 1933 to Roy Loring, who opened a car repair service and gasoline station and added a second-story garage apartment. In 1970, Ron and Candy Burgess bought the garage and began their auto body business. (Courtesy of Harold Small.)

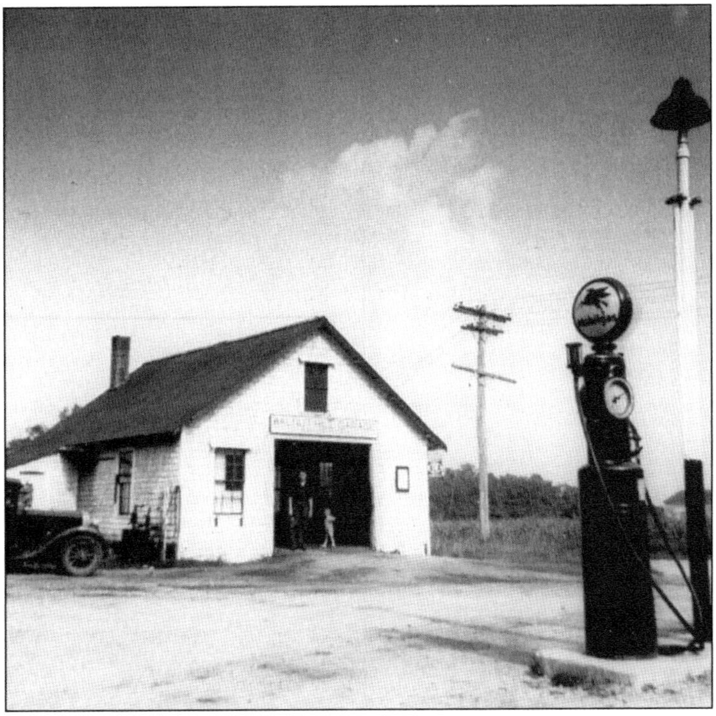

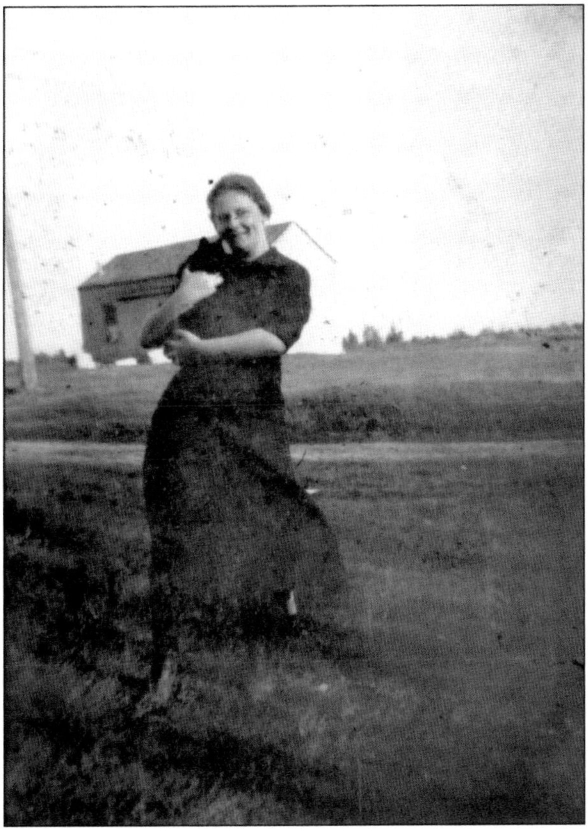

Crockett's Corner boasted an early wheelwright shop owned by Samuel Worthley Jr. He repaired wagons and wheels until at least 1871. By 1892, his space had become a workshop for monument maker Edwin Lombard, who also bought Worthley's house at the corner in 1911. Neighbors could hear Lombard's hammer ring as he chipped away the stone for local cemeteries. Some of his headstones are seen here about 1919, behind Eva Crockett. (Courtesy of Marion Reed.)

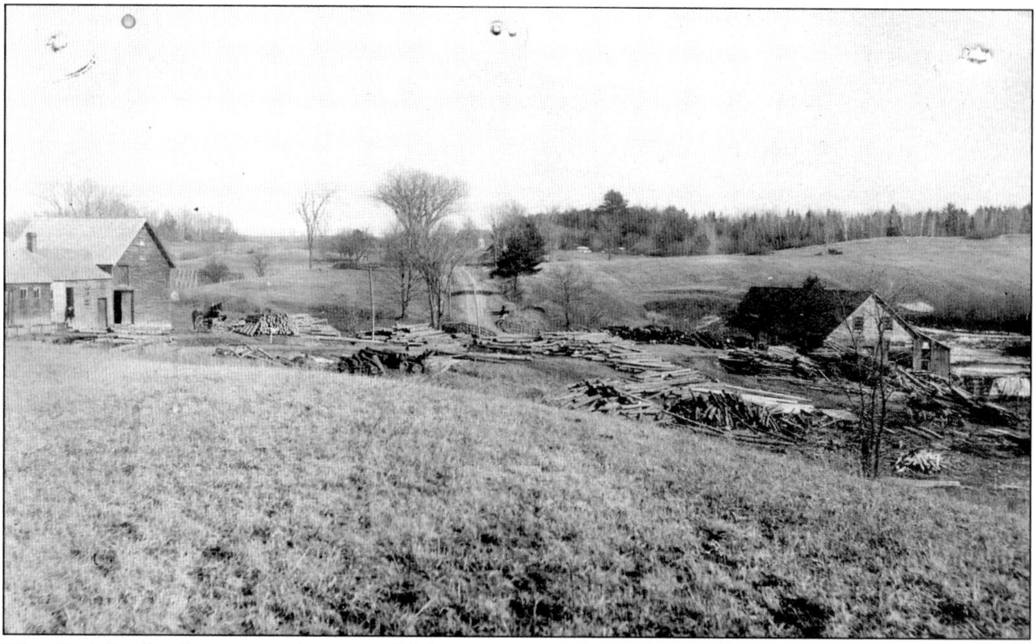

The Knight family operated successful businesses in Pownal, North Yarmouth, and Yarmouth. Frank Knight ran this sawmill on the Hodsdon Road in Pownal, pictured around 1904. His son Frank A. Knight took a similar path and completed the forestry program at the University of Maine. He worked cruising timber, cutting wood lots, and clearing roads and later became the town of Yarmouth's tree warden for many years. (Courtesy of Frank Knight.)

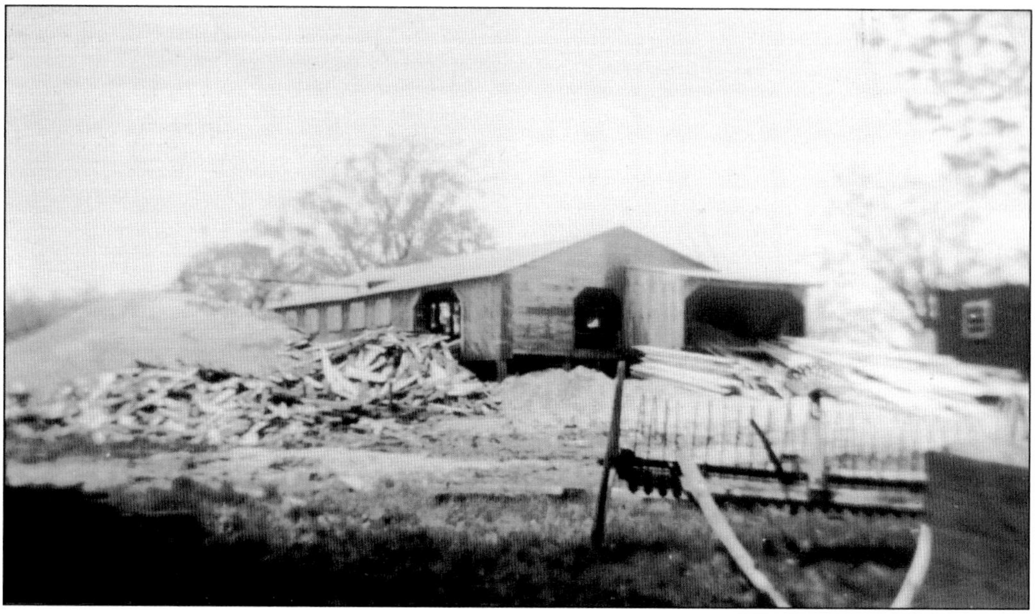

Everett L. Parker Sr., an early Maine state trooper, moved to the William B. Skillin home at 903 Sligo Road and built this sawmill, shown around 1950, across the street. He cut lumber of all types, but for lumberman Frank A. Knight he cut 18-inch-diameter elm tree trunks into wheel-shaped slices a few inches thick. Knight sold them to the Harris Company in Portland, where they were coated with rubber tires and used for rollers on fishing nets. (Courtesy of Everett Parker.)

Three

Land We Worked

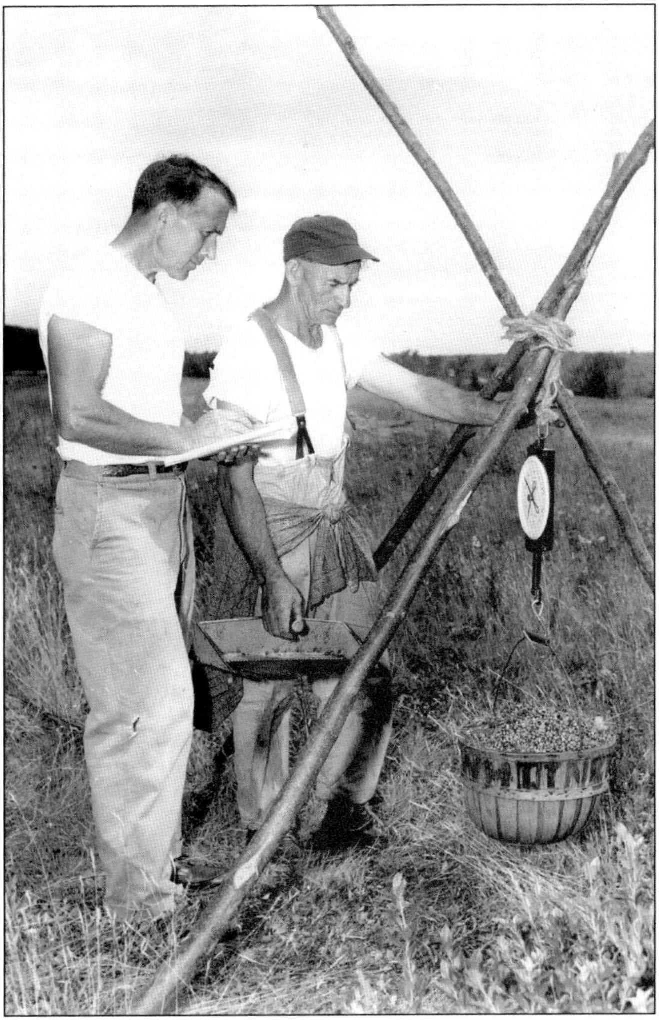

Frank A. Knight ran several large blueberry farms in North Yarmouth, Pownal, Durham, and Freeport from the 1950s to the 1970s. His business typically produced 20 tons of blueberries a year, although some good years brought in 50 tons. He hired local students to rake berries in the summer and paid them 4¢ per pound. Good rakers could do about 400 pounds per day, but Al Whitney of North Road, shown on the right weighing berries with Frank, could bring in 800 pounds. Frank also worked in the granite quarries his family owned at Royal and Hodsdon Roads in North Yarmouth and Pownal. He helped haul the granite to Yarmouth for the Orr's/Bailey's Island bridge and mixed mortar for the current Key Bank building on Main Street. He unloaded railroad cars of grain at his uncle's grain store at Dunn's Depot and worked for his cousin Philip Knight at his sawmill in North Yarmouth. Later Frank ran his own company cutting timber and clearing roadways. (Courtesy of Frank Knight.)

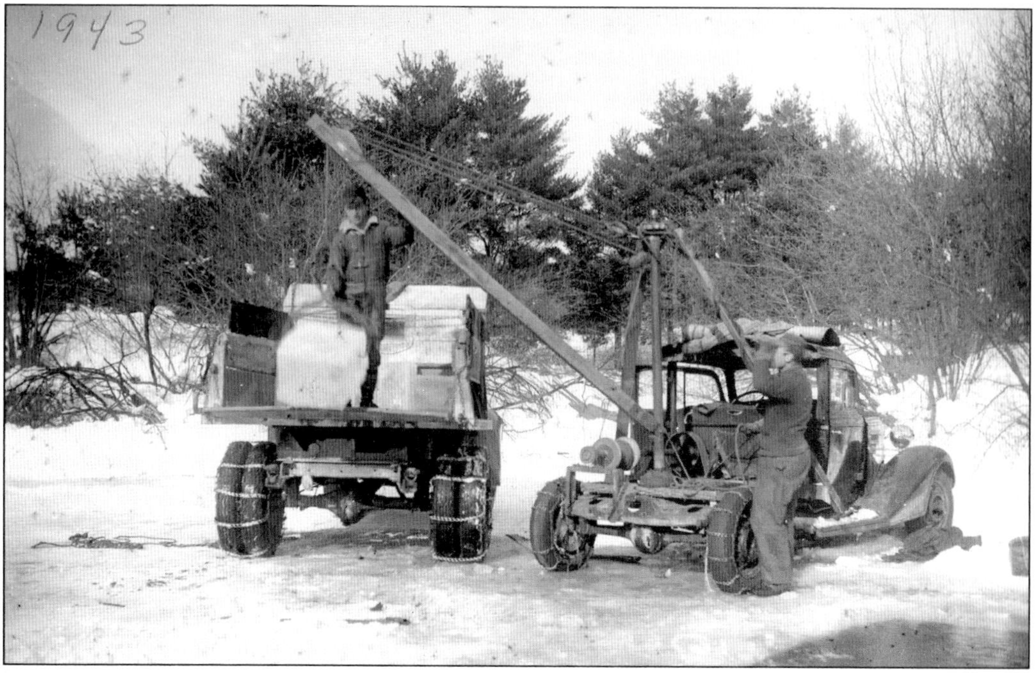

Ice cutting was an important winter activity. Without electricity to run refrigeration units, residents needed ice to keep things cool in the summer. They had insulated wooden icehouses in which layers of ice were packed with sawdust to prevent melting. In this 1943 image, dairy farmer Norman Reed (right), assisted by Oscar Braley, harvests ice from the Royal River behind his farm using machinery he built. He used the ice to keep his milk cool first in an icehouse and later in an old silo. (Courtesy of Marion Reed.)

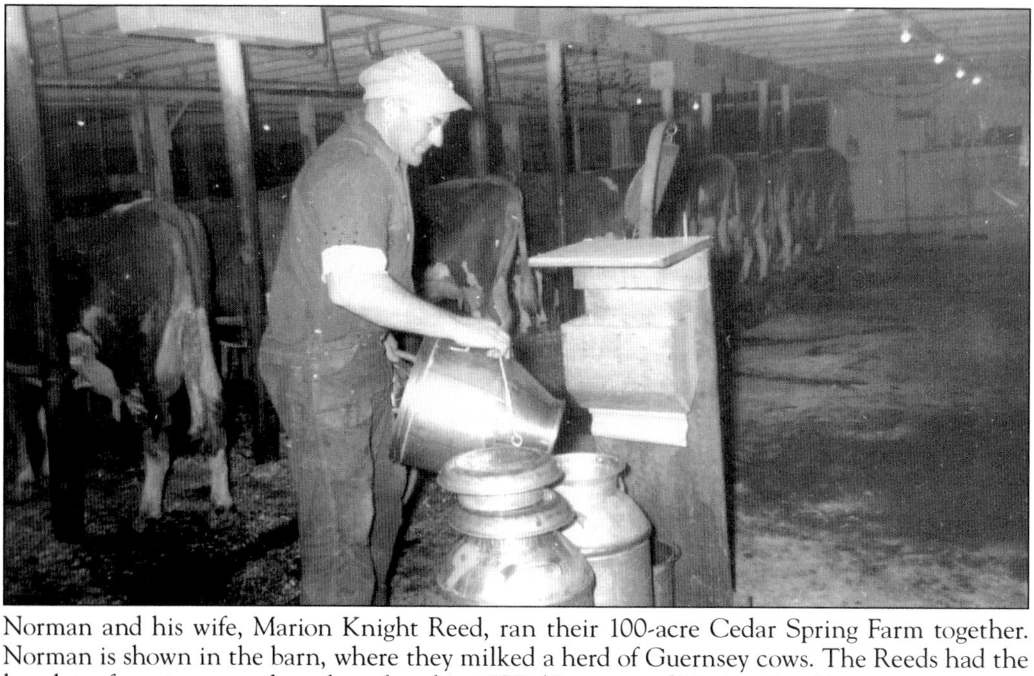

Norman and his wife, Marion Knight Reed, ran their 100-acre Cedar Spring Farm together. Norman is shown in the barn, where they milked a herd of Guernsey cows. The Reeds had the last dairy farm in town when they closed in 1977. (Courtesy of Marion Reed.)

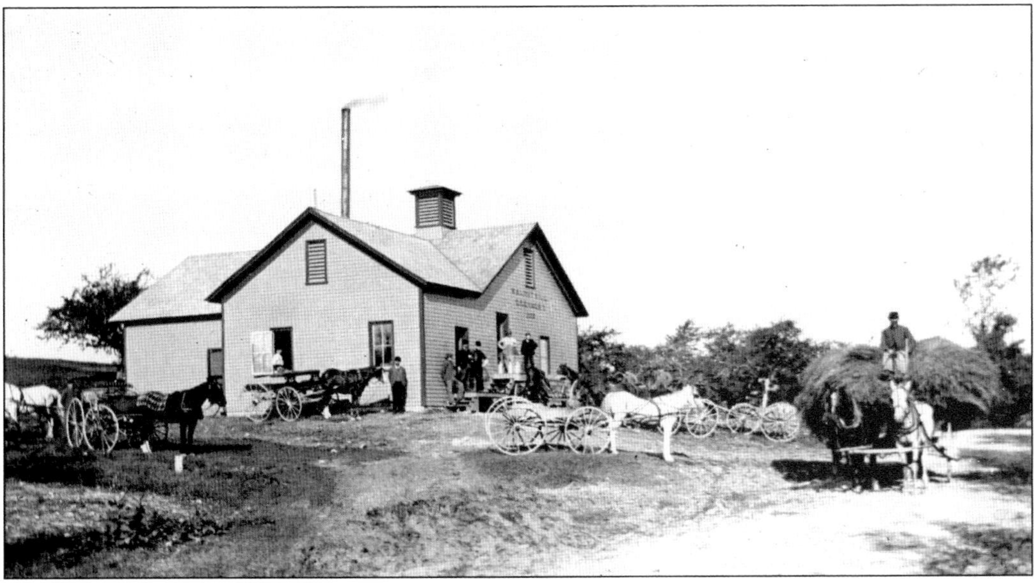

Native Henry S. Osgood (1834–1903), a Portland businessman, started the Walnut Hill Creamery in 1892. Built near the headwaters of Toddy Brook along Walnut Hill Road, it manufactured butter using local farmers' milk and water from Hobart Spring. The business failed in less than two years, and the building was used as a dance hall and corn-canning factory. Older residents recall that the structure (torn down in the early 1900s) was painted yellow.

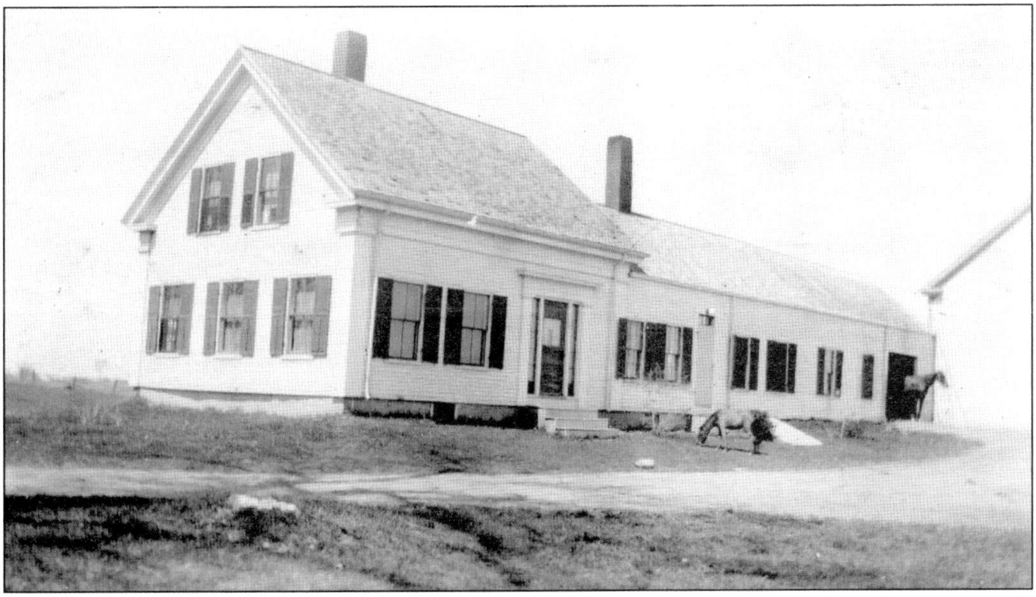

This *c.* 1920 photograph shows the home at 809 North Road owned by Charles Lewis, a cattle dealer and Yarmouth butcher shop owner. In the 1930s and 1940s, the O'Donnell family ran North Yarmouth Dairy here, bottling and delivering milk on routes that included Portland. They had their own cows and also bought milk from other farmers. The O'Donnells sold the business to Oakhurst Dairy, and the tenant-occupied property burned in 1945.

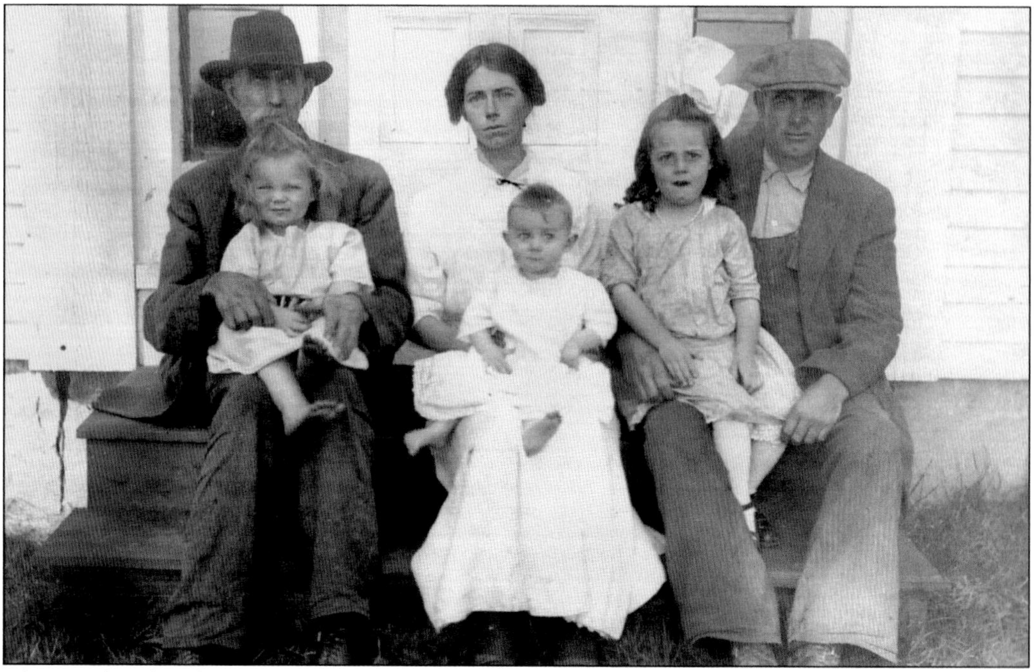

The Joseph Hilton family moved to North Yarmouth and lived in the home at 352 Memorial Highway. This 1915 photograph shows, from left to right, Joseph, with his grandson Stanley Hilton on his lap; his daughter-in-law Bertha Gooch Hilton, with her son William Hilton; and Joseph's son Frank Hilton, a dairyman and cream separator salesman, with his daughter Clara Hilton Small, at Frank's Ledge Road farm. (Courtesy of Charles Small.)

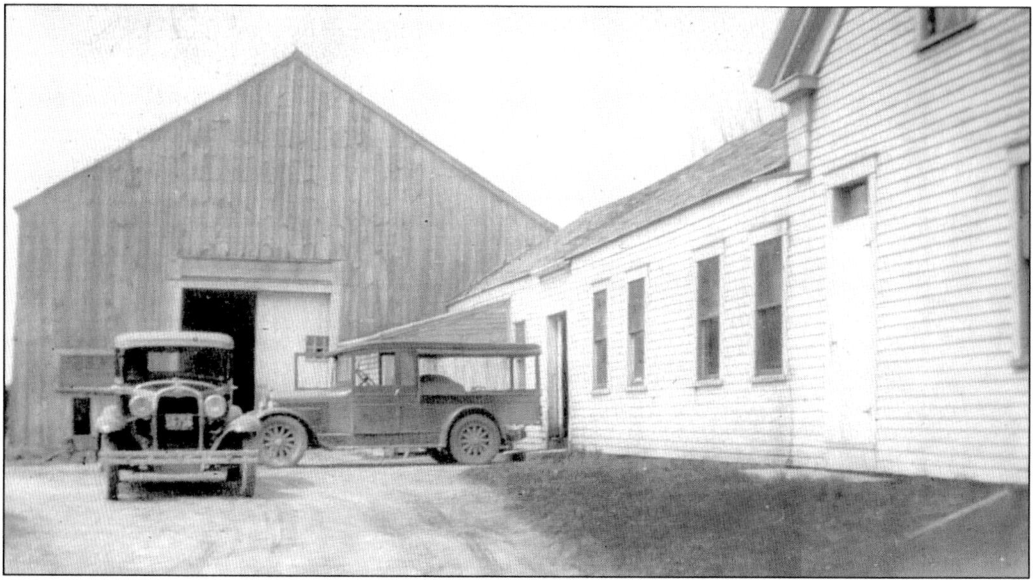

Frank Hilton and later his son Kent E. Hilton Sr. ran Elm Farms Dairy at 414 Ledge Road from 1910 to 1946. After buying milk from local farmers, they pasteurized, bottled, and delivered milk six days a week in the area between Portland and Lewiston using the truck shown on the right in this 1931 image. Orinn Hamilton helped Kent make deliveries of up to 1,500 units per day. Kent sold to Hood Dairy in 1948 and later bought Stevens Insurance. (Courtesy of Charles Small.)

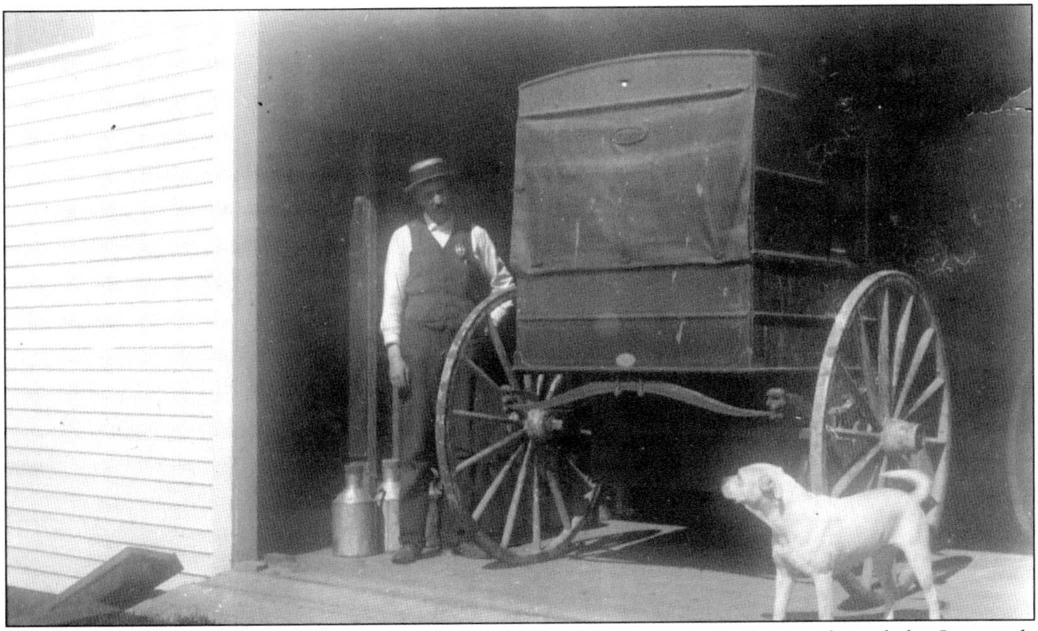

George Roberts was a city person who decided to become a farmer. He purchased the Jeremiah Walker farm on West Pownal Road, across from the Methodist church, in 1913. According to lore, the Roberts family nearly starved to death, as George was not experienced in farm life. He is shown here at the farm with his milk cans and wagon. George moved to Lisbon Falls in 1918 and became a pharmacist, inventing Roberts' Reliable Salve, a liniment used by both humans and animals for dry skin. (Courtesy of Noyes Lawrence.)

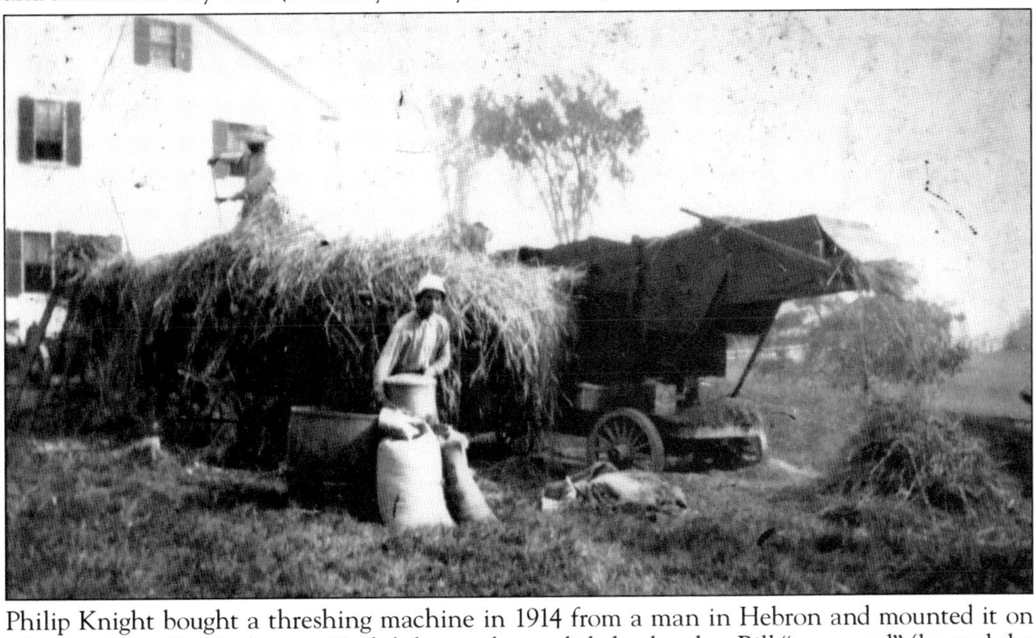

Philip Knight bought a threshing machine in 1914 from a man in Hebron and mounted it on wheels to be pulled by horses. He fed the machine while his brother Bill "measured" (bagged the grain). He threshed 35,000 to 40,000 bushels of grain each year in Pownal, Durham, Freeport, and North Yarmouth from 1914 to 1916. Here the machine operates at the Roberts Farm about 1915. The house burned down in 1925. (Courtesy of Noyes Lawrence.)

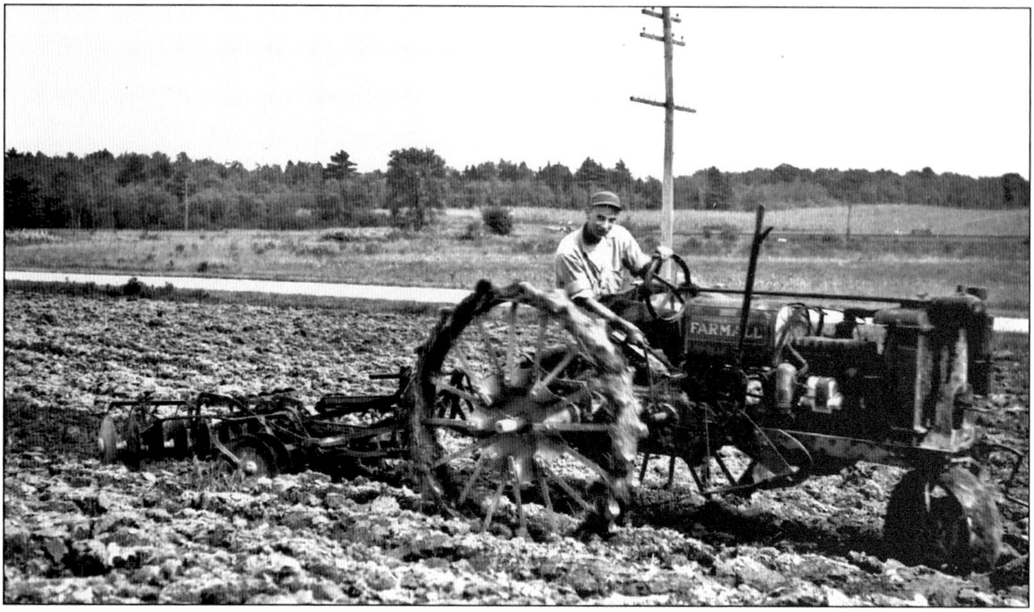

Robert and Margaret Anderson bought the Annie May Bacon farm, at 352 Memorial Highway, in 1957 (now Toddy Brook Golf Course) and became potato farmers. Bob had been a County Extension agent. He is shown harrowing his fields on an iron-wheeled Farmall tractor in this early 1960s photograph. The couple also had a potato-packing operation at the farm, where local residents Maureen Wentworth, Verdell Barter, and Elsie Moreau worked. Margaret ran the local Cheerful Workers 4-H Club. (Courtesy of the Anderson family.)

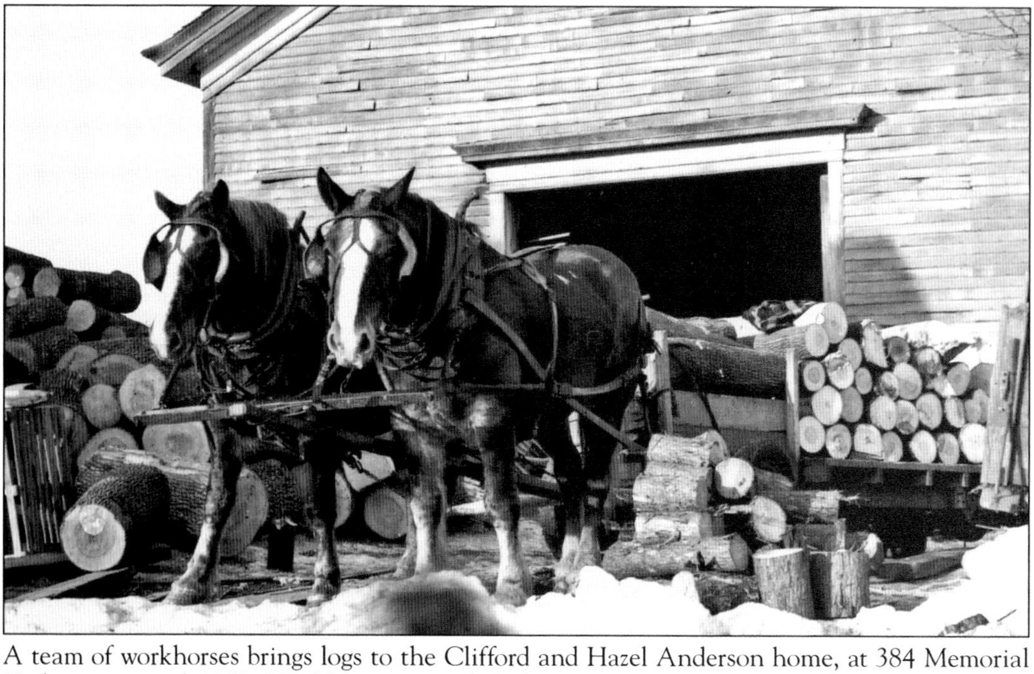

A team of workhorses brings logs to the Clifford and Hazel Anderson home, at 384 Memorial Highway, around 1950. Workhorses provided the power on many local farms until tractors became commonplace. Anderson produced wooden stock for lobster traps, snowshoes, and baseball bats here. This barn is no longer standing. (Courtesy of the Anderson family.)

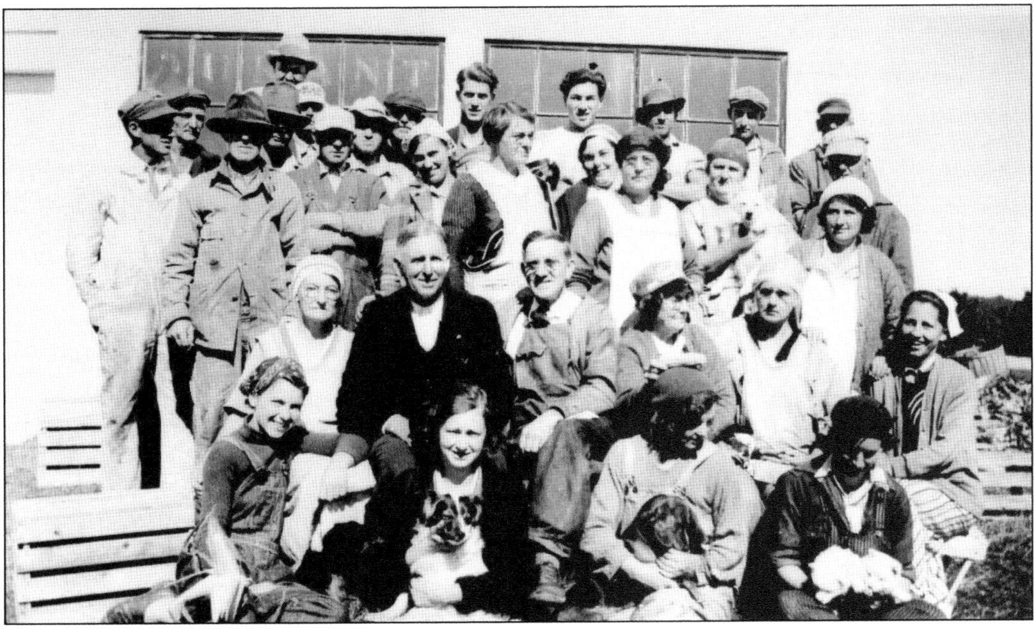

This September 1935 photograph depicts the H. L. Forhan sweet corn factory on Hallowell Road in Pownal, near the town line. Owner Clarence Harmon paid farmers to grow corn for him. Charles L. Dunn ran the business, employing local people during harvest season. Corn was weighed, cut from the cob, and shipped to Gorham to be canned. Dunn and Harmon are seated in the second row.

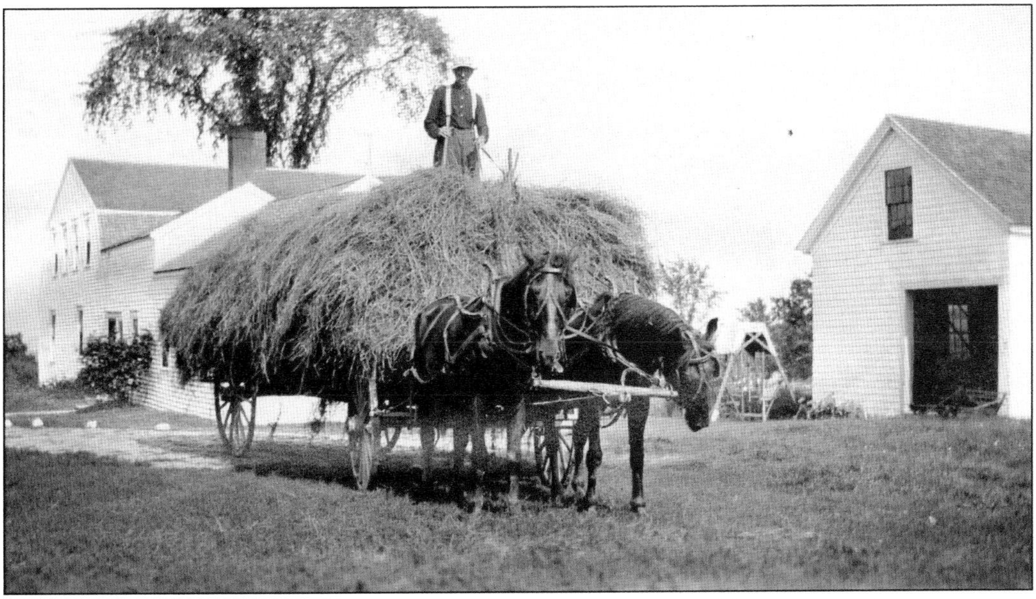

The Ammi Loring farm, at the corner of New Gloucester and Mill Roads, is pictured around 1930, shortly before it would burn. The fire was started when the boarding teacher from the Hicks School across the street fell asleep while smoking. Ammi Loring (1803–1881) was the grandson of Congregationalist minister Nicholas Loring, but was a devout Methodist and left his money to various Methodist societies. This farm was once considered for purchase by the town as a poor farm. (Courtesy of the Nelson family.)

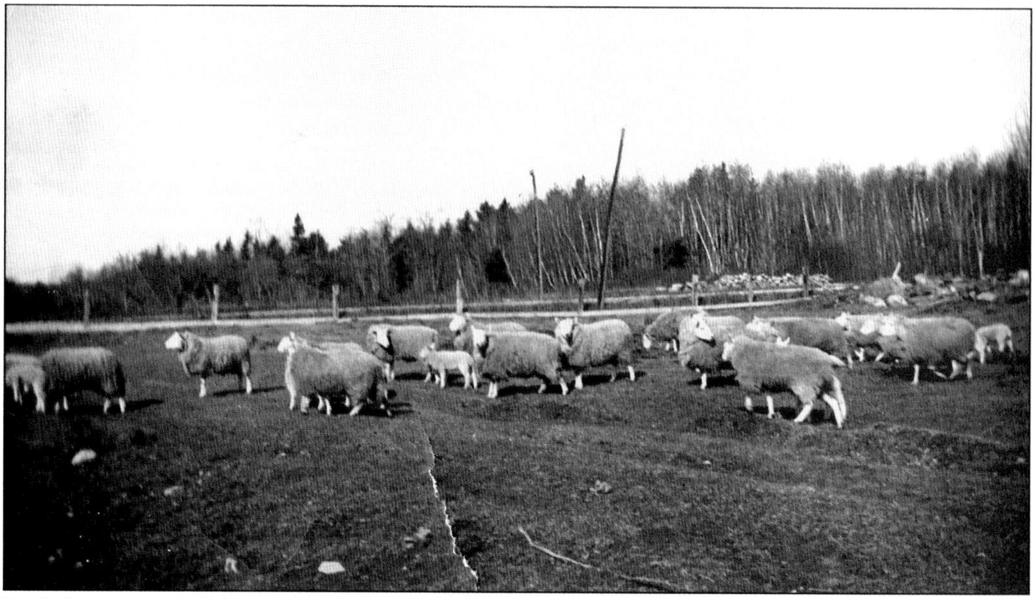

Early farmers raised sheep as part of their diverse operations. They often sold wool to the Shakers in New Gloucester or Mayall Mill in Gray. They raised lamb for their own food or sold them to others. More recently, poultry farmers like Norman and Sidney Smith raised sheep to keep the grass down in the range-raised chicken pastures. In this *c.* 1930 photograph, sheep appear near the intersection of Mill and Gray Roads.

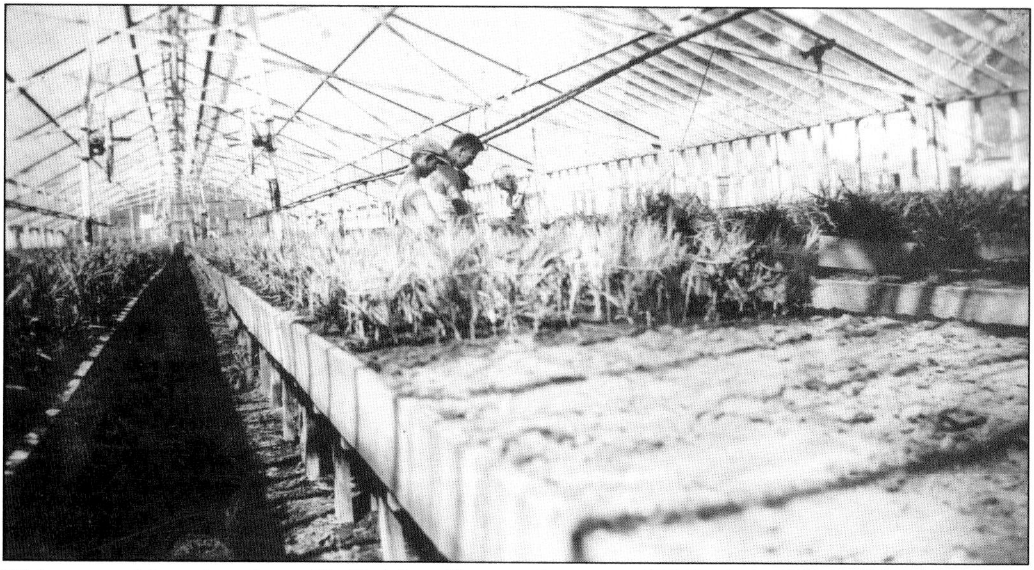

This unusual interior view of F. D. Morrill's greenhouse at 525 Walnut Hill Road, taken about 1935, shows where carnations and snapdragons were grown and then shipped by railroad to markets in Boston and Bangor. Fred Morrill ran the business from 1927 until his death in 1939. Arthur Dunn then operated it until about 1959. The greenhouses were sold and moved to Allen Farms on Gray Road in West Cumberland. (Courtesy of Carol Black.)

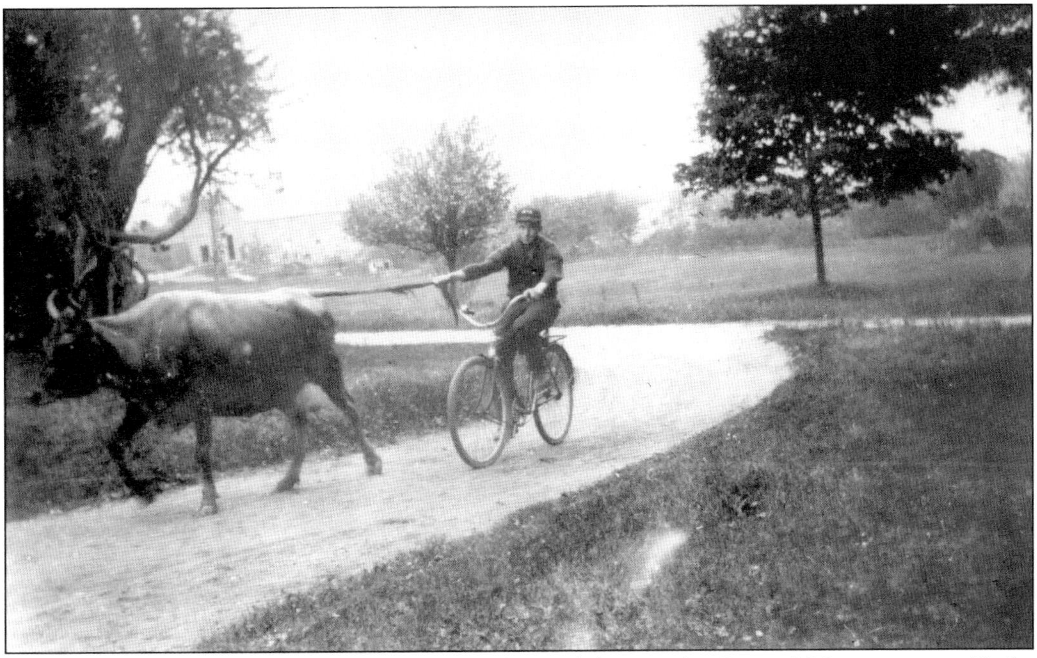

Frank Knight was raised by his grandparents on the Hodsdon Road in Pownal. He was responsible for taking the cows to his uncle's pasture each day and leading them to the barn at night. In this *c.* 1924 image, Frank, a student at North Yarmouth Academy (see cap), brings home the Jersey cow Reddy. He would hold Reddy's tail and let the cow pull him on his bike. (Courtesy of Frank Knight.)

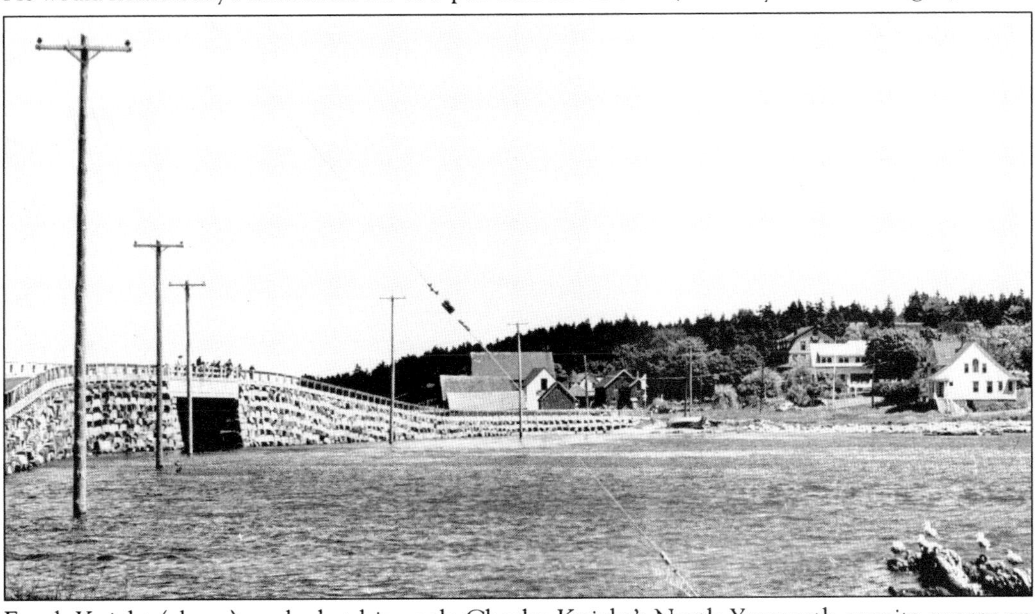

Frank Knight (above) worked at his uncle Charles Knight's North Yarmouth granite quarry on Royal Road where the stone was cut to build the crib-stone bridge that connected Orr's and Bailey's Islands in 1927. Knight and others hauled the granite to the Cousins River in Yarmouth, where it was loaded on barges and delivered to the construction site. This bridge is unique, as only one other span worldwide incorporates a similar design. Granite was laid crosswise to allow water movement when the tide changed.

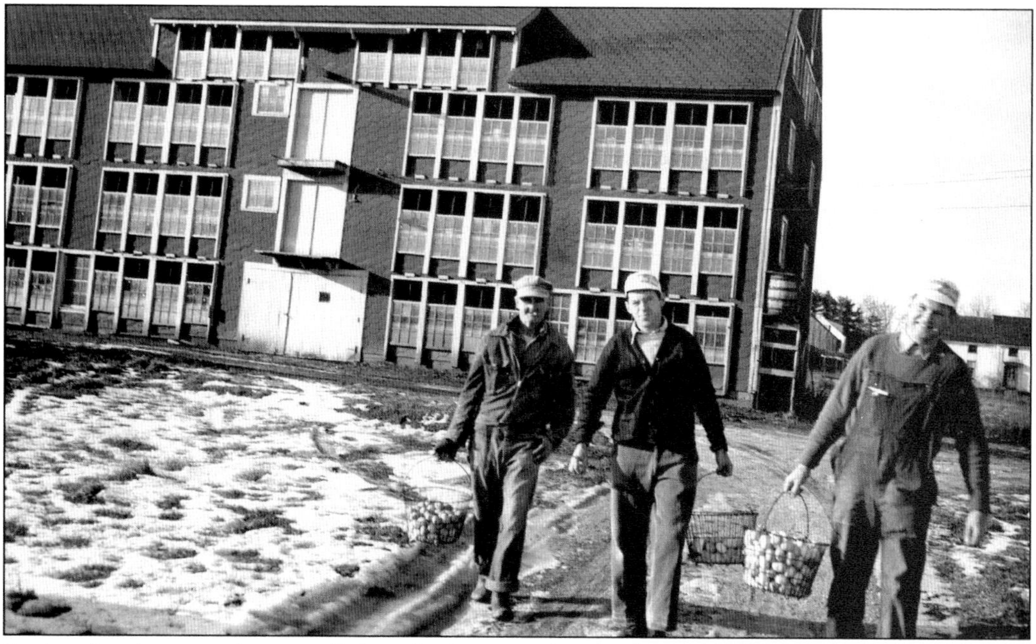

Poultry farming grew from small farm flocks into a large industry, and by 1909, North Yarmouth had over 12,000 chickens. It remained that way for many years until the 1980s, when the industry moved to the South because the cost of heating the barns became prohibitive. Gardiner Leighton owned the first major poultry farm, about 1910, and North Yarmouth quickly became one of the largest poultry producers in Cumberland County. Initially eggs were the main product; then shipping fertilized eggs called hatching eggs to other farmers became a big business. Eventually the market changed to meat birds called broilers. Metal broiler houses could be seen all over town in the 1960s and 1970s. Above, John Hayward (left) carries an egg basket, along with Smith brothers Sidney (middle) and Norman, in front of their poultry barn. Donald Smith is seen below (left) about 1955 with Harland Drowne, his Wirthmore Feed representative. (Courtesy of the Smith family.)

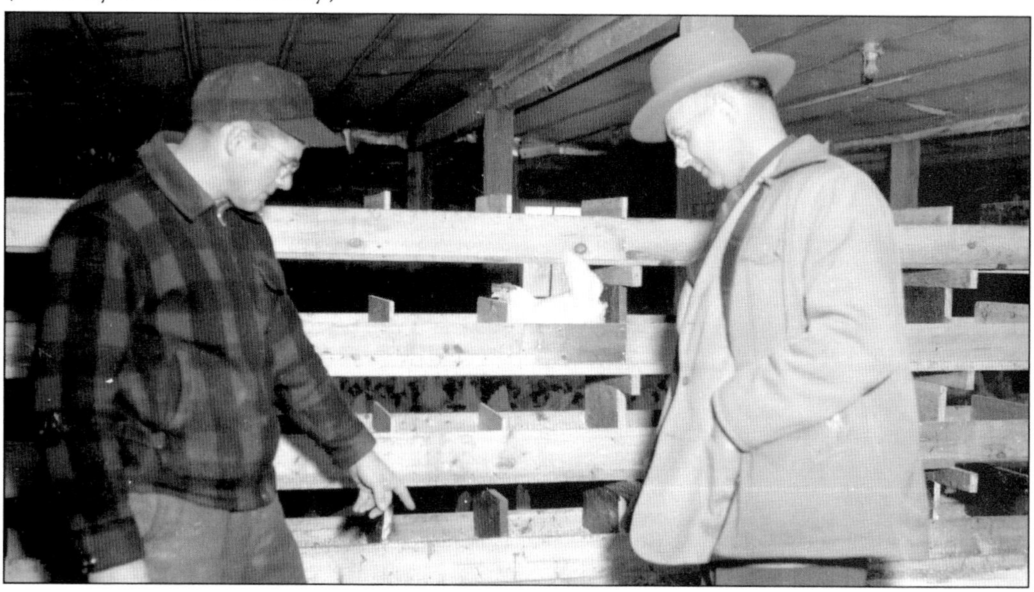

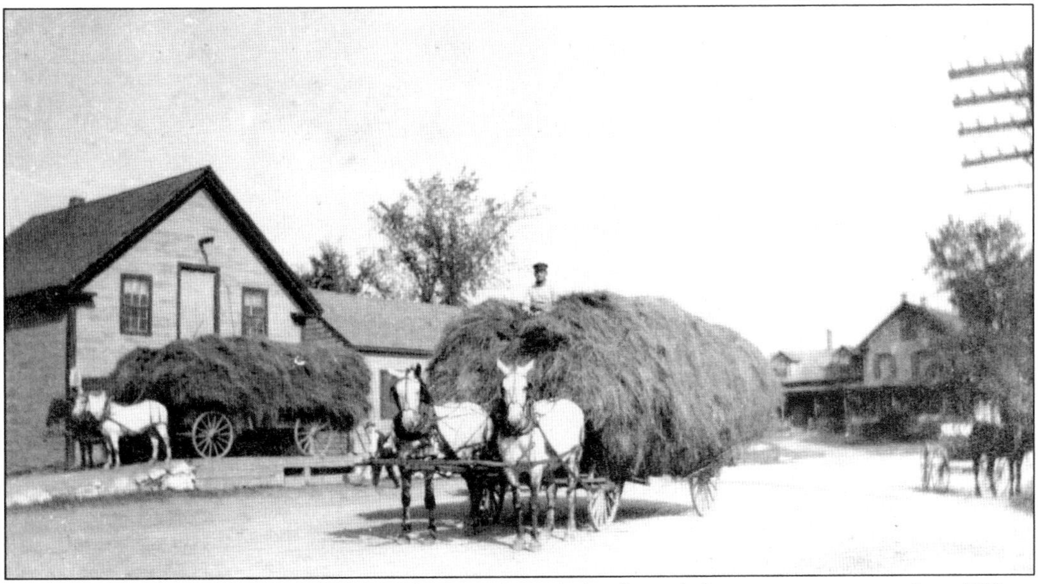

Local farmers sold hay and also pressed it into large bales for rail shipment to city markets. When it was sold in loose form, it was weighed on hay scales like those shown on the left. The weight was recorded on a signed slip and given to the driver. The building behind the hay wagon is still standing at Falmouth Corner, at the intersection of Bucknam Road (once Depot Road) and Middle Road (Route 9). (Courtesy of Frank Knight.)

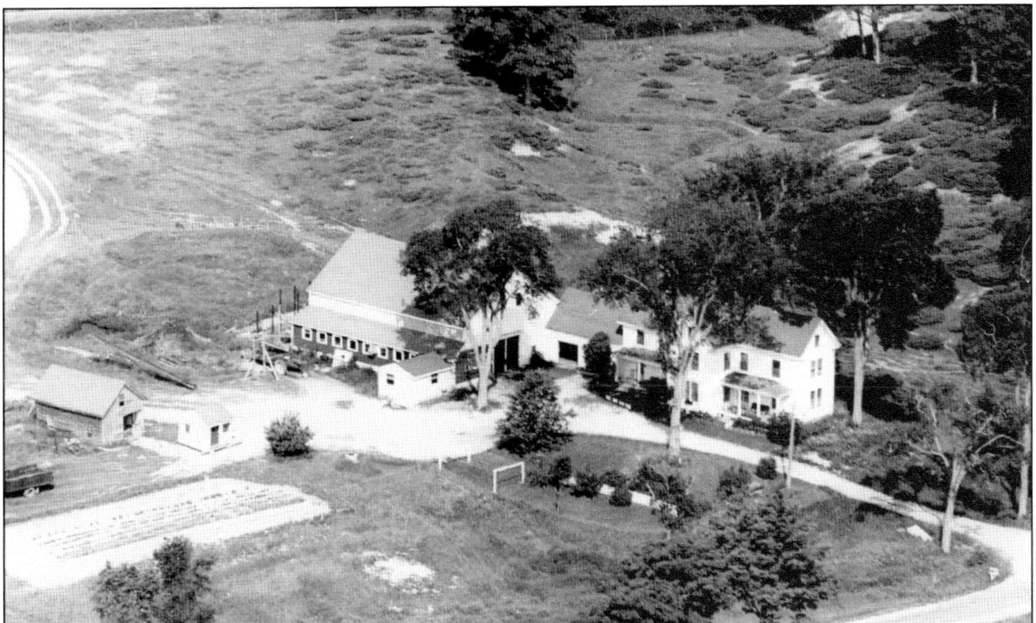

This aerial view shows the Weston and Sherman Grover dairy farm, at 774 Sligo Road, in 1962. Originally Enos True's residence prior to 1871, the property was used to raise mules for military pack animals during World War I. The Grovers were industrious farmers who worked the land efficiently and always maintained their land. The milk room, with its cooler, is attached on the left side of the barn. The machine shed is at the far left. (Courtesy of Norene Grover.)

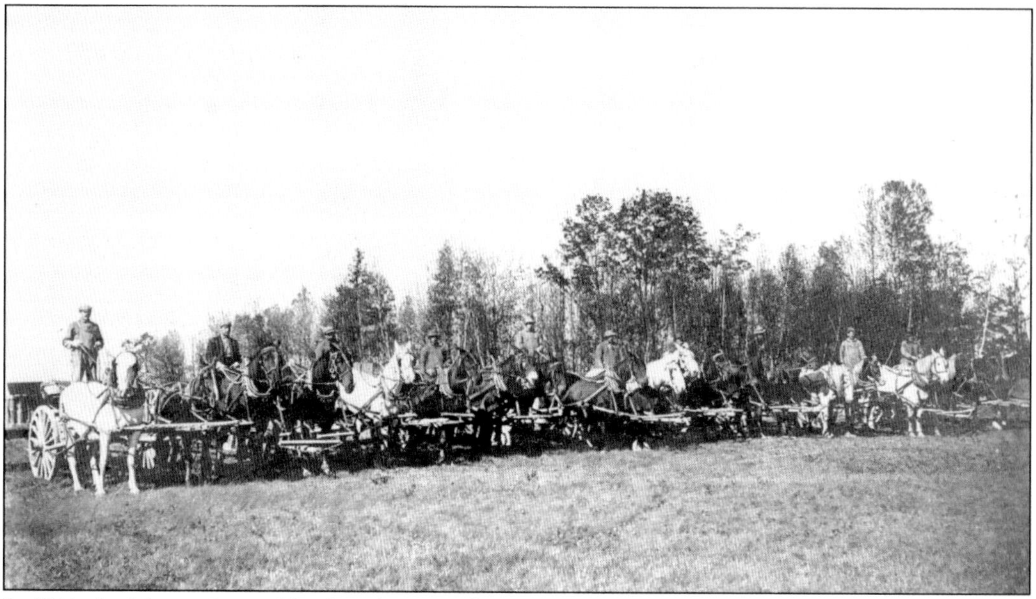

In 1911, the Maine Central Railroad rerouted its track through North Yarmouth and Cumberland to avoid a long uphill grade that made it difficult for the steam engines to haul heavy loads of freight cars. The new route passed near the Old Town House on Route 9. The construction project involved a general contractor and a crew of construction workers from Portland known as "the Italians." Local farmers were hired to help clear the new rail line using their wagons and horses. The farmers are shown above with their teams near the Route 9 crossing. Hazel Anderson's father, Robert Hoey, appears on the far left. The temporary trestle in the below photograph allowed a small railroad engine to carry gravel up, dump it, and bury the trestle, thus building the Memorial Highway approach to the overpass. This overpass is still there today. (Above, courtesy of the Anderson family; below, courtesy of Ginger Collins.)

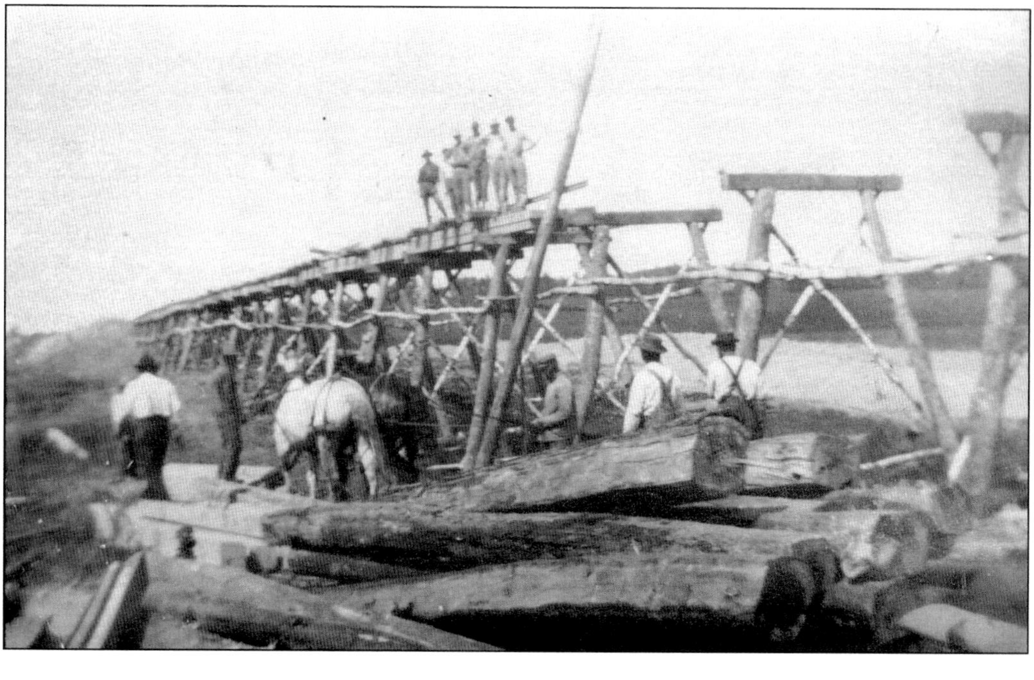

Farmers with oxen—and later residents with dump trucks—were paid by the town to work on the roads. Payment was often made through a credit on their property tax bill. Here local dairy farmer Frederick Titcomb's oxen pull a wooden drag to smooth Mountfort Road in the spring of 1937. (Courtesy of Dick Knight.)

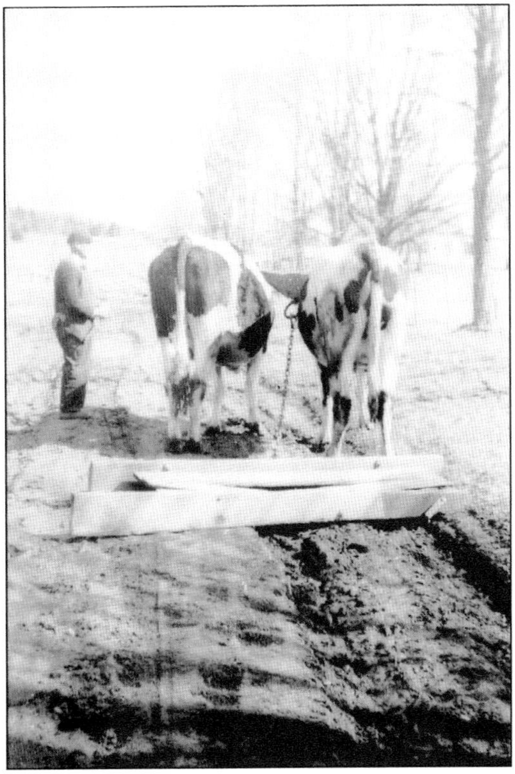

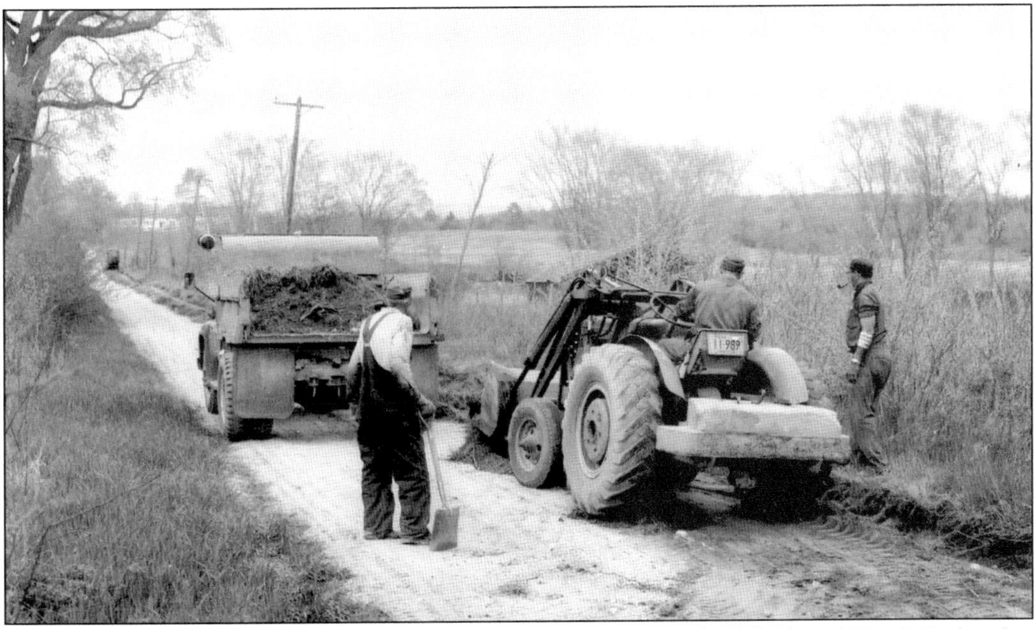

Road commissioner Herman Smith (right) works with Arthur Cluff (left) and Frank Parker (on the tractor) widening and ditching The Lane around 1965. At that time, there was no public works department, and so town voters elected the commissioner who often had his own dump truck and other construction equipment. Snowplowing was contracted out and the town hired drivers and laborers on a temporary or seasonal basis. (Courtesy of Phyllis Smith.)

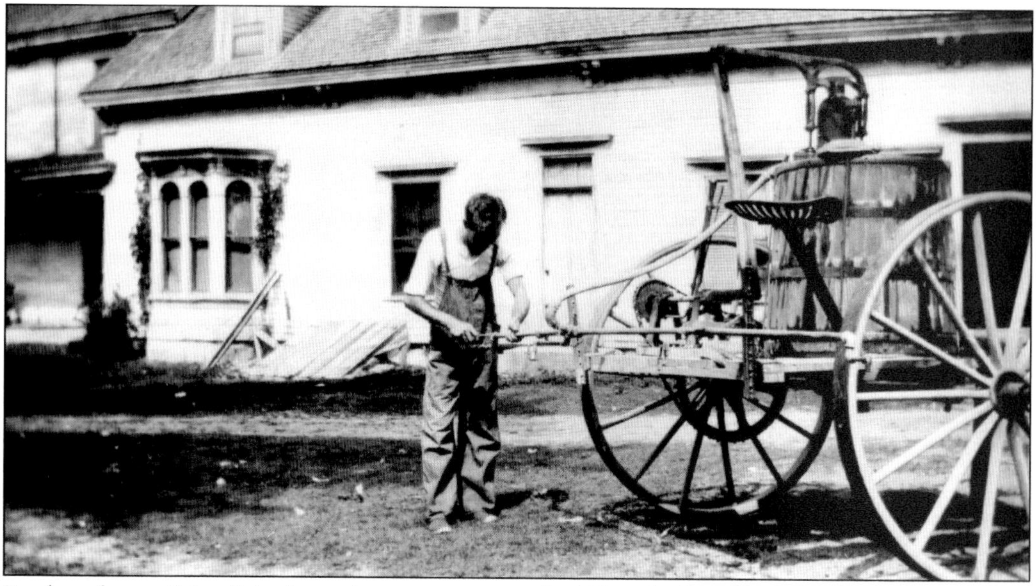

Produce farmer John Britt Jr. works on a sprayer at his Thunder Road home, where he lived with his parents. The horse-drawn sprayer would protect Britt's vegetable fields from insect damage. The Britts raised beans and possibly potatoes and also sold milk. He married Abbie Pervier of Pownal in June 1914 but died in August 1915 from diabetes complications.

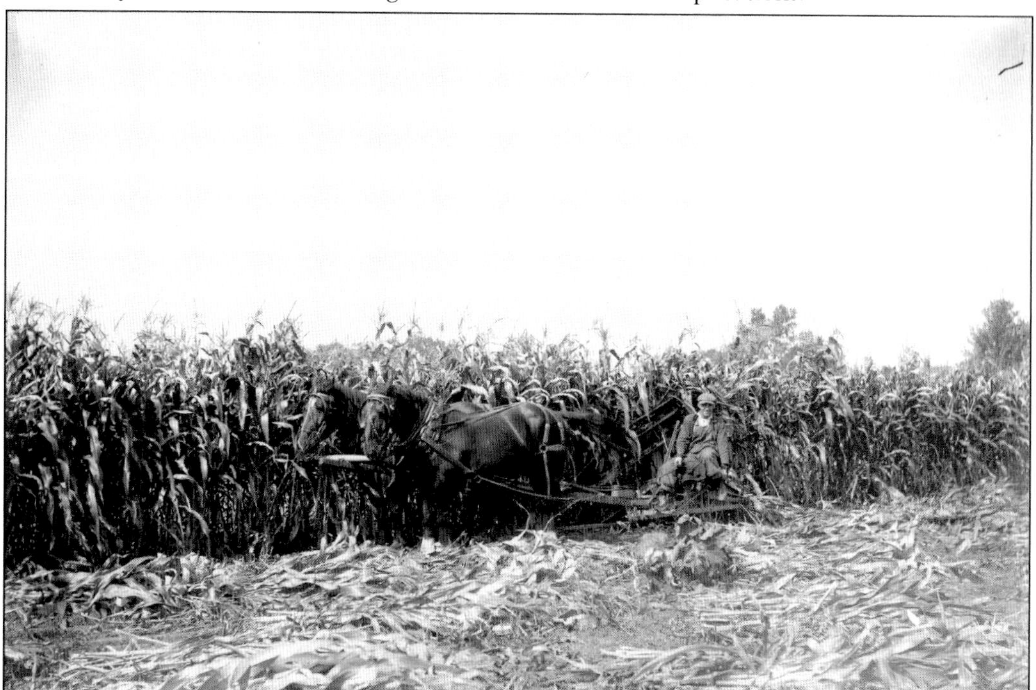

Oscar Braley, an employee at the Reeds' Cedar Spring farm, drives a horse-drawn corn picker about 1945. The Reeds used horse-drawn machinery on their farm until 1955, when they switched to tractors and trucks. The corn picker cut down the corn with a blade and then bundled the stalks, which were then chopped up to make silage for the farm's dairy cows. This diet produced milk with a high fat content. (Courtesy of Marion Reed.)

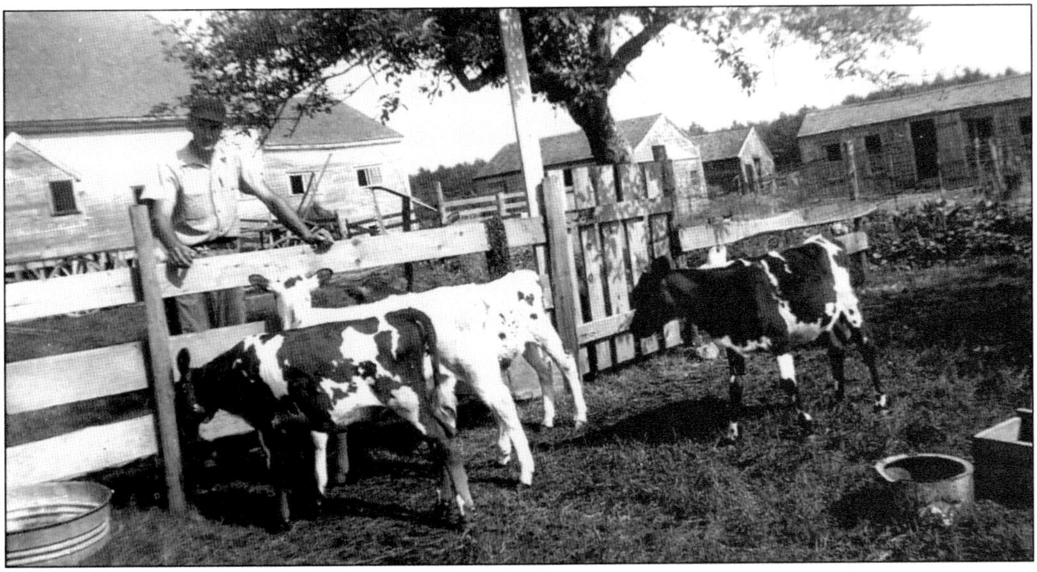

The George and Olive Loring Small farm, next to the Congregational church, was an active dairy and vegetable farm. Since the property included land on the Lufkin Road, sons Harold, Maurice, and Charles would ride a horse over there to bring cattle home to milk. The area was called "Pumpkin City" as early as 1872 and Small helped preserve the name by growing them in the gardens behind the vestry. Maurice (with cat) and Harold, who appear on the pile of squash around 1925, continued to farm as adults. Harold eventually took over his father's farm and raised Ayshires and Holsteins. Shown above, surrounded by farm buildings, Harold looks at some of his calves about 1954. Maurice was a wholesale florist with several greenhouses in Cumberland, and Charles had a dairy farm in Yarmouth. (Courtesy of the Small family.)

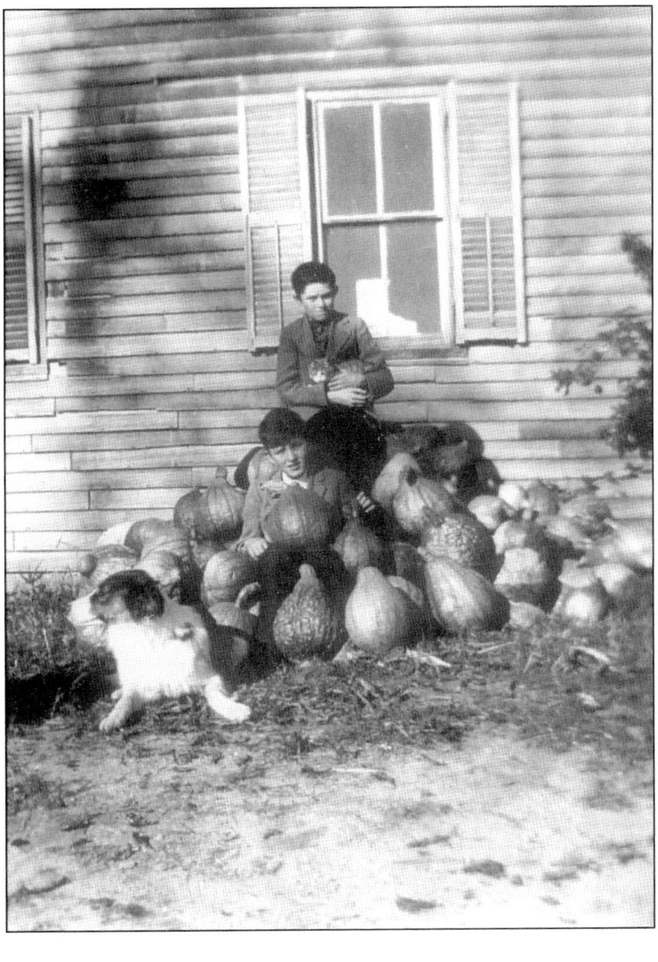

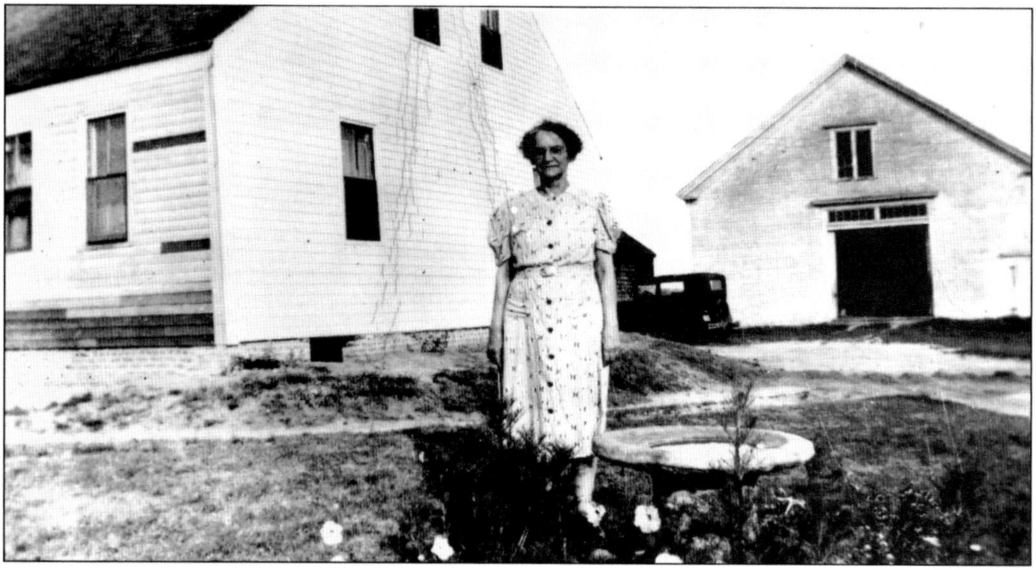

Fannie Baston (above) and her husband, Fred, lived at this 129 Baston Road home, currently Beckwith's strawberry farm. Fred and his brother Willard, who lived next door, were farmers who shared the pastures around their homes for raising cows. This structure, although likely built around 1800, sits on a brick foundation that is much newer, suggesting it was moved from its original site. The brothers moved their father's house to Willard's farm from the Range (Sweetser) Road, which once extended all the way to Yarmouth before about 1920.

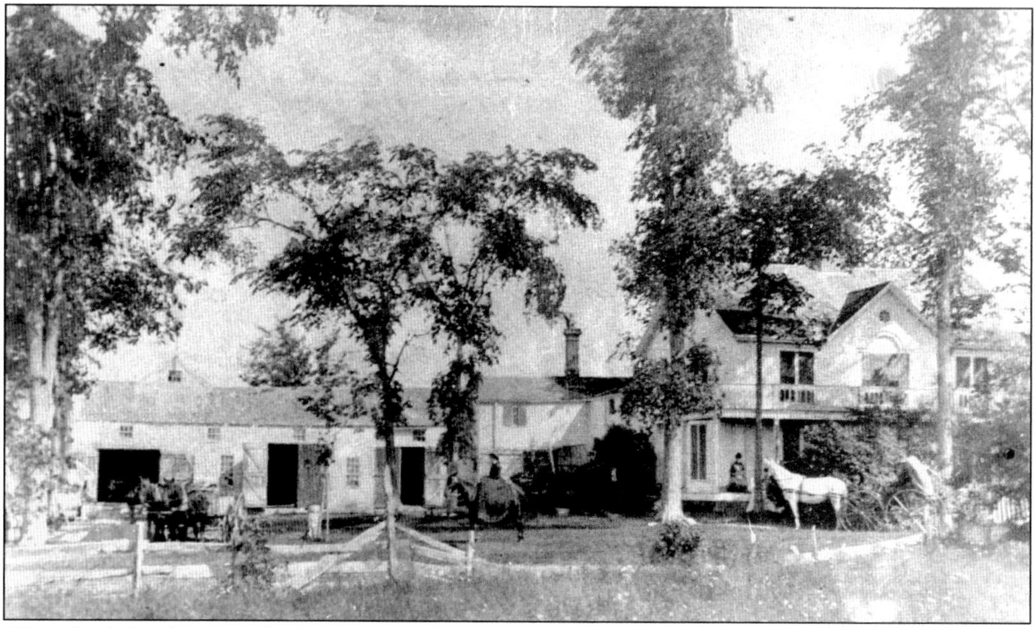

The ell of this house, which once stood at 512 Memorial Highway, was the original structure and the connected farmhouse grew over time. The Italianate details were added in the 1860s. The Sawyer family bought this property in the late 1800s and owned it until 1979, when it was demolished to make way for the Gillespie Farm Market. Lawrence Gillespie operated the market until 1997. The girl riding sidesaddle is likely Winifred Sawyer, shown around 1900. The Old Town House property was originally part of this farm.

Four

FUN WE HAD

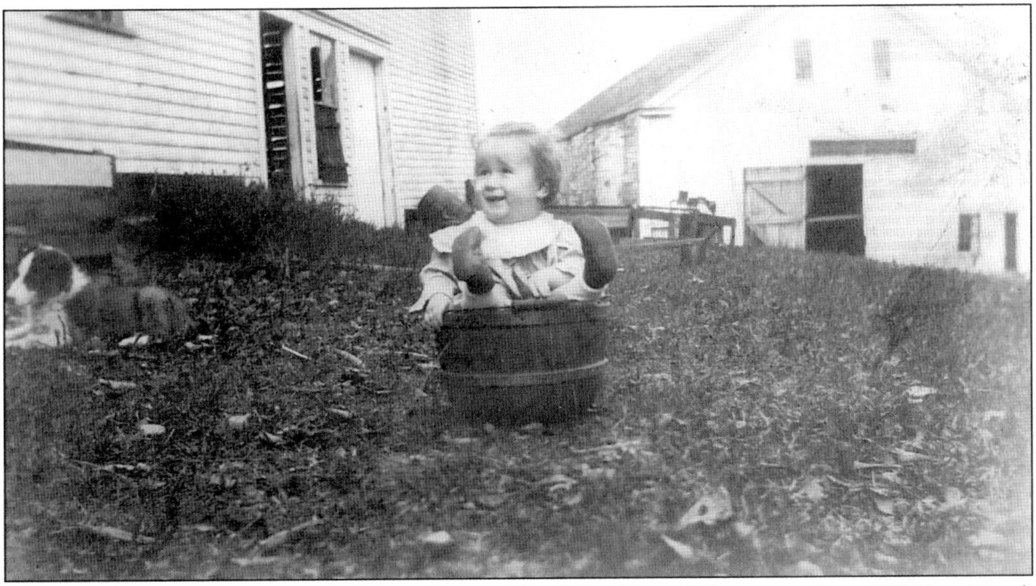

Esther Chadbourne Walker appears in front of the John Herrick homestead, at 407 Gray Road, where she and her twin brother, Lester, were born in 1920. When previous owner Charles B. Herrick, farmer and lumber dealer, passed away, Esther's parents rented and then owned the farm from 1923 until 1925. Esther, a lifelong resident who has lived in many different houses throughout town, worked making boxes at Knight's Mill for a penny apiece. She also built Liberty ships at the South Portland shipyard during World War II. The Herrick home burned once in 1898, was rebuilt, and burned again about 1930. This is the only known photograph. The barn was spared but soon fell into disrepair. Arthur and Irene Lavoie constructed a new home on the foundation in the 1940s and converted the barn into a poultry house. It burned in the late 1940s, when a brooder warming baby chickens burst into flames. Lavoie ran from the barn just ahead of the spreading fire. (Courtesy of Esther Walker.)

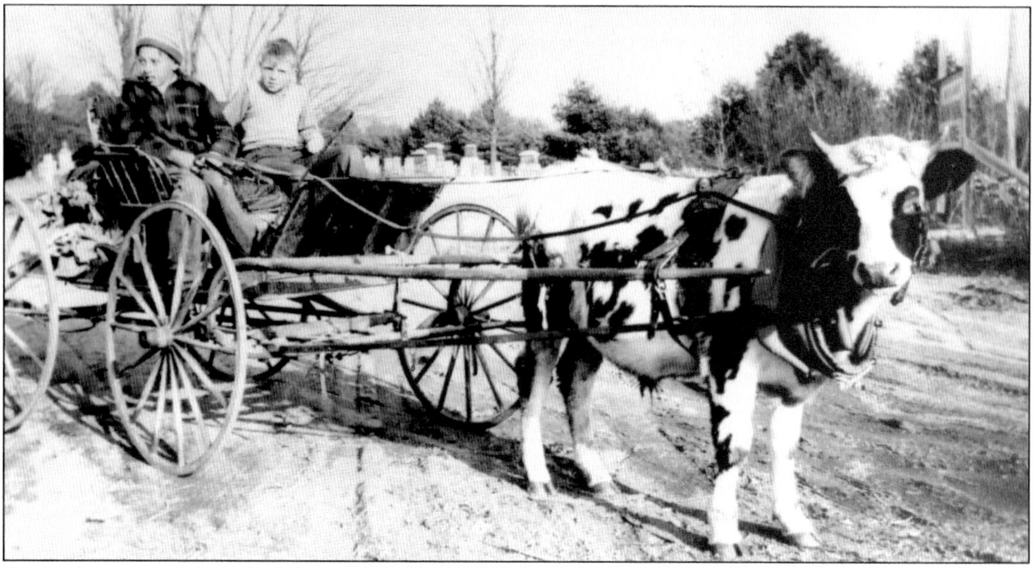

Elwood Bearce (left) of 1473 North Road had a disability that affected his leg. To make it easier to get around, he had a wagon drawn by a pet Holstein steer named Popeye. It was an unusual sight that many older residents recall with amusement. Here Elwood and his brother Roland are in the yard at Knight's Mill around 1943. The Pine Grove Cemetery on Hallowell Road is in the background. (Courtesy of Marion Reed.)

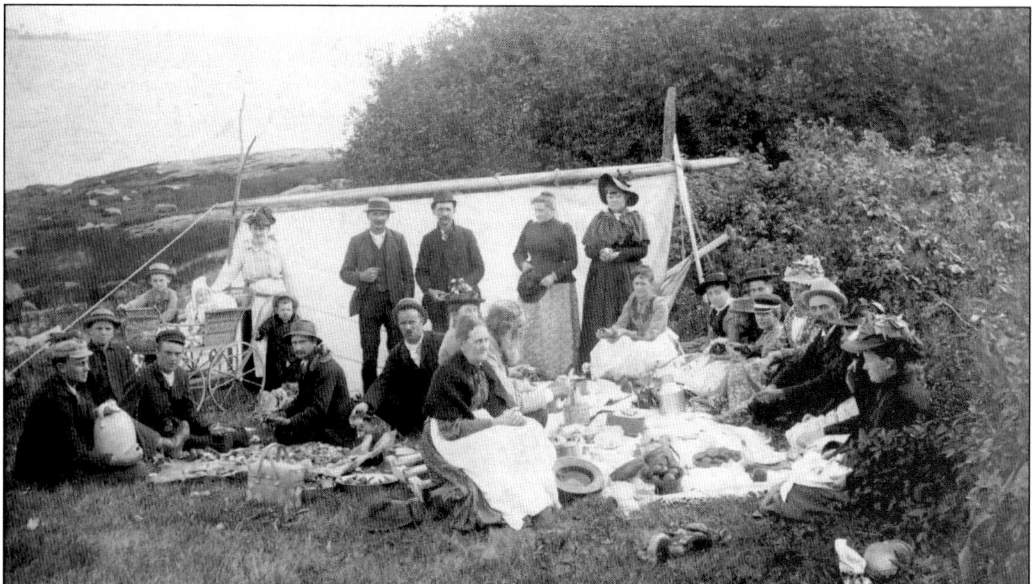

The great-grandparents of lifelong resident Marion Knight Reed, Nicholas and Mary Drinkwater, attend a family reunion in the summer of 1892 at Princes Point in Yarmouth, near where they lived. North Yarmouth townspeople often visited Princes Point, Cousins Island, and Chebeague Island to picnic and enjoy the shoreline. Wescustogo Grange members held several clambakes at the ocean. (Courtesy of Marion Reed.)

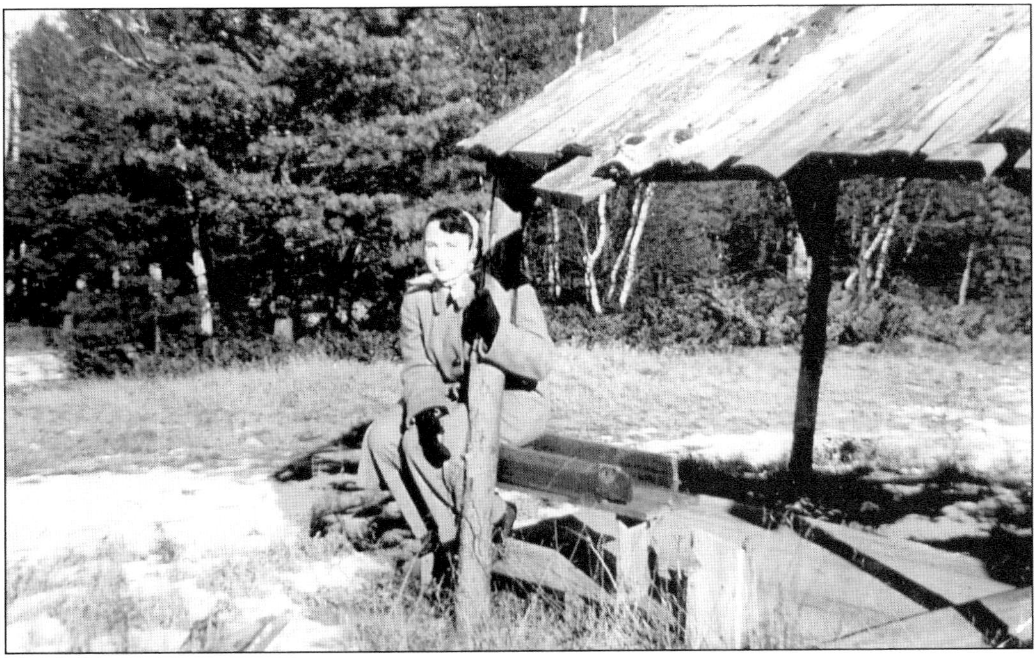

The North Yarmouth Community Club was formed in 1930, after the town's 250th anniversary celebration, for the purpose of improving the town. Eventually 140 members joined the club and developed a community center on land owned by George Smith. At the recreational area on Memorial Highway, across from the current fire station, the group built a baseball field, tennis courts, and an outdoor bowling alley. Here Norma Fountain Grover sits under the slab roof that protects the wooden alley from rain. (Courtesy of Norma Grover.)

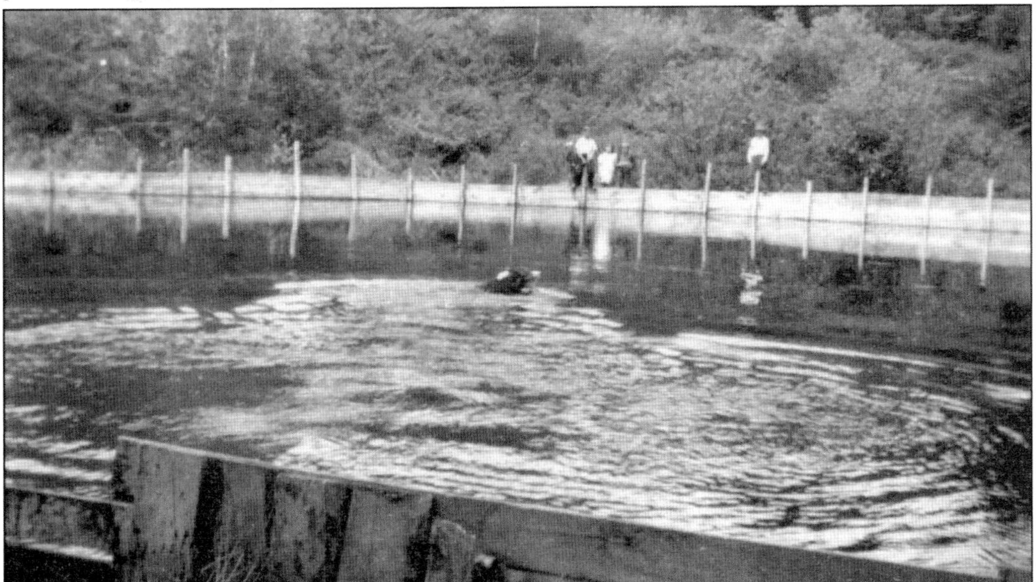

The club's most ambitious undertaking was the swimming pool it made in Toddy Brook. Local men with their teams, trucks, and equipment dammed the brook and hauled in sand to line the bottom. The group built a changing house with seven rooms and hired a swimming instructor. Many residents learned to swim in the five-foot-deep pool.

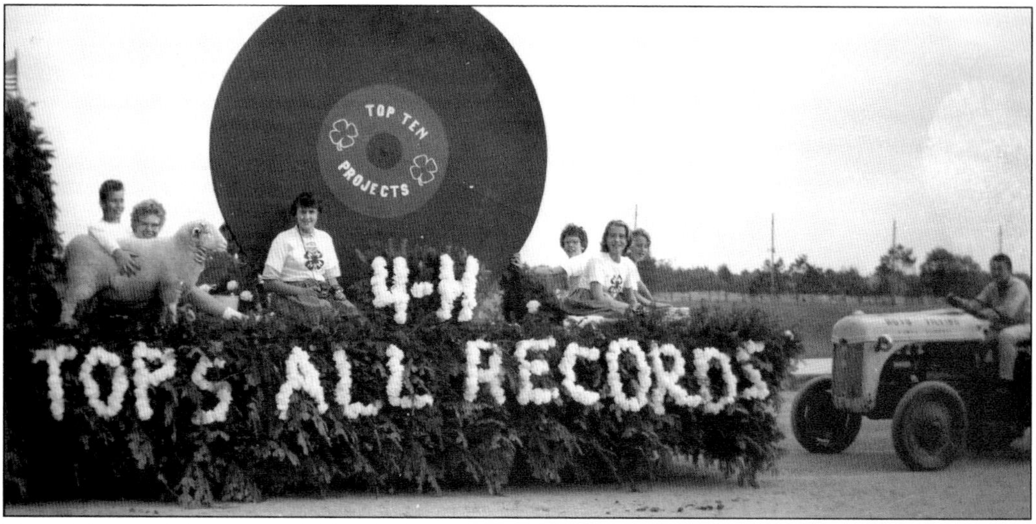

North Yarmouth had many 4-H clubs from the 1930s to the 1970s, including the Willing Workers and the Happy Workers. Members of the Cheerful Workers 4-H Club, under the leadership of Hazel Hoey Anderson, ride their parade float at the Cumberland Fair in 1961. Pictured here, from left to right, are John North, Jane Dunning, Joan Blackstone, Shelly North, Judy Bowie, and Dixie Hayes. (Courtesy of Harriet Bowie.)

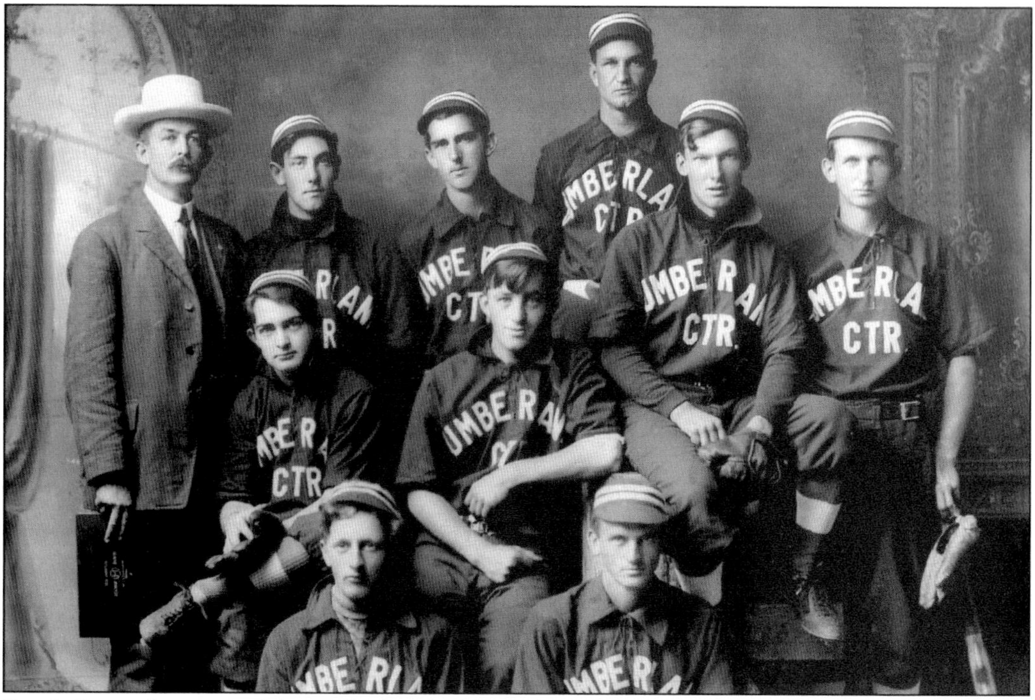

Baseball was the sport of choice for local athletes from the late 1800s to the 1960s. Almost every Maine town had its own team that competed against neighbors for bragging rights. The games often drew hundreds of spectators. North Yarmouth had a team that played against Pownal and Cumberland, but no images have yet been found. In 1909, North Yarmouth and Cumberland formed a baseball association, which included residents Maurice Hayes (lower left) as shortstop and Everett Sweetser on third base. The team poses here in 1910.

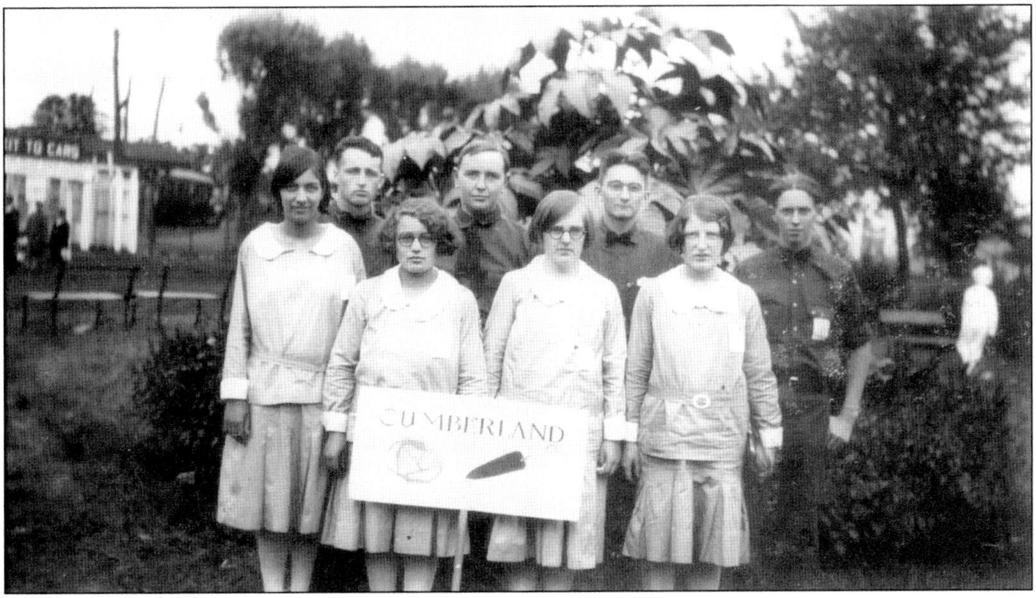

Each year, North Yarmouth 4-H members compete to attend the Eastern States Exposition in Springfield, Massachusetts, with their livestock projects. This 1929 photograph of the 4-H representatives from Cumberland County shows Charles Small (in the back left) and Paul Merrill (second row, third from left) of Cumberland who went on to found Merrill Transport Company. Recent competitors have been from the Merrill, Champlin, Dahlgren, Barter, Furey, Hayward, Moreau, and Grover families. (Courtesy of Charles Small.)

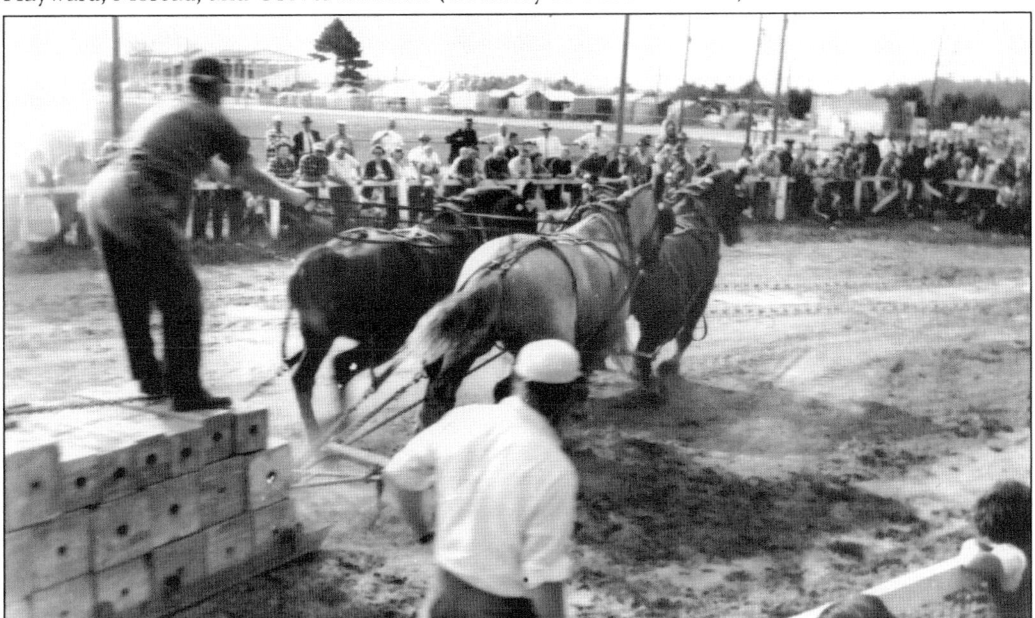

The Cumberland Fair has been held almost every year since 1868. Many North Yarmouth farmers were founding members of the Cumberland Farmers Club, which owns the fairgrounds in West Cumberland and sponsors the fair. Now held during the last week in September, in the early years the fair often occurred in October. Horse pulling has always been a crowd favorite, as evidenced by this *c.* 1950 image of an open ring.

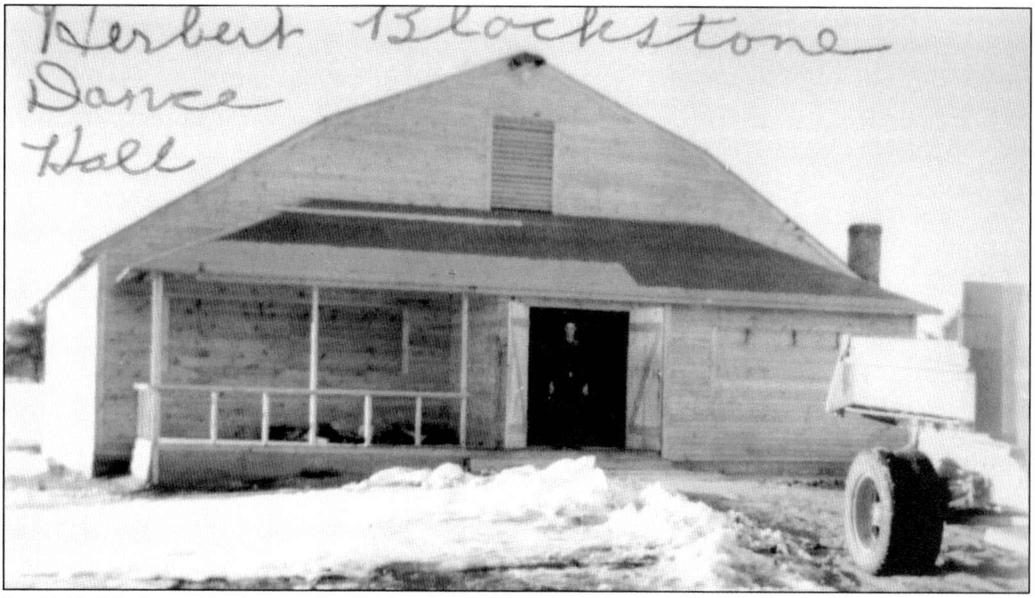

In 1941, Herbert Blackstone built this hall on Hallowell Road near Pownal and held dances every Saturday night. The Charmers, a band featuring piano, banjo, saxophone, clarinet, and drums, entertained audiences from surrounding towns. According to patron Kenneth "Diddy" Allen, the hall was "safe inside but a little rough outside," as patrons had to go outside to drink alcohol in their cars. Fights were not out of the ordinary. In the 1960s, the structure became an antique shop and is now the Northern Lights Auction Hall. (Courtesy of Marion Reed.)

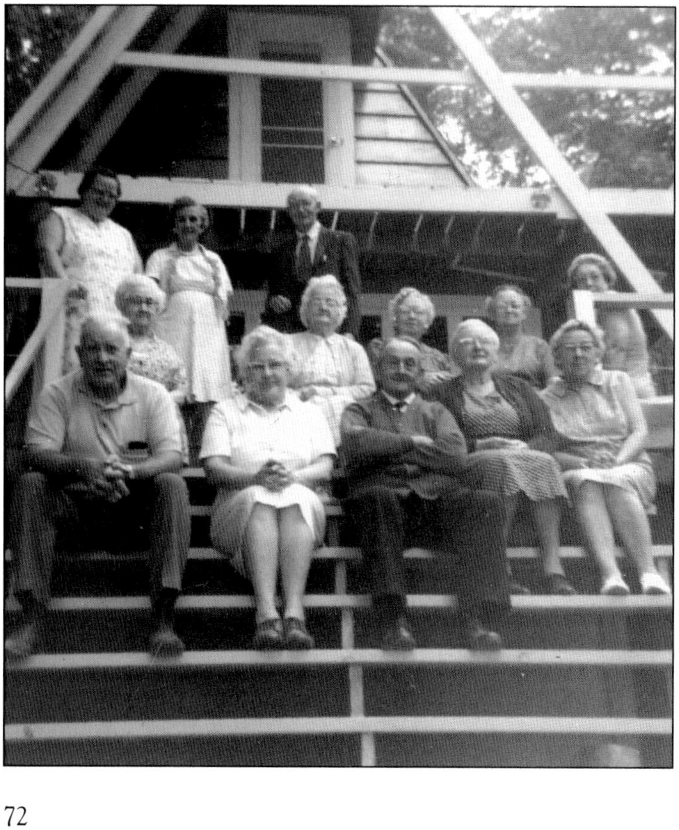

Shirley Fountain formed the North Yarmouth Senior Citizens group in 1967. Members enjoyed their first summer outing, in August 1968, at Marjorie Scott's cottage on Raymond Pond. Pictured here, from left to right, are the following: (first row) Ernest Allen, Shirley Fountain, Elmer Sawyer, Helen Sawyer, and Gladys Hamilton; (second row) Beulah Crichton, Myra Barter, Madelyn Freeman, Floyd Goff, and Vida Arbo; (third row) Eleanor Sawyer, Helen McLean, and James Crichton. In April 1970, the senior groups from North Yarmouth and Cumberland merged, forming the North Yarmouth/Cumberland Senior Citizens, a group still active today.

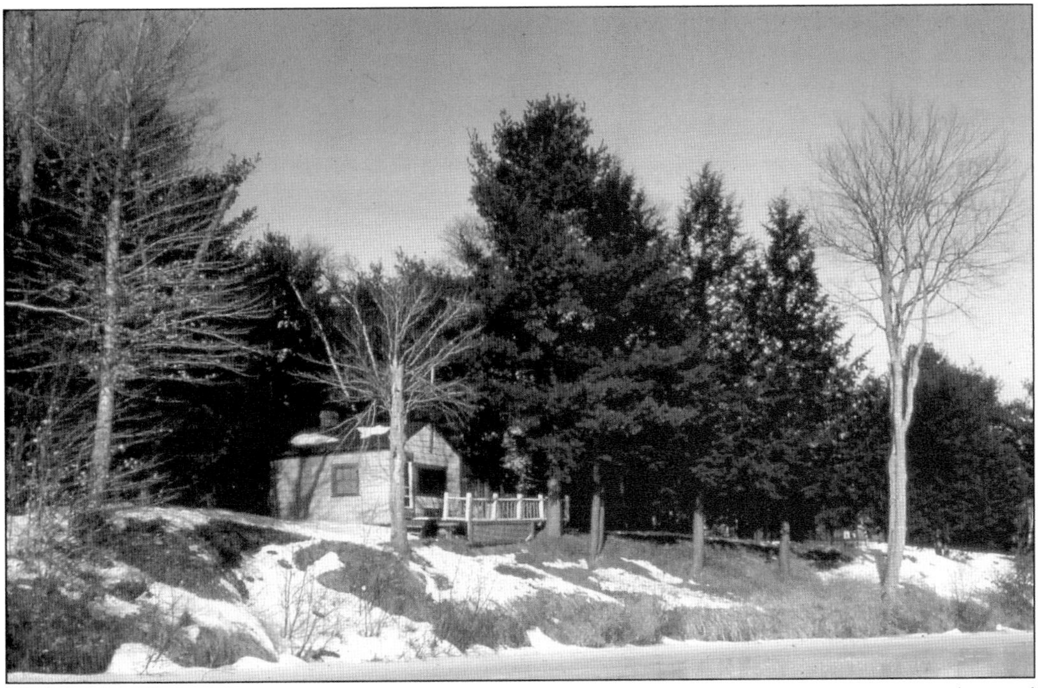

Since the early 1800s, the Ring family has owned land along the Royal River off North Road near Deer Run Road. The Atlantic and St. Lawrence Railroad took some of the property when the line was built through in 1849. This photograph, taken from the frozen river, shows the Ring family camp in February 1962. Numerous camps were set up along the river, used like lake camps for fishing and swimming. (Courtesy of Virginia Davis.)

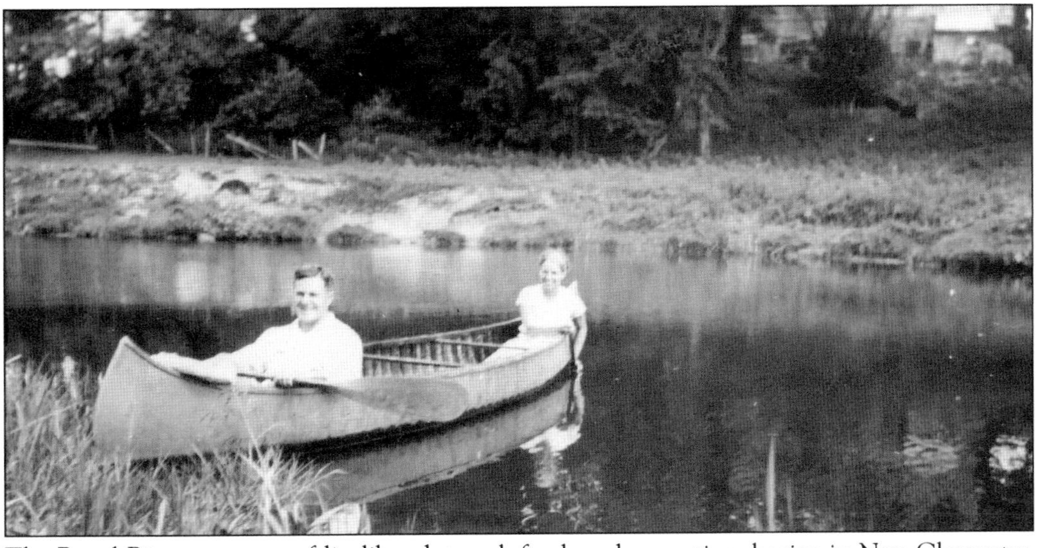

The Royal River, a source of livelihood, travel, food, and recreation, begins in New Gloucester, travels through Gray and North Yarmouth, and empties into Casco Bay in Yarmouth. Ice racing on the river by sleigh or sulky was popular around the start of the 20th century. Ice-skating and canoeing have also been enjoyed by residents for many years. Luther Lawrence and his cousin Ruth Dunn DeRoche go for an afternoon canoe ride in 1940. (Courtesy of the Hathaway family.)

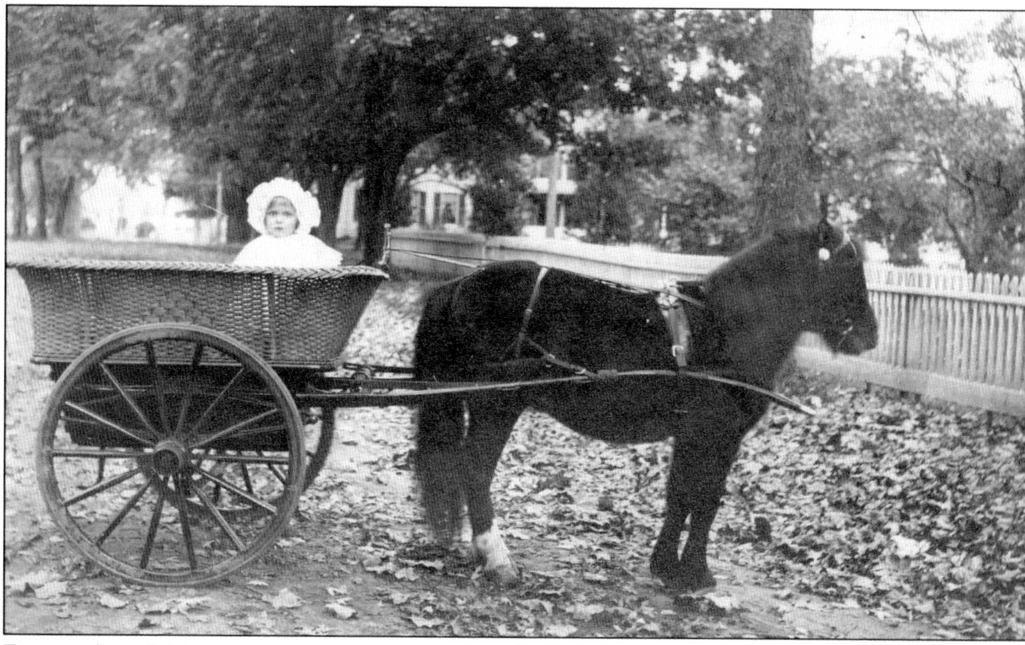

Frances (Fran) Mann sits in a governess cart in her Yarmouth yard about 1910. Descended from Benaiah Titcomb and Joseph Hicks, two of the earliest settlers in East North Yarmouth, she inherited her uncle Fred Titcomb's farm on Mountfort Road. Frank Knight of Pownal met her while shingling the farm's barn roof. When he fell off and broke his back, Fran ran to the next farm for help, which ultimately led to romance and marriage. (Courtesy of Frank Knight.)

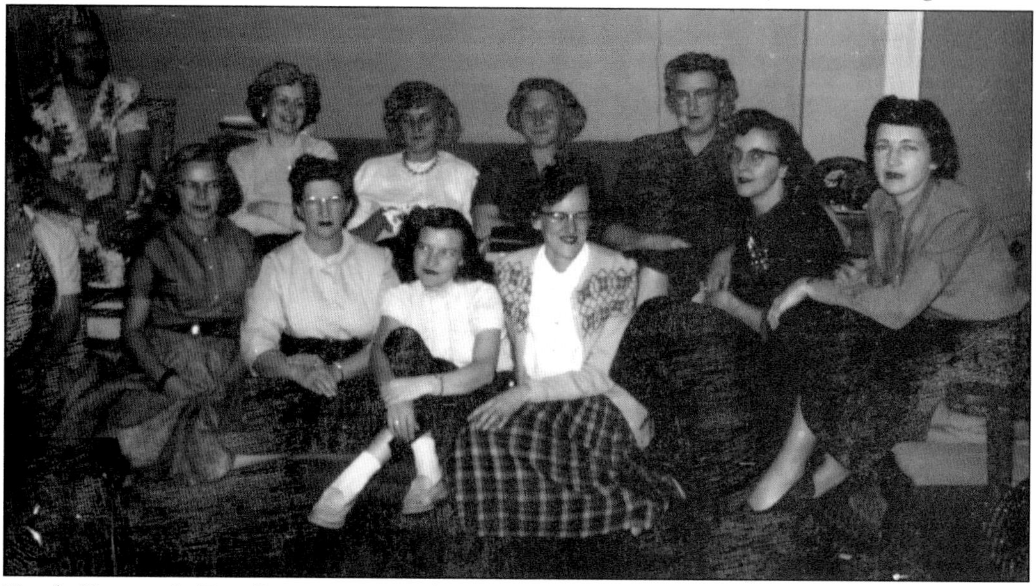

North Yarmouth Fire Department Ladies Auxiliary members gather at Ann Smith's for a Christmas party in 1956. The auxiliary raised money for the department by putting on harvest suppers and chicken pie suppers, conducting raffles, and helping run Fun Day. The ladies would bring food and dry clothes to the men fighting fires. Members in the front row from left to right include Ann Smith, Theona Blackstone, Barbara Parker, Edith Atkins, Verdell Barter, and Norma Smith. (Courtesy of Phyllis Smith.)

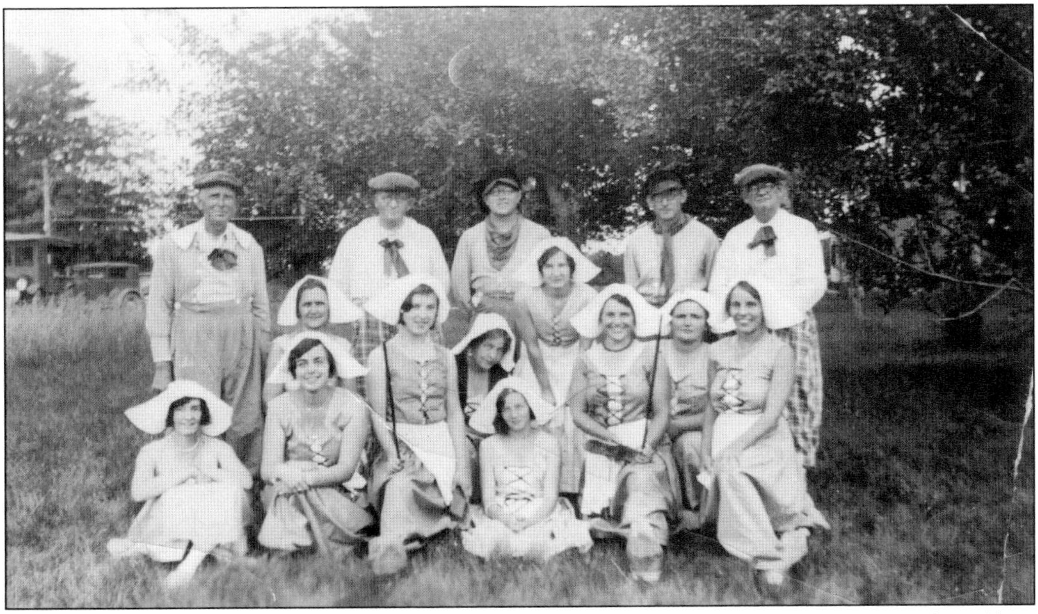

In the 1930s, Pres. Franklin Roosevelt developed the Works Project Administration (WPA) to create employment by funding public works projects and employing artists. A woman from the WPA came to town and directed a show that starred community members (standing in the back, from left to right) Charles Dunn, Bert Lawrence, Lester Smith, and Lewis Hatch. Clara Hilton Small is in front row, second from left; Ruth Dunn is on far right; and Charlotte Lawrence is standing in the center. The performers wore Dutch costumes including large wooden shoes and danced onstage at the church vestry. (Courtesy of the Hathaway family.)

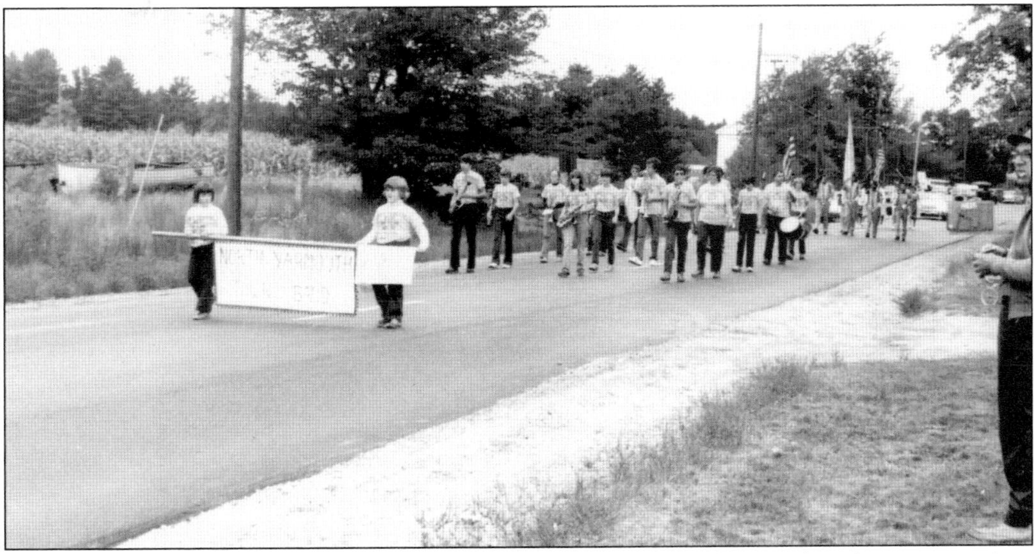

The North Yarmouth Community Band, so named because it includes members from surrounding towns, was started in 1975 just before America's bicentennial. Shirley Fountain asked George Warchol to organize the group using funds left over from the Memorial School Band. Members have ranged in age from students to retirees. They have marched in parades and entertained at the town Christmas party. Elaine Rooff, marching on the right in the September 1980 tricentennial parade, was an original member and still plays in the band today.

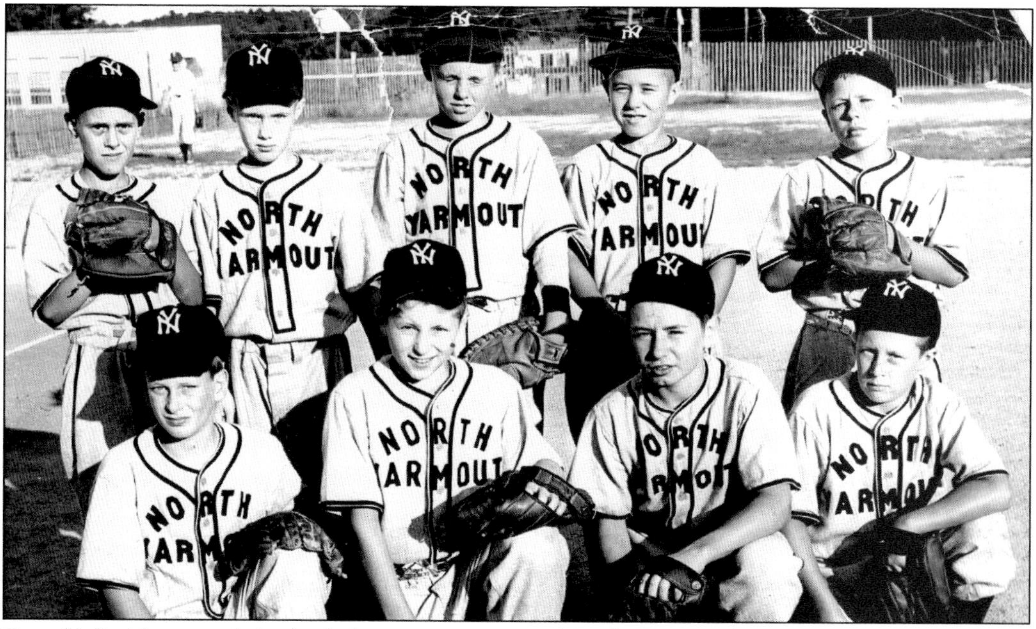

Donald Smith started the little league program in North Yarmouth in 1953 so his sons could play baseball. Marvin Beckwith served as assistant coach. Forming one of the earliest teams in the area, members had uniforms their first year. In 1954, they joined the Tri-Town League in Freeport and became perennial champions. The players in this 1955 image are as follows, from left to right: (first row) Jeff McConnell, Jerry Emery, Ronnie Allen, and Bruce Verrill; (second row) Eddie Schulte, Butch Goff, Dennis Beckwith, Gerald Tetreault, and Gerry Smith. (Courtesy of Marion Goff.)

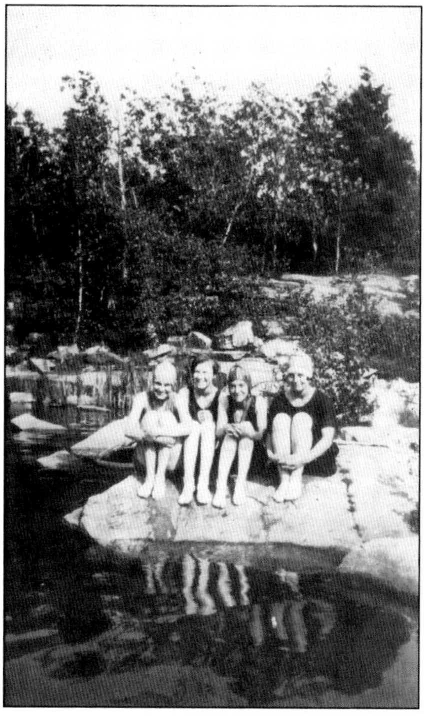

In this *c.* 1920 photograph, Frances Mann Knight (left) swims with her girlfriends at Charles Hodsdon's granite quarry, between Royal and Hodsdon Roads in Pownal. As the granite was removed, the hole began to fill with water, which made it a popular spot on a hot day. The water was about five feet deep, so residents could swim here safely. The quarry is overgrown today. (Courtesy of Frank Knight.)

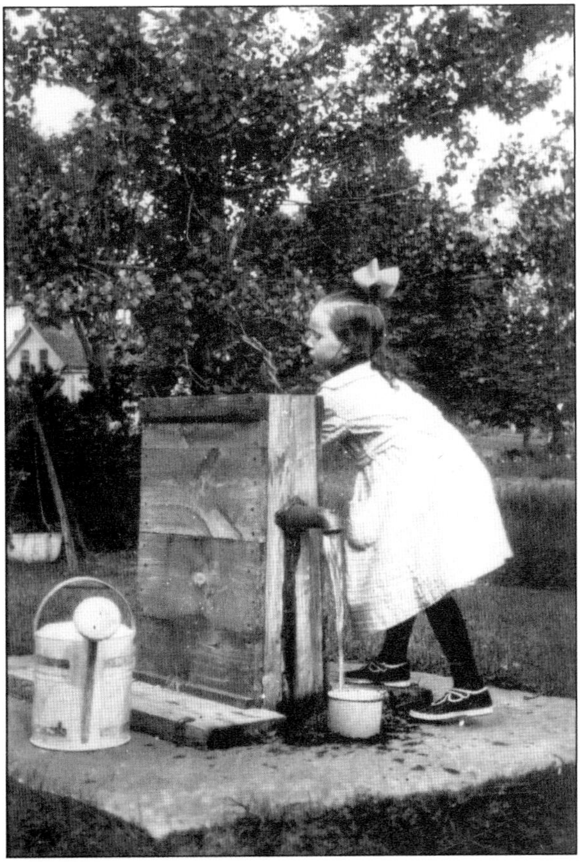

These images show scenes from a Memorial Day party at Capt. James Mountfort's home, 546 Walnut Hill Road, on May 30, 1929. Right, an unidentified young girl earnestly pumps water from the Mountforts' well. The men below are engaged in a game of croquet, a popular recreational activity in the country following the Civil War. Men and women played it in their yards and at summer hotels throughout Maine, including at the Wescustogo Hotel. (Courtesy of Dick Baston.)

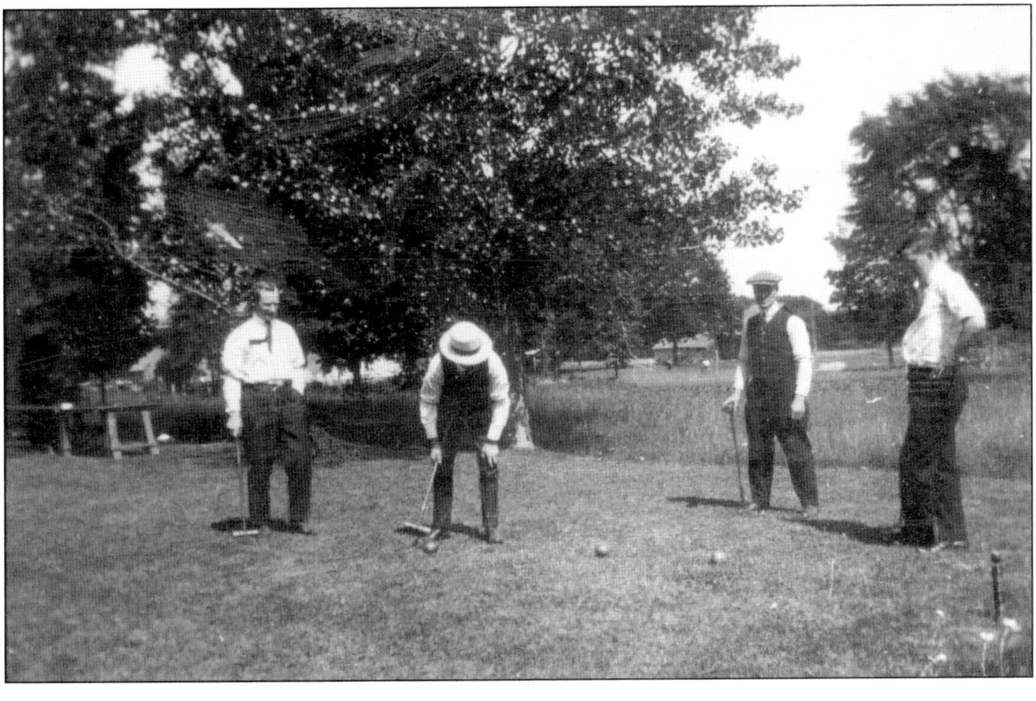

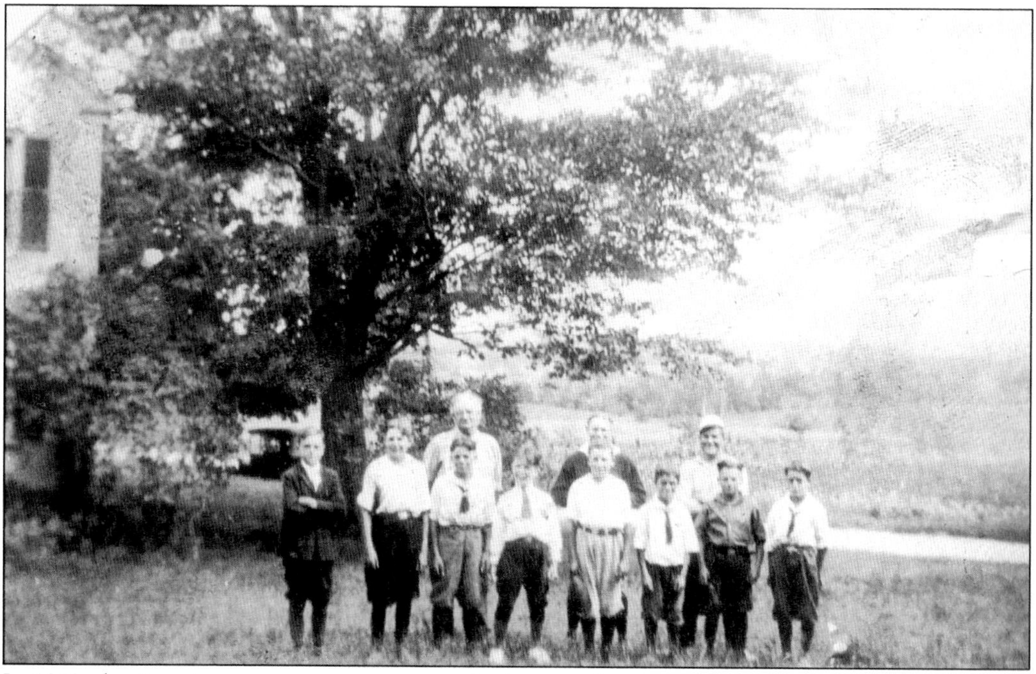

In 1910, the Boy Scout movement came to the United States from Britain and North Yarmouth started an early troop. This *c.* 1920 photograph shows the first troop at Charles Dunn's home, at 1264 North Road, with an automobile parked on Hallowell Road in the background. The boys wear kerchiefs but not the official uniform, as money was scarce for many families. Charles Dunn Jr. is the boy second from the left. (Courtesy of the Hathaway family.)

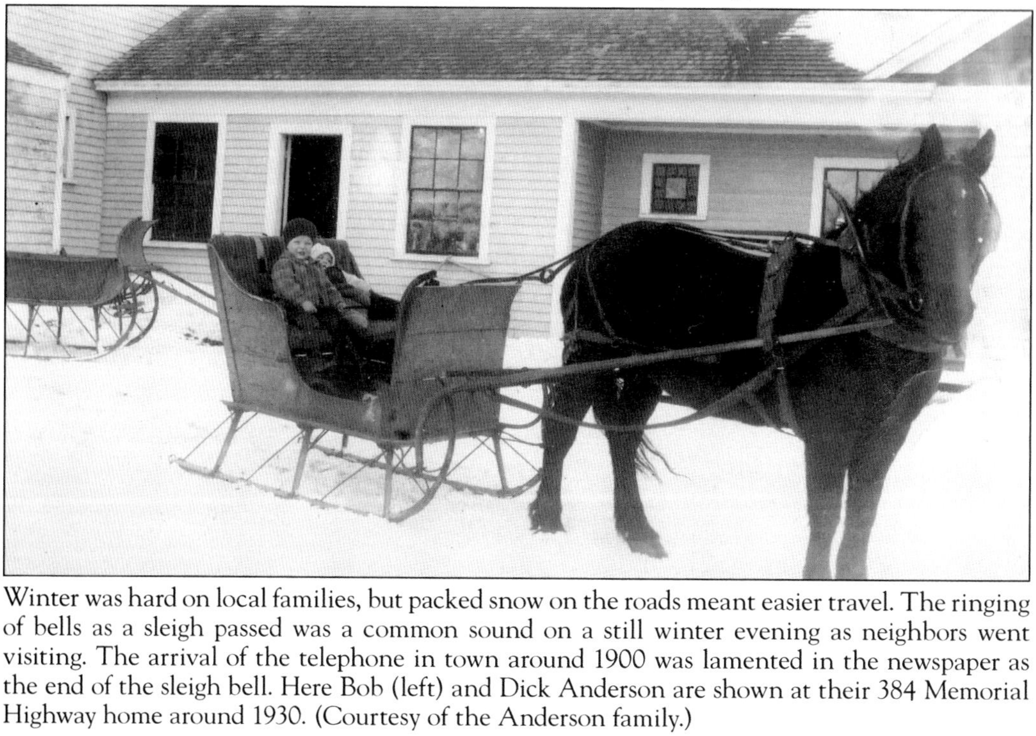

Winter was hard on local families, but packed snow on the roads meant easier travel. The ringing of bells as a sleigh passed was a common sound on a still winter evening as neighbors went visiting. The arrival of the telephone in town around 1900 was lamented in the newspaper as the end of the sleigh bell. Here Bob (left) and Dick Anderson are shown at their 384 Memorial Highway home around 1930. (Courtesy of the Anderson family.)

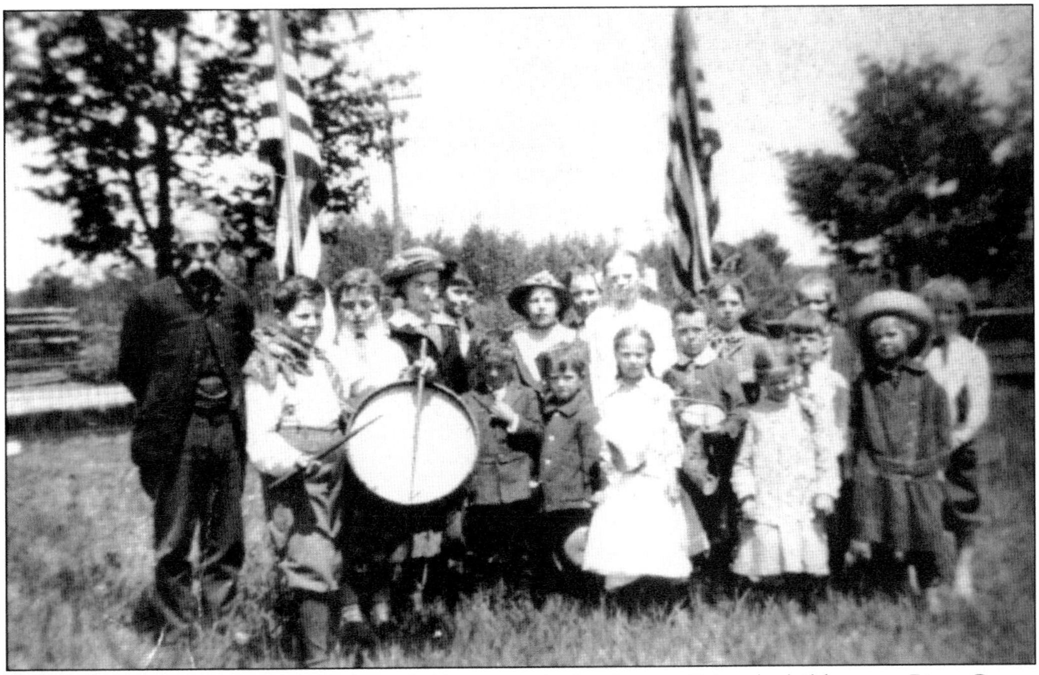

Civil War veteran Charles Colley (left) paraded the Dunn School children to Pine Grove Cemetery each Memorial Day. In this 1912 image, one can see the iron fence that still stands today. Identified are Arthur Lawrence with the drum and baseball glove on his shoulder, his sisters Charlotte (left) and Shirley both with braids in the first row, Charles Dunn Jr. behind Shirley, Ruth Dunn with a hat in the rear center, and Lucy Dunn to the right of Ruth.

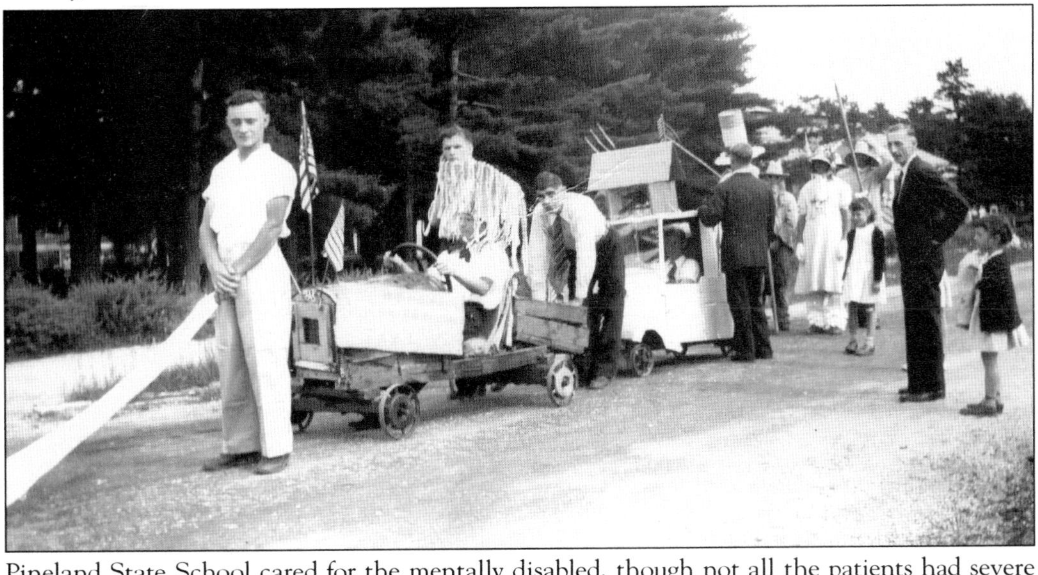

Pineland State School cared for the mentally disabled, though not all the patients had severe handicaps and so were allowed to work for local poultry farmers. In the 1970s, the school had a basketball team that played junior high school teams such as Greely. One runaway patient burned several hay barns in North Yarmouth as he made his way through town. Pineland celebrated the Fourth of July each year with fireworks that drew people from all over and a parade such as this one, likely around 1945. (Courtesy of Kenny Allen.)

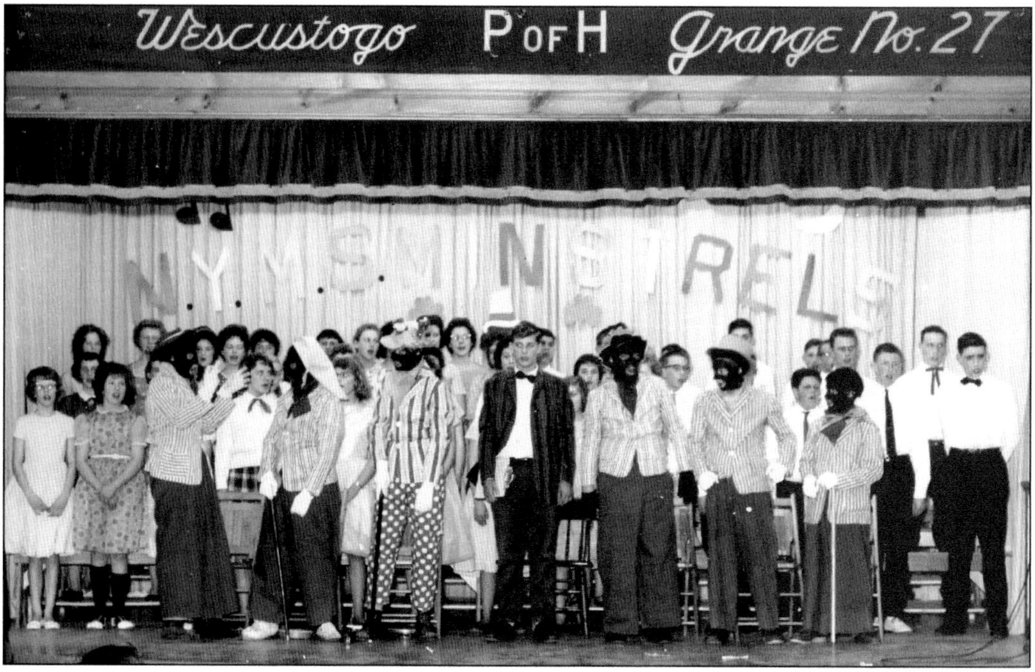

North Yarmouth Memorial School students put on a minstrel show for their parents and the public each year. This image shows a traditional blackface show held at the Wescustogo Grange Hall in the early 1960s. Run by the Grange, the shows continued into the 1970s and 1980s, although without the blackface. Local residents helped with the Thursday and Friday night shows, which were fund-raisers for the Grange organization.

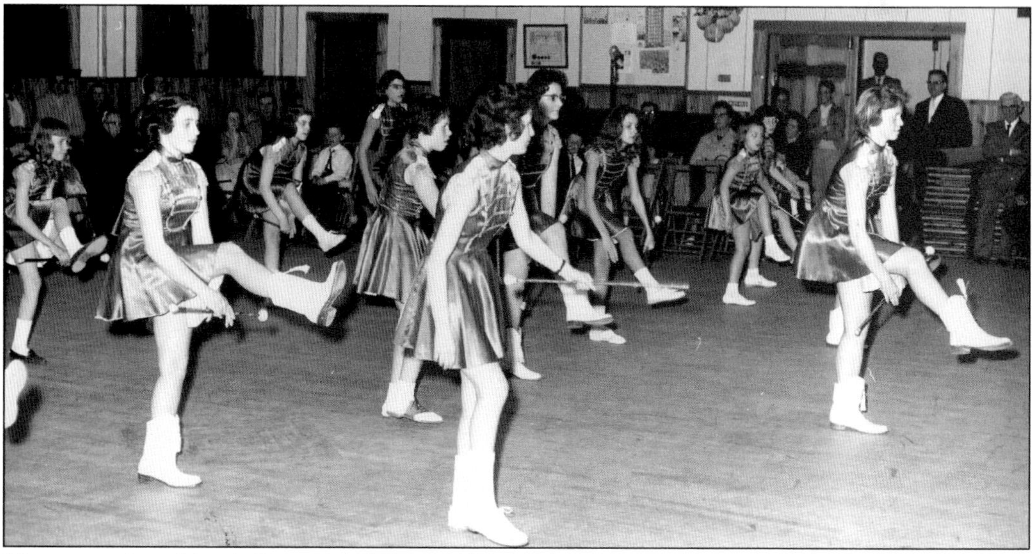

Majorettes from North Yarmouth Memorial School perform in Wescustogo Grange Hall about 1965. The mothers of the students sewed the uniforms and made hats from satin placed around cardboard forms to hold the shape. The girls regularly marched in parades in Yarmouth and Gray, as well as in North Yarmouth. The Grange assisted the majorettes and the school band financially. Here they appear to be performing for Grange members at one of their Thursday night meetings.

Five

PLACES WE LEARNED

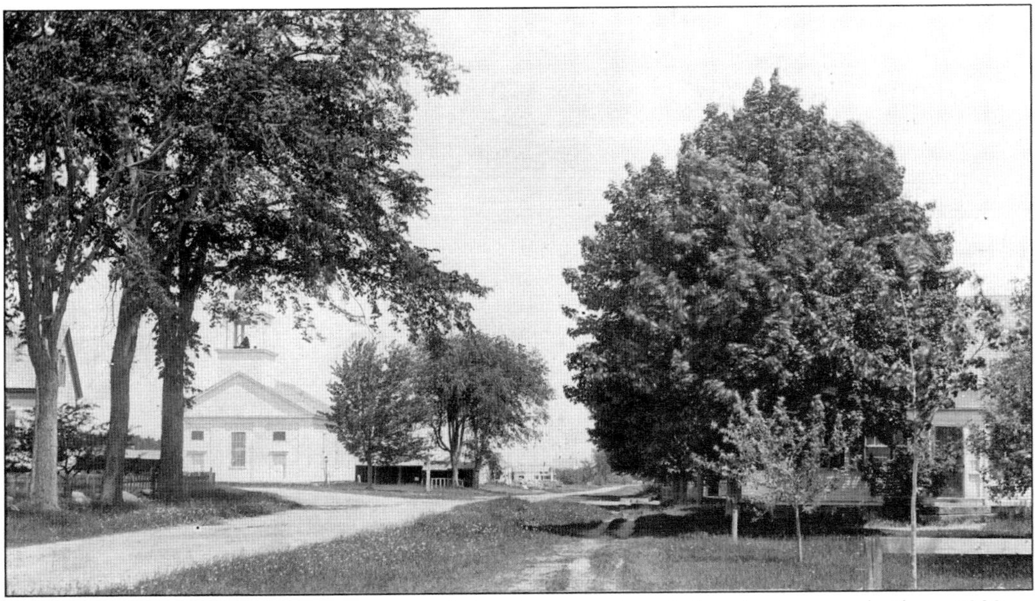

This *c.* 1900 view shows the area around the Congregational church that was built in 1839 to replace the 1794 meetinghouse on the same site. It includes an elm-lined street and a fence next to the church vestry, which was built in 1866. Directly across the street from the vestry, James Doten's blacksmith shop operated from 1877 to 1918. The front is visible on the right, behind the large maple tree and the J. Dunn house. It is no longer standing. On the left of New Gloucester Road in the distance is the Daniel Skillin house, which was struck by lightning and burned on August 20, 1917. Horse sheds behind the church were used to shelter members' horses and carriages during services. Early deeds show sales of small land plots and refer to blacksmiths, a school, and a store near the meetinghouse, suggesting that this area was the first village center. The coming of the new stagecoach line around 1800 redirected traffic to the intersection of Routes 9 and 115, thus creating a new center of commerce.

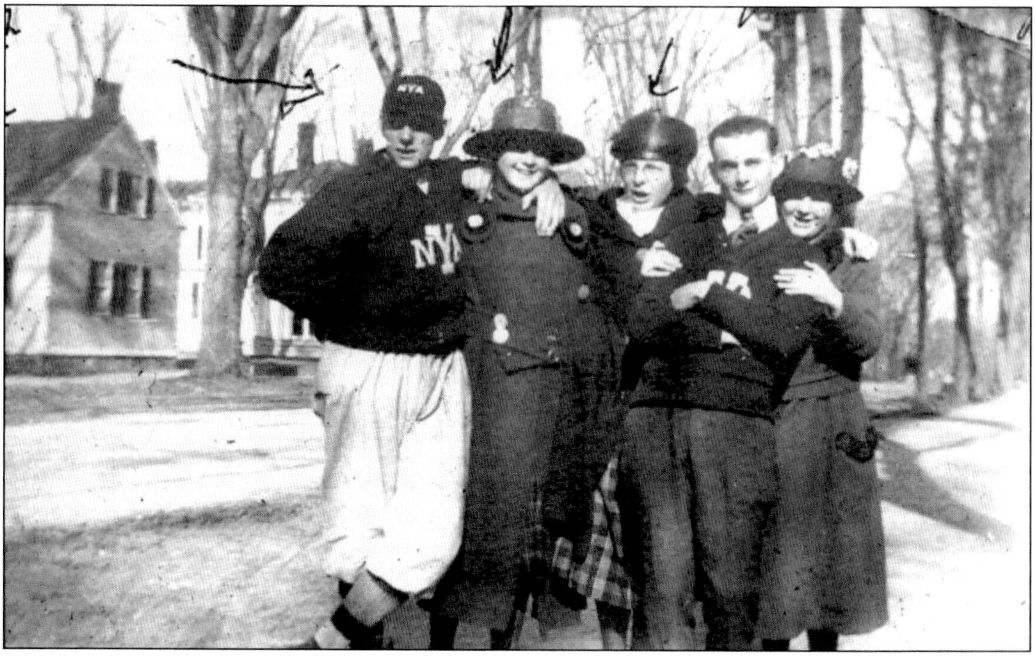

Since North Yarmouth did not have a school beyond eighth grade before 1965, students were tuitioned to the high school of their choice. Typically residents who lived in East North Yarmouth or whose parents had attended North Yarmouth Academy (founded 1814) chose to go there. In this 1919 image, Clifton Sargent appears on the left in an academy sweater while his future wife, Lucy Dunn, is in the middle. They are standing on the lawn in front of Academy Hall. (Courtesy of the Hathaway family.)

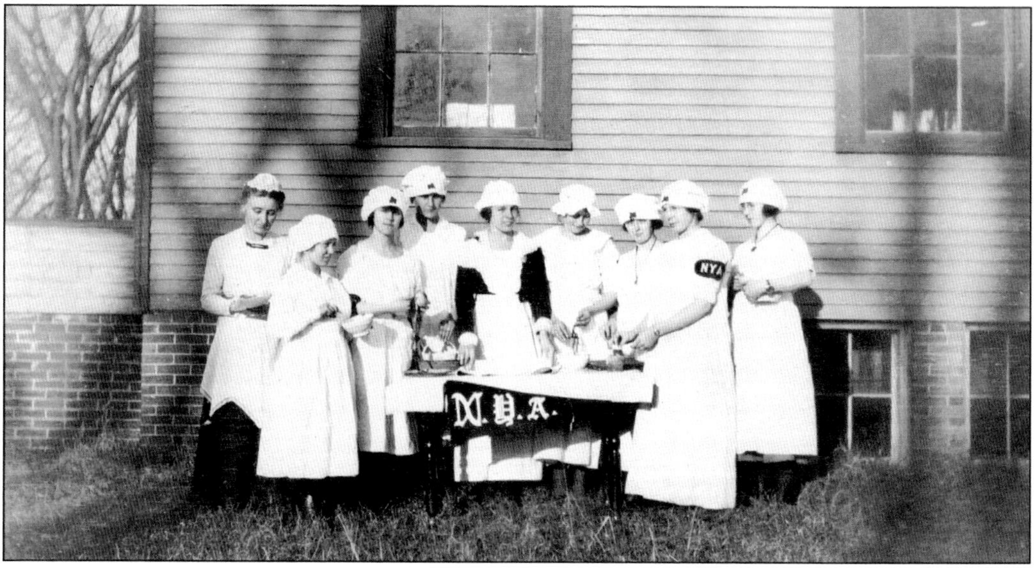

This 1919 photograph of North Yarmouth Academy's Cooking and Housekeeping Club shows advisor Mrs. Hall on the left and North Yarmouth residents Lucy Cushman Searles, Inez Merchant Pulsifer, Ruth Dunn DeRoche, Lucy Dunn Sargent with NYA armband, and Ellen Cushman Allen, along with other students Mabel Leighton and Helen Knight. The club appears to be engaged in food preparation. (Courtesy of Dick Baston.)

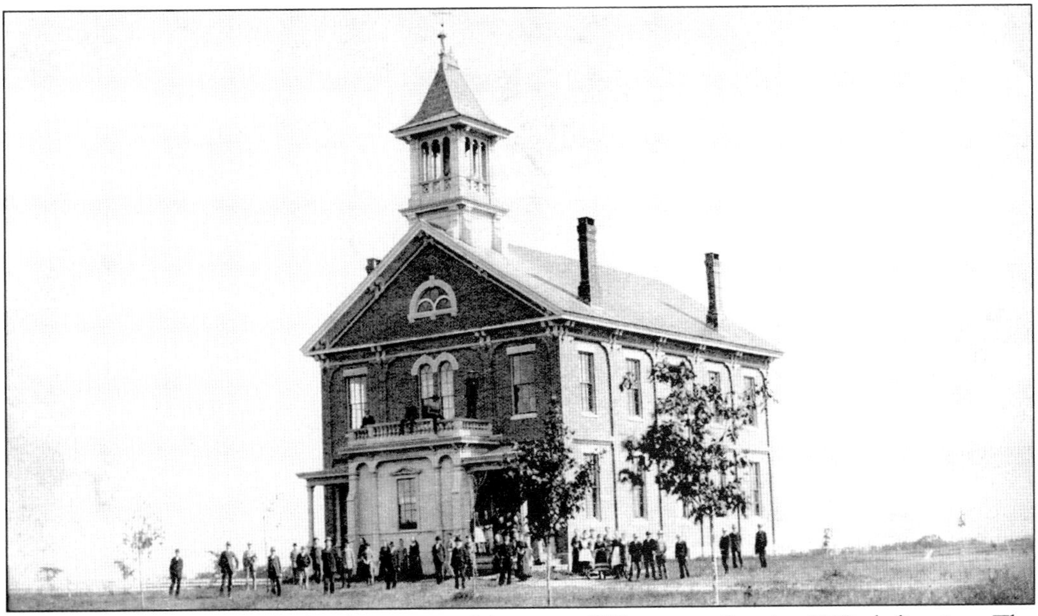

Greely Institute in Cumberland is pictured here in 1872, soon after its 1868 dedication. The Cumberland Fairgrounds, including a track for harness racing, were located behind the school at this time. The West Cumberland Fairgrounds were also operational and the two competed for several years. The institute building was financed by a bequest from Eliphalet Greely, a Portland businessman from Greely Road. Walnut Hill residents of North Yarmouth generally chose to attend high school here before MSAD 51 was formed in 1965. (Courtesy of the Cumberland Historical Society.)

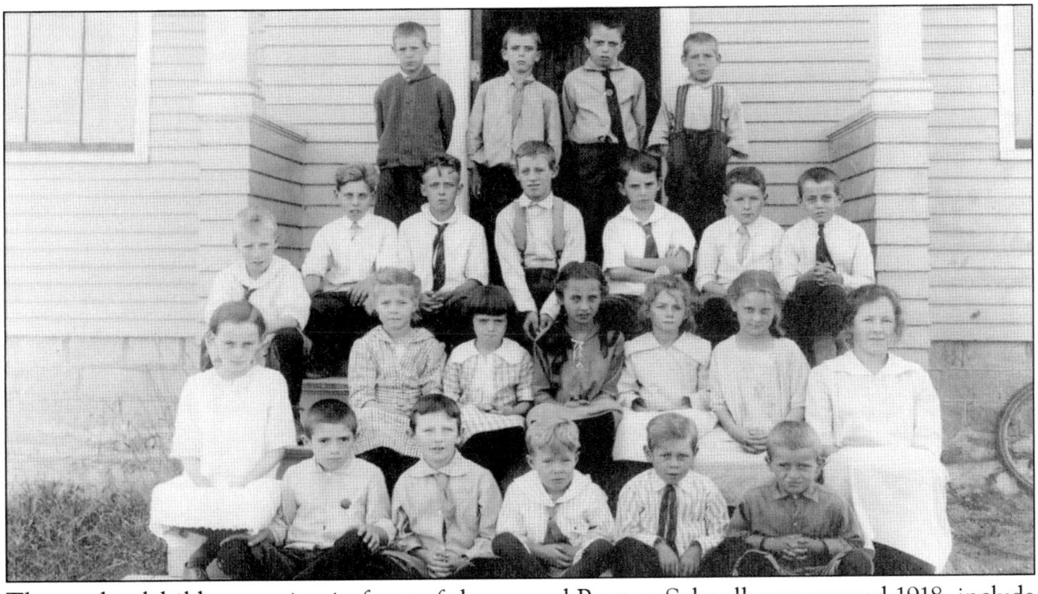

These schoolchildren, posing in front of the second Buxton Schoolhouse around 1918, include (second row) Nellie Smith Leighton (third from left) and Shirley Hamilton Fountain (far right). Built in 1909 at the corner of Pea Lane and Route 115 (308 Yarmouth Road), the school smelled of wet wood, sawdust, and old wool, according to Leighton. The building was sold to Phil Coffin on the condition that he destroy it; he used it for storage for a few years until the town burned it down around 1970.

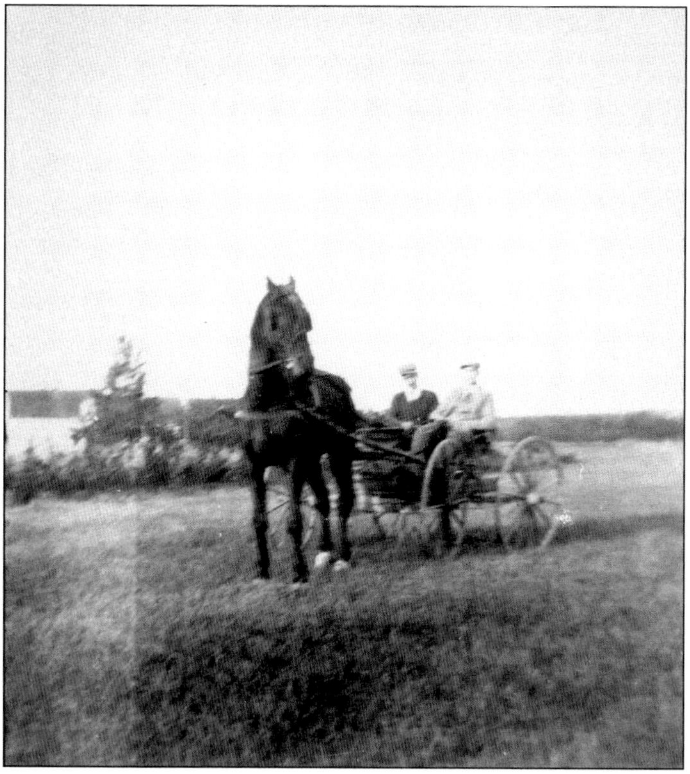

Charles Small (right) and one of the Lowe boys drive a horse and buggy from Walnut Hill to high school at Greely Institute in 1926. Charles grew up on the dairy and produce farm of his parents, George and Olive, on Gray Road near the Congregational church. He became a dairy farmer on Ledge Road in Yarmouth, eventually retiring to North Yarmouth, where he held the Boston Post Cane for being the oldest resident.

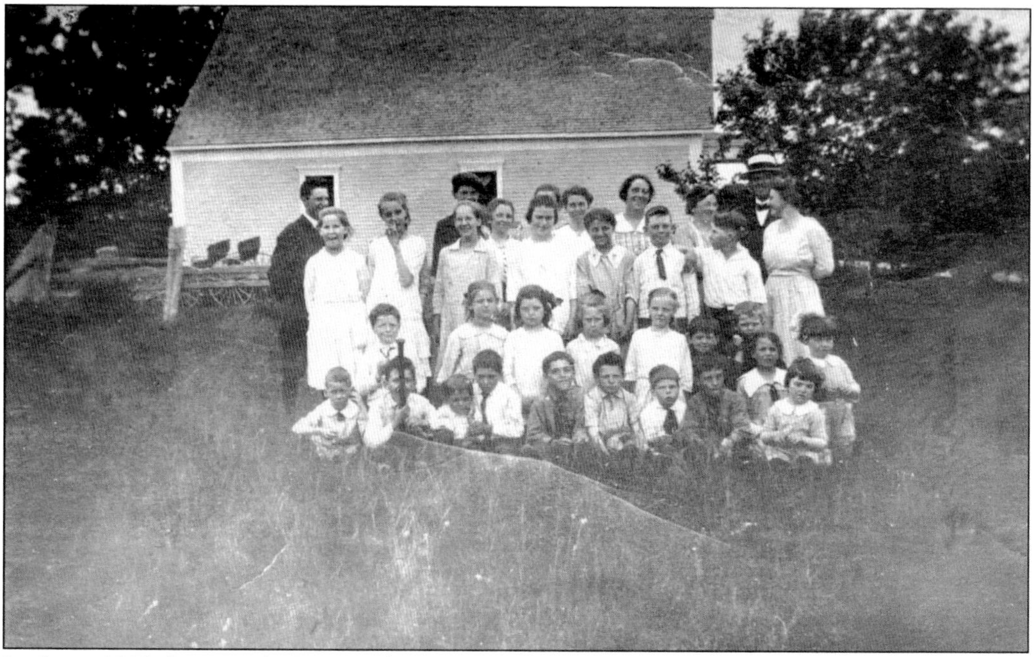

In this *c.* 1915 photograph, Dunn School students attend the end-of-year picnic in the yard of the Old Town House, down the road from their school. The Old Town House was built in 1853 as the first town hall. This view shows the early windows that were later changed in the 1940s when it became a schoolhouse. It is now the home of the historical society. (Courtesy of Ginger Collins.)

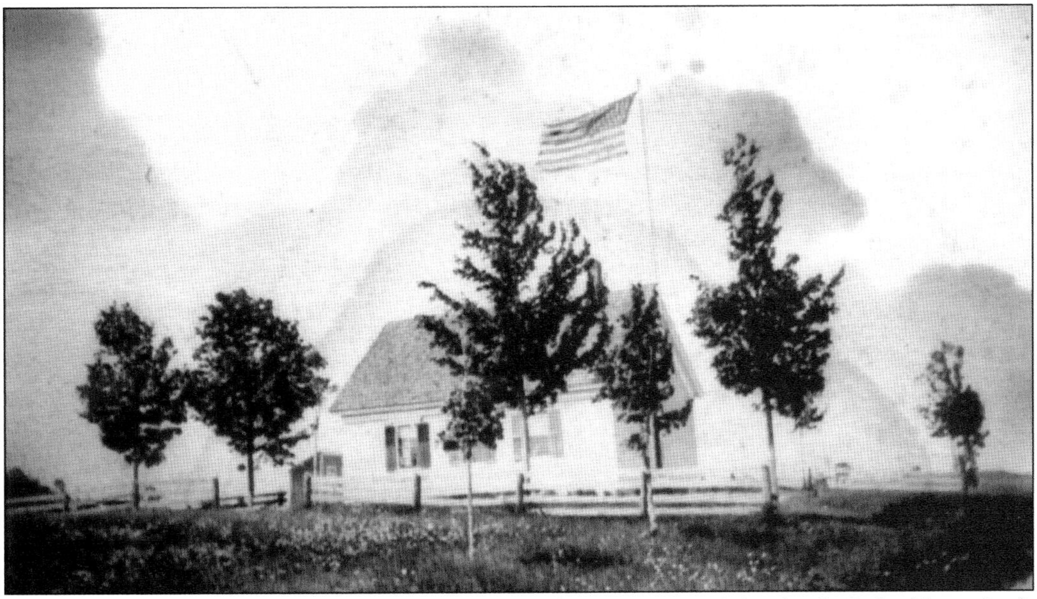

In December 1884, School District No. 6 opened the new Dunn School, which had been built on property bought from Charles Dunn on Hallowell Road. The privy is behind the schoolhouse in this *c.* 1910 scene. It replaced a *c.* 1805 red schoolhouse that local lore says originally stood near Crockett's Corner and was later moved to Dunn's Corner across from the James Dunn house. The red schoolhouse was struck by lightning on July 15, 1891, and burned after it was no longer in use as a school. (Courtesy of Ginger Collins.)

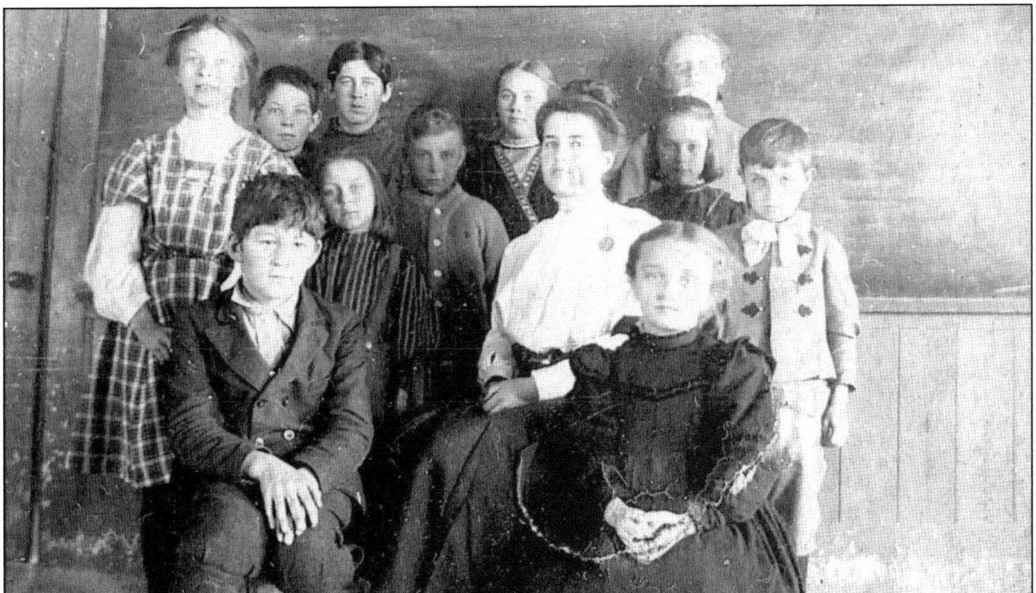

This Dunn schoolhouse image is the only known inside view of a one-room schoolhouse. The teacher and her students, including Susie Sawyer in the plaid dress, are gathered in front of the blackboard. Marion Knight Reed attended school here and later served as the janitor. She remembers the older boys going to the neighbor's well to bring a bucket of water, since the school had none. (Courtesy of Ginger Collins.)

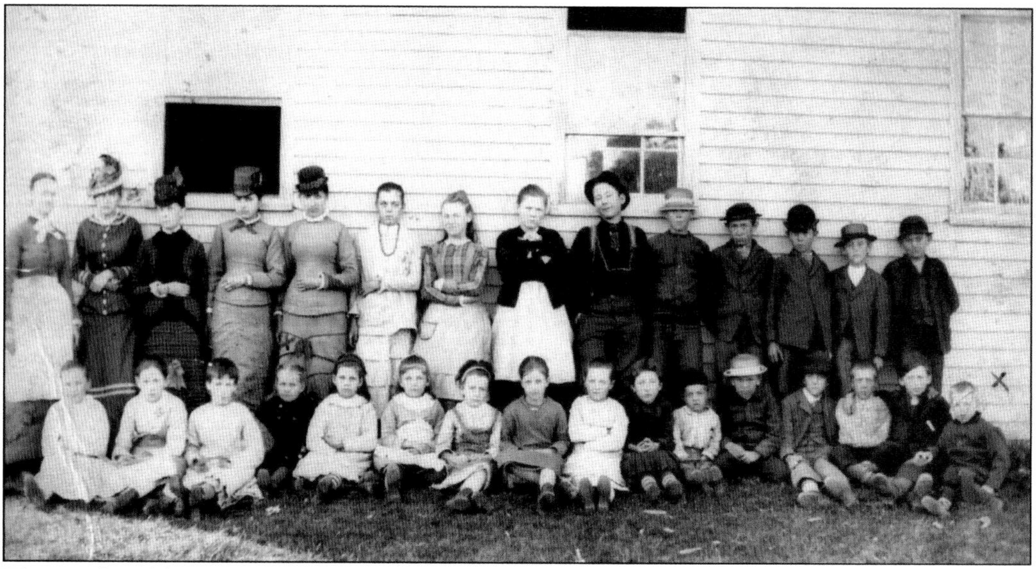

This is the oldest known image of a North Yarmouth school class, taken in October 1880 at the original District No. 2 Walnut Hill School. This building stood on the east side of New Gloucester Road, just past Lufkin Road. Mabel Skillin, age seven, is fourth from the left in the first row, and her brother Isaac Skillin, age four, is at the right end of the same row.

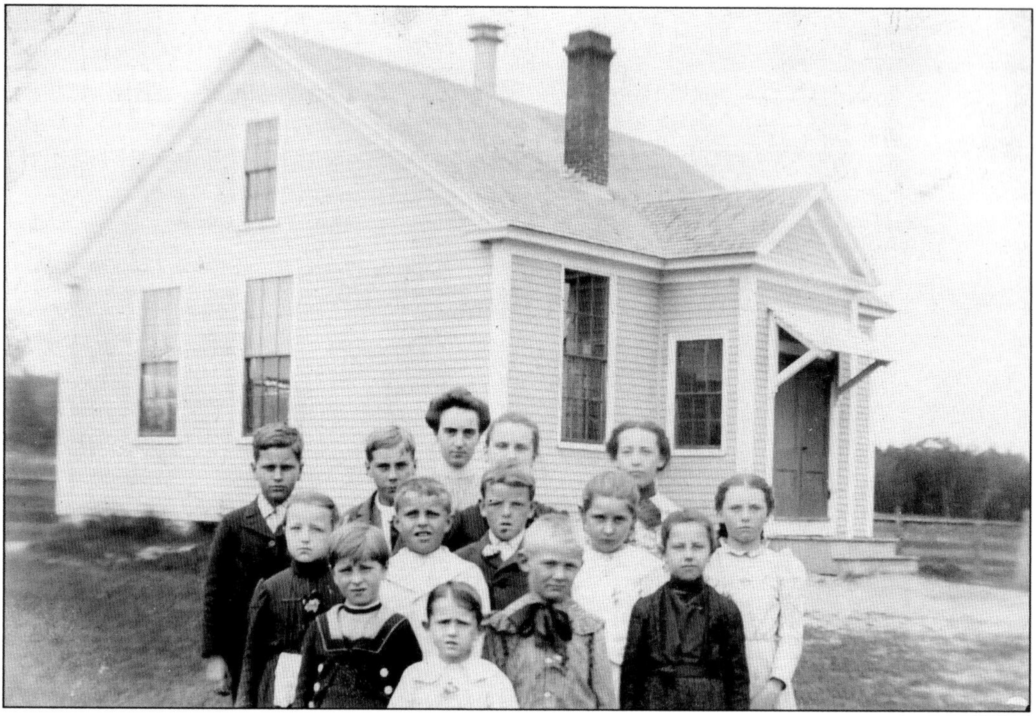

The more modern Walnut Hill School, replacing the original building in 1895, was built on the west side of the road. This c. 1897 class photograph includes Myra, Guy, and Harvey Lovell in the second row and Arthur Hayes and Ernest Hamilton (back row, from left). When the schoolhouse was no longer being used, it was moved across the street to 23 New Gloucester Road and converted to a home.

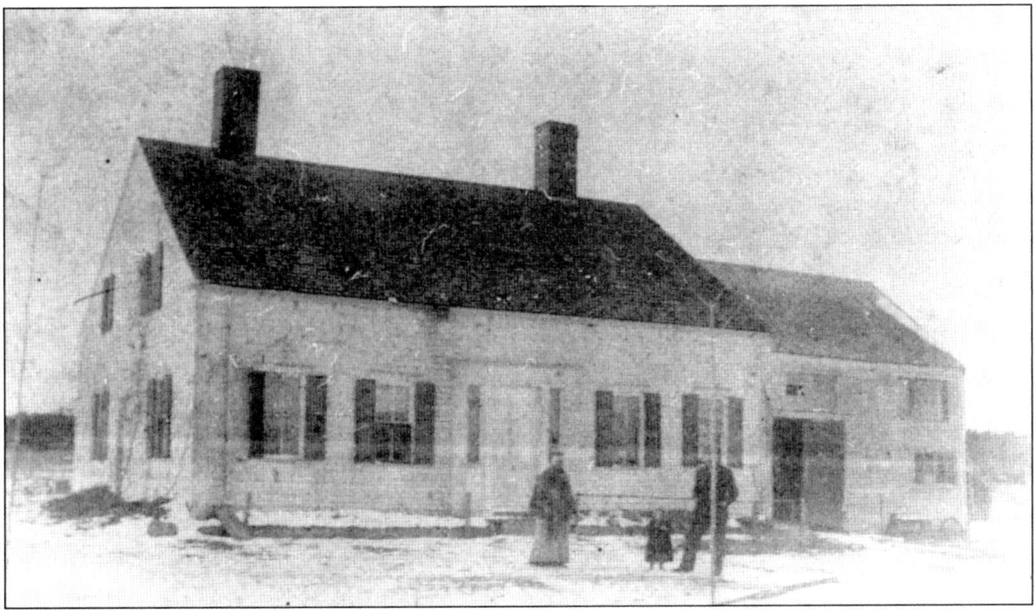

This house, adjacent to the Walnut Hill School at 10 New Gloucester Road, was purchased by Frank Sawyer in 1892. Each school district bid off boarding of the teacher for the lowest cost, and often the District No. 2 teacher boarded here with the Sawyers. This 1895 image shows Frank, his wife, Abbie, and their son Elmer. In 1900, the barn was replaced with the current one, which then served as a stable.

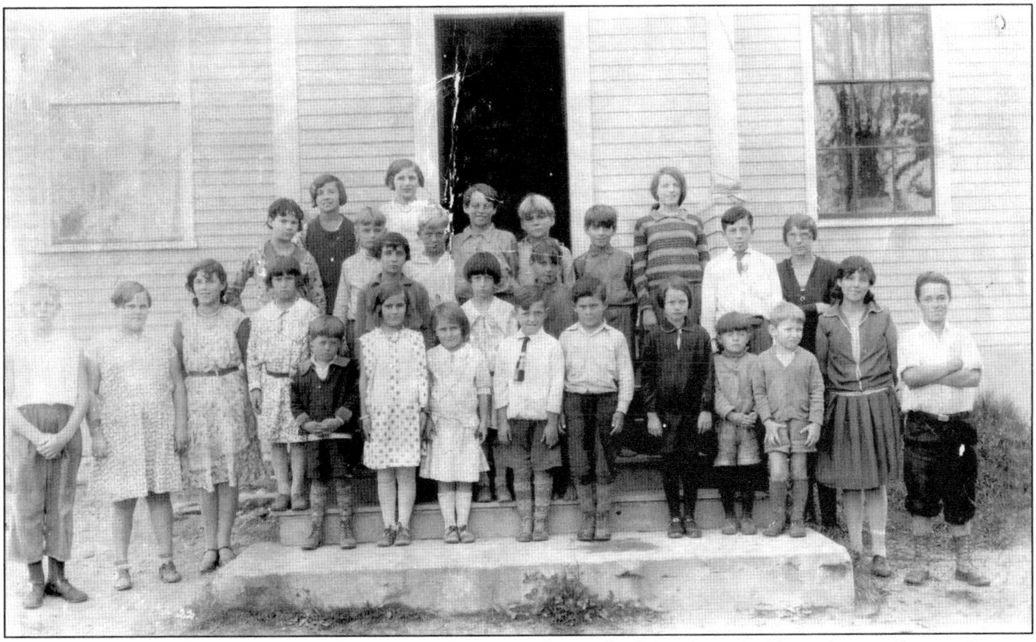

The schoolhouse in District No. 4 was originally called Ryder's Hill and was located near 612 New Gloucester Road. In 1895, a new District No. 4 School was built on land from the Hicks family at the corner of Mill Road and was dedicated by a tipsy minister. In this 1933 image, Hicks School teacher Cora Fox poses with her class of 27 pupils. Twelve children are from the Liberty family and four are Jewetts. The house serves as a private residence today at 442 Mill Road.

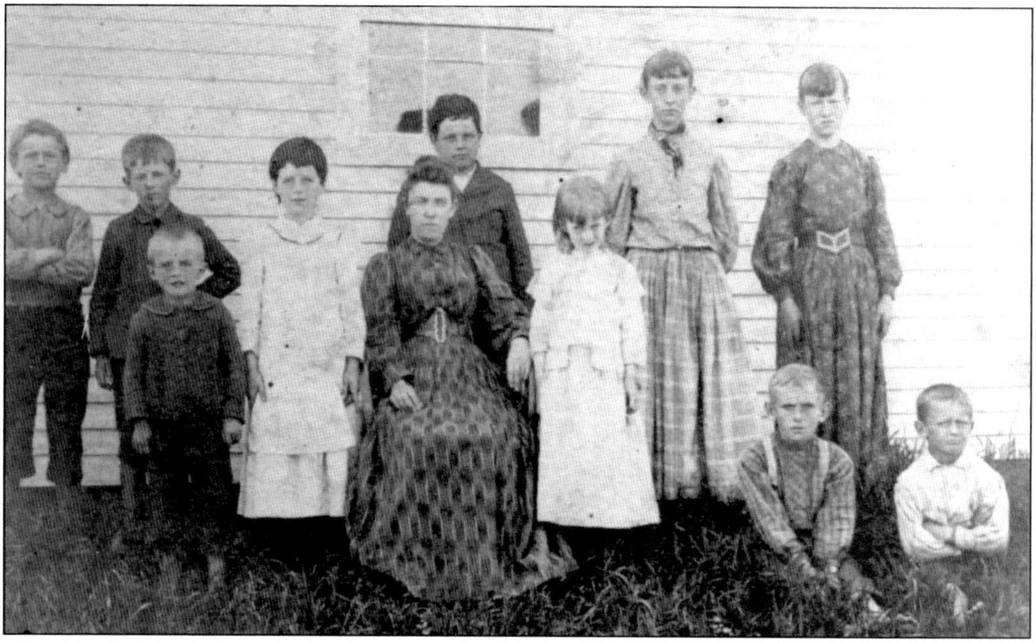

The District No. 9 School, also known as the Washington School, stood next to the 1871 Lowe residence and across the street from the home at 881 Sligo Road. When it closed in 1903 after many years of declining enrollment, the students were sent to the Walnut Hill School. The building was torn down and the wood was used to build horse sheds at the Old Town House. This c. 1892 photograph includes six Pullen children, Guy (third from left), Josephine (fifth from right), Leon (far right), Will (second from left), Maude (fourth from right), and Grace (second from right), with their teacher (seated, fifth from left). (Courtesy of Ruth Ristich.)

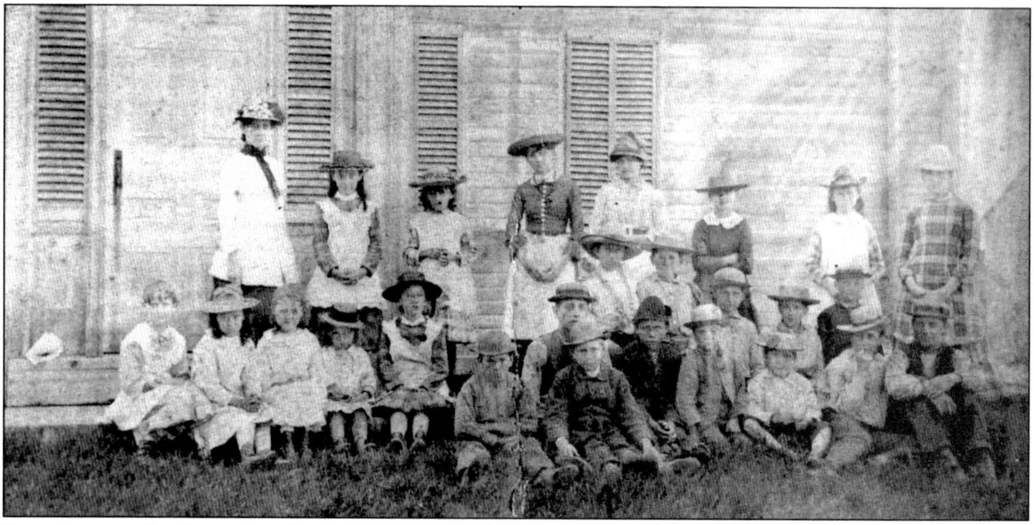

Seen here is the last school group to attend the original red schoolhouse across from the James Dunn house, where this image was taken in the spring of 1884. The new Dunn School opened in December 1884. Charles Dunn is the second boy from the left in the first row, while Herbert Lawrence is the second boy from the right in the second row. They must have been told to wear their hats! Of the town's seven one-room schoolhouses, three closed and four were replaced between 1884 and 1910.

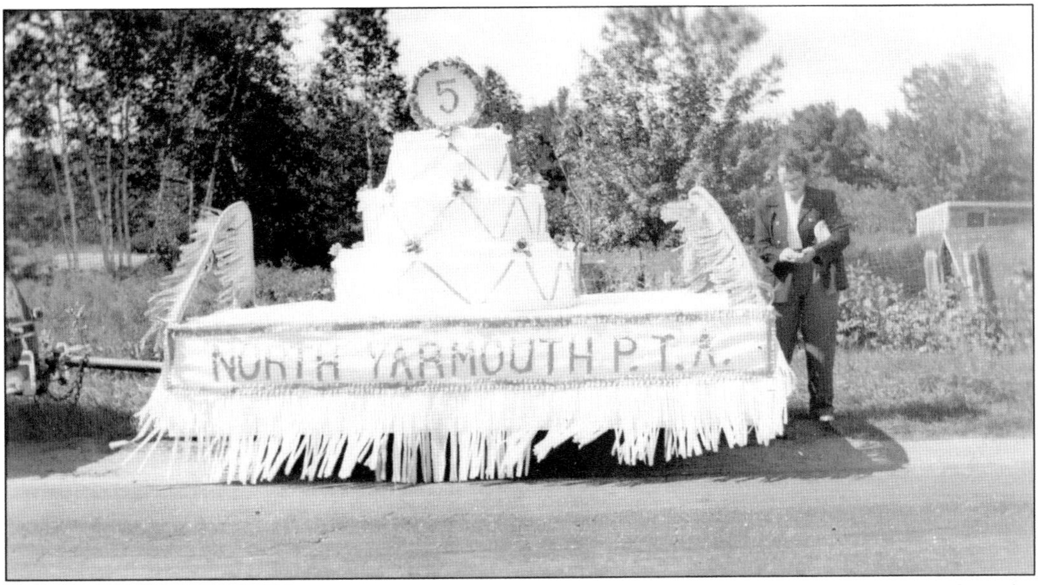

The Parent Teachers Association of the North Yarmouth Memorial School made a float for the 1957 Wescustogo Grange Fair parade. The birthday cake is topped with the number 5, apparently indicating the fifth anniversary of the organization. The Memorial School opened in 1950 and consolidated the one-room schools, leading to the creation of this new association. The float is on Walnut Hill Road in front of the Grange Hall.

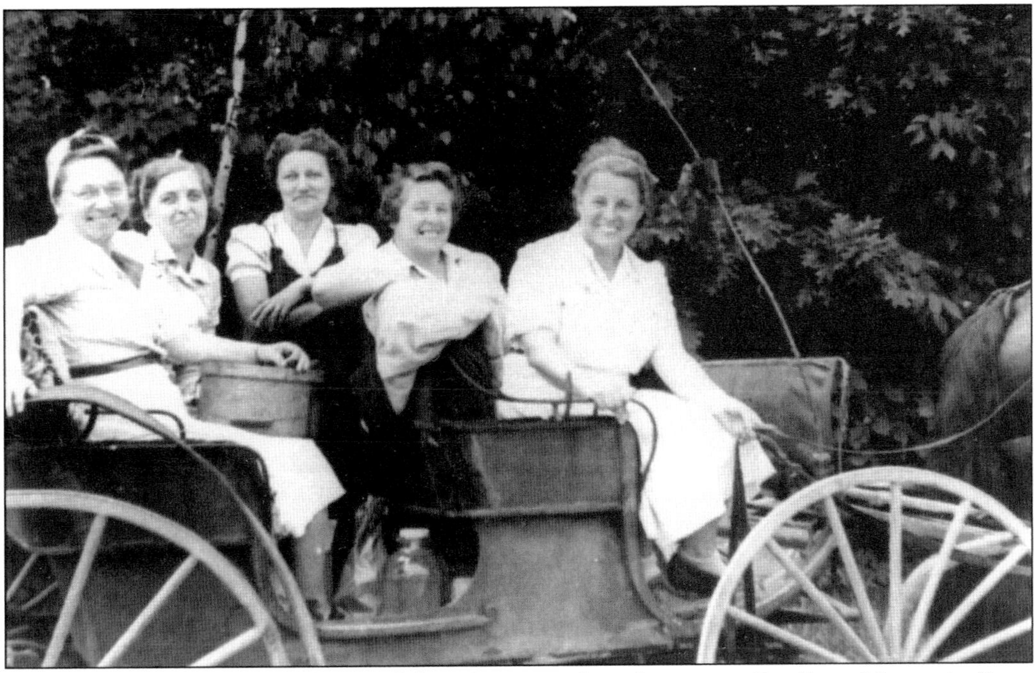

One-room schoolhouse teachers and friends set out for a day trip to Bradbury Mountain State Park in Pownal around 1945. They have borrowed Charles L. Dunn's blind horse and wagon and are leaving from his house at Dunn's Corner. Pictured here from left to right are Velma Ames Bornheimer, Maude Small, Florence Richards Ames, Shirley Hamilton Fountain, and Ruth Dunn DeRoche.

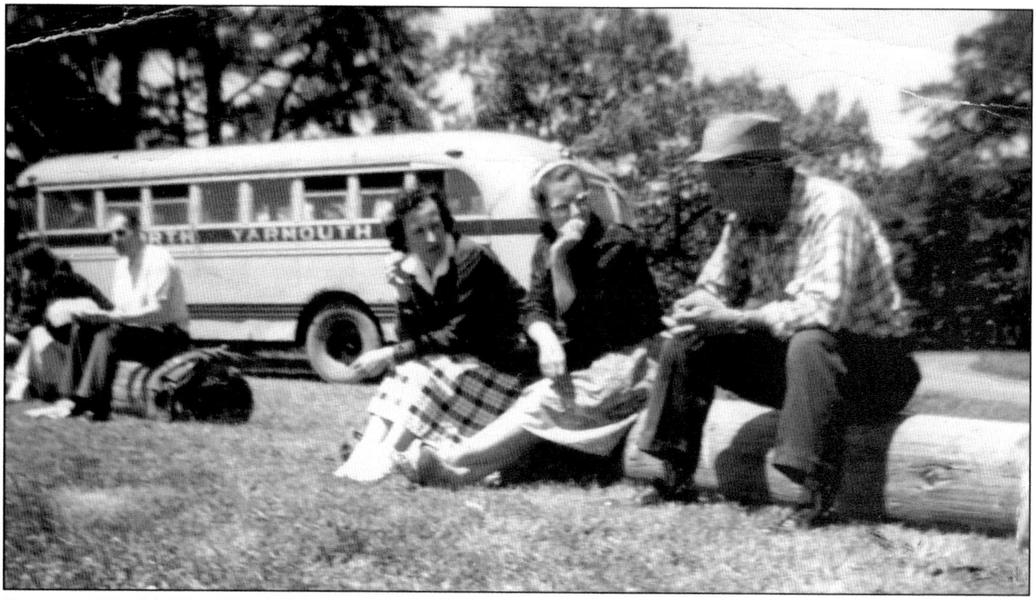

Prior to World War II, children attended the one-room schoolhouse closest to their home and were generally able to walk there. After that time, the schools were reorganized and grouped by age, which made transportation necessary for many students. Residents like Bert Lawrence were hired to drive students to school. The opening of the consolidated Memorial School required busing throughout town. This photograph, taken in June 1960, shows driver and owner Carleton Semmes with schoolchildren and teachers, including fifth-grade teacher Mr. Kane at the far left. (Courtesy of Elaine Gallant.)

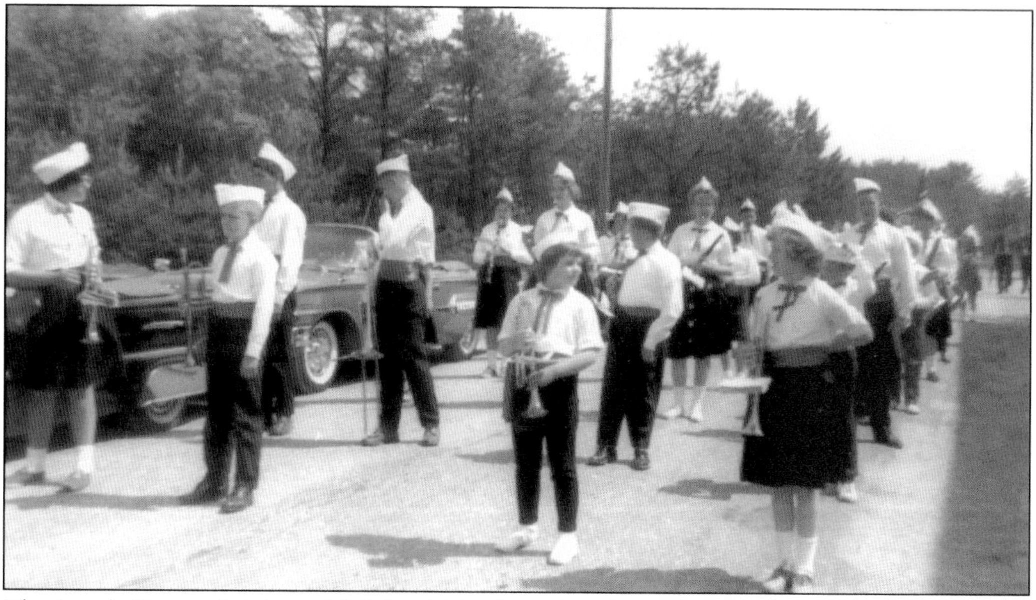

The North Yarmouth Memorial School Marching Band was popular during the 1960s, as not many other recreational activities were available to young people in town. Members marched in many parades each year in Gray and North Yarmouth. Shirley and Henry Fountain were active boosters of the band. When Henry died in 1966, the band dedicated a plaque to him that hung in Wescustogo Grange Hall. (Courtesy of Harriet Bowie.)

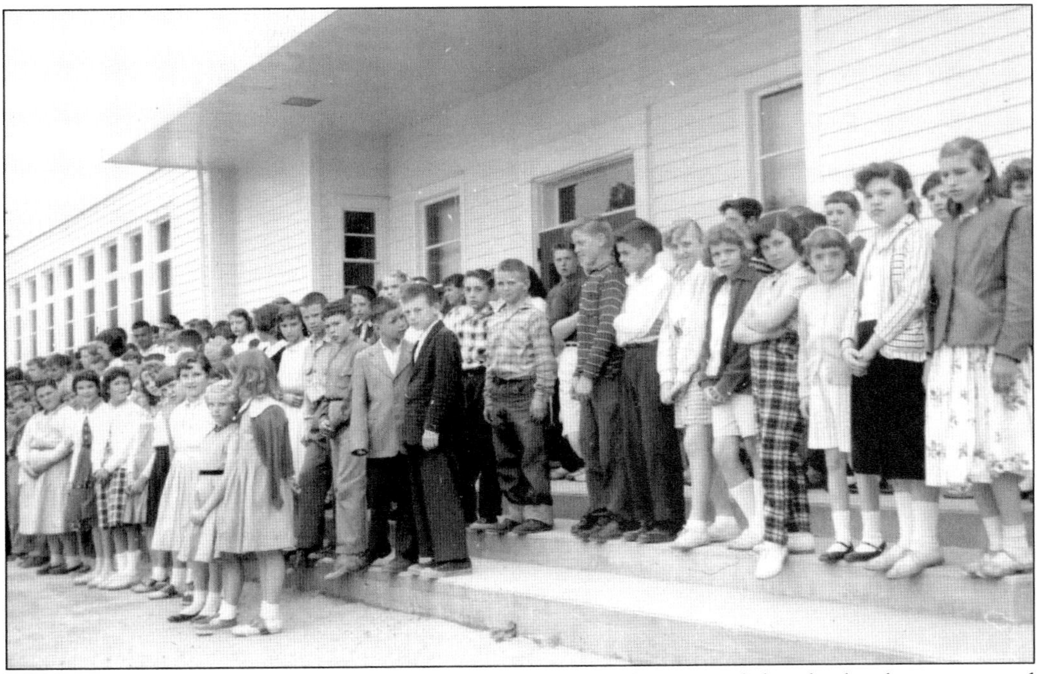

When it opened in 1950, the Memorial School was the first consolidated school in town and housed kindergarten through eighth grades. Multiple grades shared rooms, and after a few years it was necessary to build an addition to house the growing number of students. Each grade then had its own room and the kindergarten was moved into the Congregational church vestry. Memorial School students are gathered on the front steps in 1958.

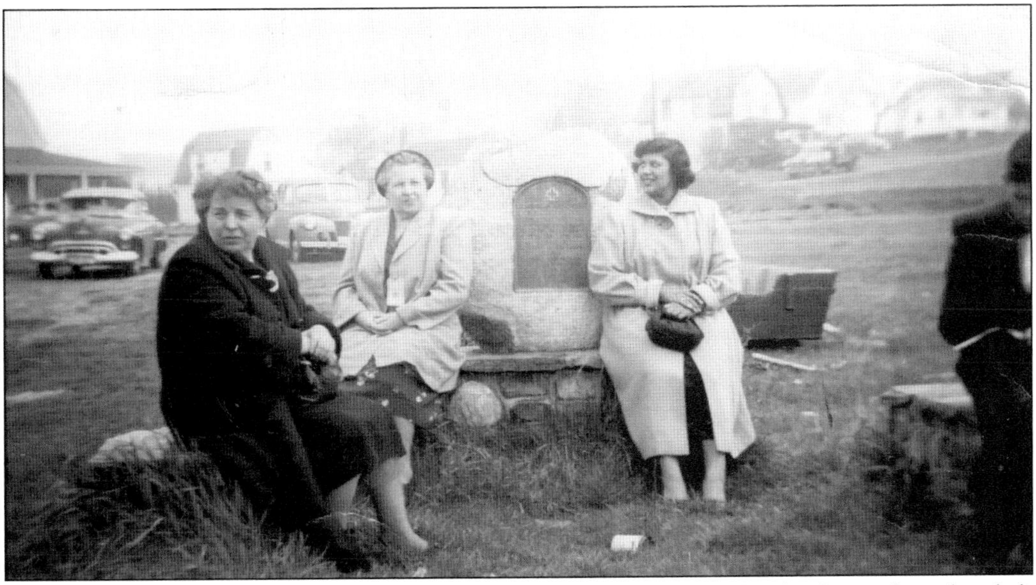

Teachers enjoying an outing are, from left to right, Ruth Dunn DeRoche (seventh and eighth grades), Shirley Hamilton Fountain (fifth and sixth grades), and Ann Cummings (first grade). Cummings, the first black teacher in North Yarmouth, taught at the Memorial School from 1951 to 1953. Her weekly salary in 1952 was $65.38. She was reportedly well liked by her students. (Courtesy of Ginger Collins.)

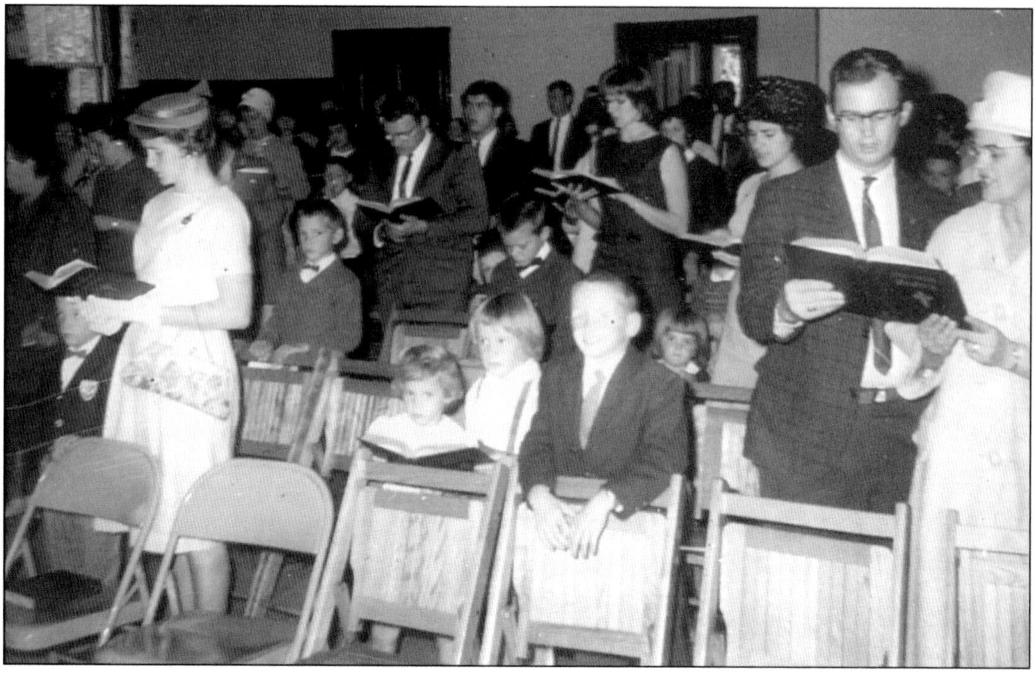

In 1965, the Congregational church was lifted to install a basement for classrooms. Sunday services were held in the vestry for months during the construction. This 1965 image shows people dressed up for church. Ladies wore hats and dresses and men and boys wore coats and ties. Pictured here, from left to right, are the following: (first row) Glen, Fran, Diane, Cindy, and Peter Freeman, and Vernon and Marion Goff; (second row) Scott, Linc, Lorna, and Barbara Merrill; (third row) Jay Rogers, Bruce Doyle (behind), Jay Jr., and Dot Rogers. (Courtesy of Ruth Faut.)

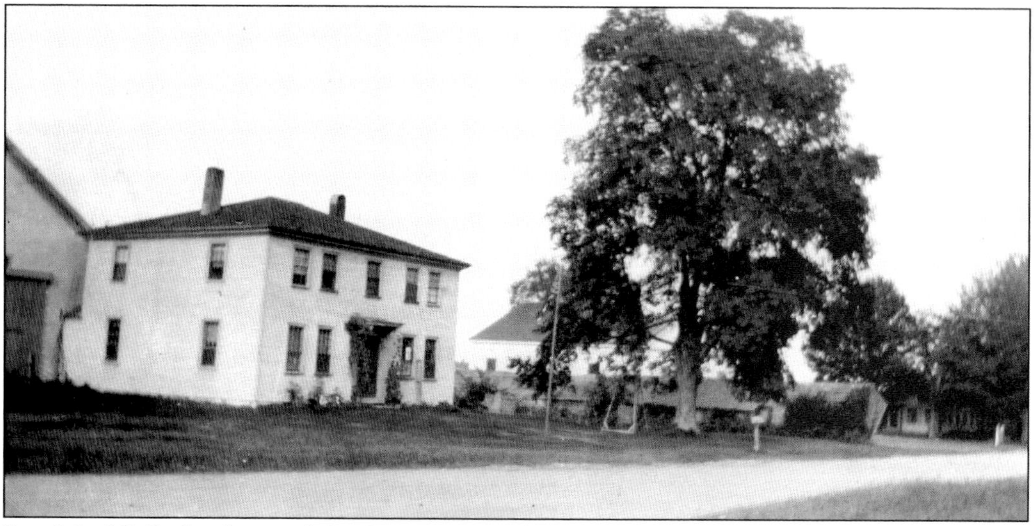

Rev. Jehiel S. Richards served the Congregational church from 1901 to 1907. He retired to North Yarmouth and lived in this home adjacent to the church, shown about 1930 with its lone elm tree and the church's horse sheds behind. His daughter Annie lived here after her parents died and was an active church member. In 1961, the church bought the house for a parking area and sold the residence to Robert Verrier, who had it moved to its present location on Wescustogo Lane in 1964.

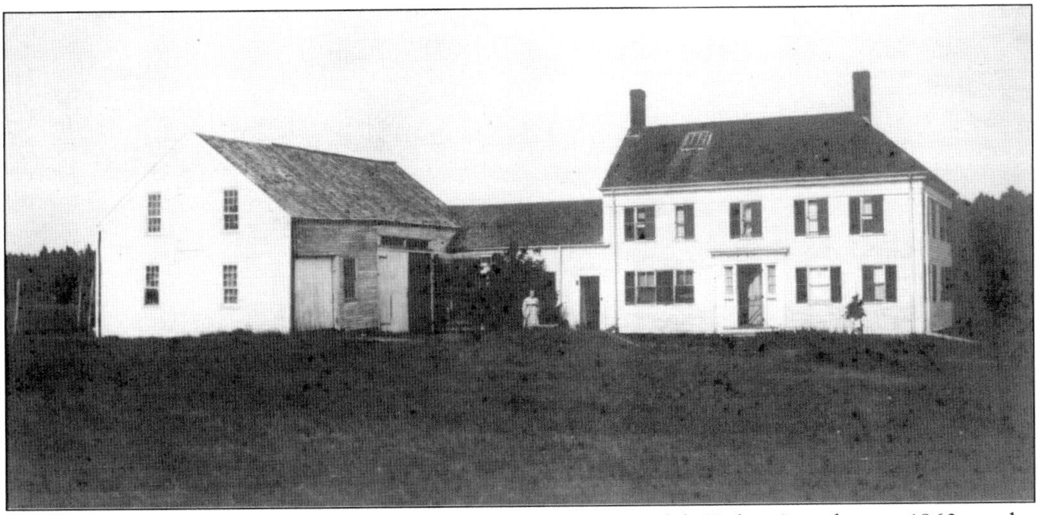

The Congregational church bought this house from Rev. Caleb Hobart's widow in 1860 on the condition that it be used "forever" as home for the minister. Parsonage Road takes its name from this unusually shaped Federal building constructed prior to 1857, which did indeed serve as a parsonage until it was sold in 1978. The church had decided to pay the minister an allowance to buy his or her own home to avoid the continual repairs on the aging building, shown here around 1920.

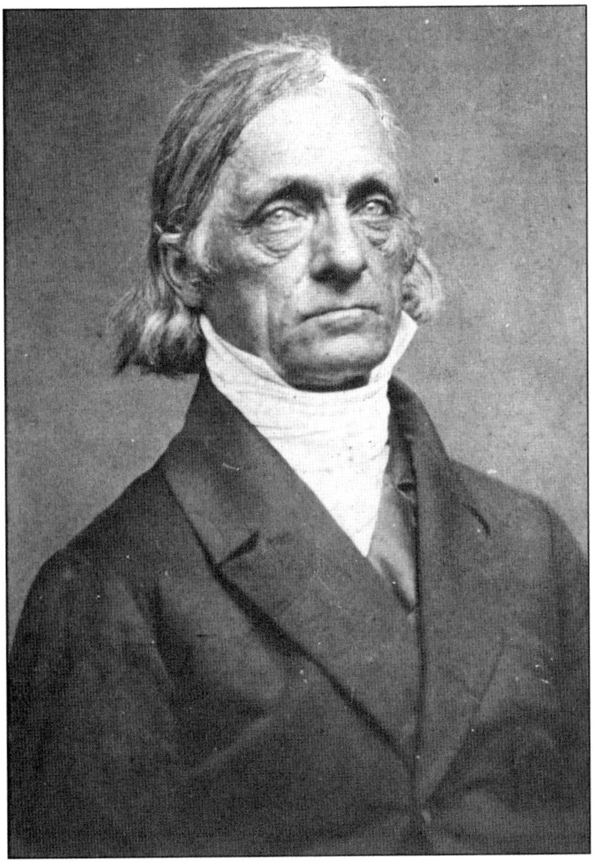

Rev. Caleb Hobart, depicted in this c. 1850 daguerreotype, served the Congregational church for 36 years from 1823 to 1859, longer than any other pastor in its 200-year history. Hobart was known as a strict disciplinarian, and his correspondence describes grievances, trials, and accusations against members for not attending church or for disagreeing with his views. Although some left the church during his pastorate, his lengthy service suggests his parishioners were largely content with his role as religious teacher.

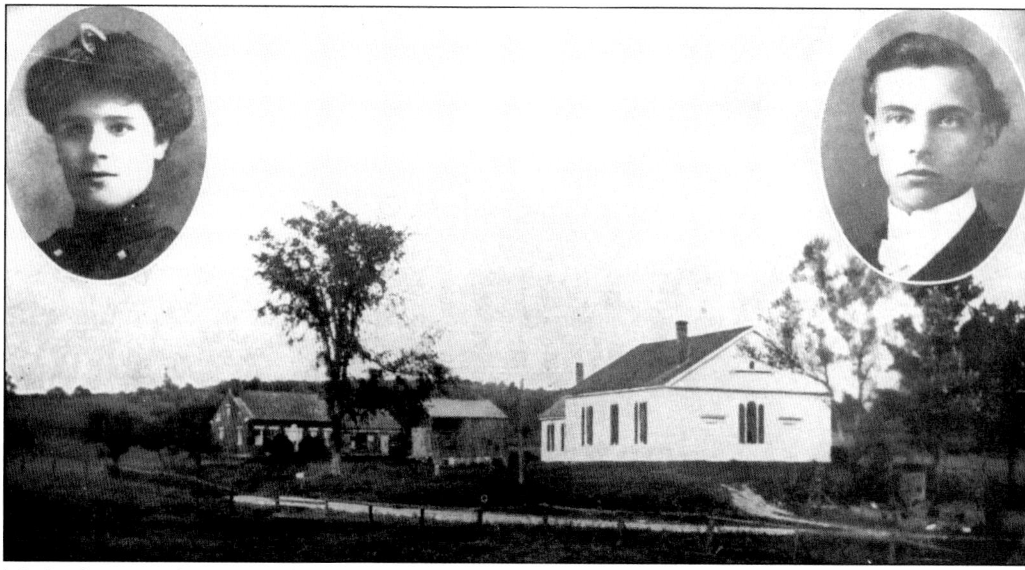

Methodist preachers visited East North Yarmouth as early as 1814. This early church was built in 1831 at the intersection of West Pownal and Lawrence Roads. Rev. Benjamin Burnham built the brick house seen behind the church in 1830 and served as minister until 1870. It became the parsonage, but burned in 1914, and the current residence was built. As a policy, the Methodist Conference changed ministers at local churches every two years, so church members struggled to build strong relationships with their ministers. The congregation weakened after World War II and by the 1960s, was nearly dormant. The building was sold for salvage in 1979. The 1906 postcard above shows the Methodist minister Joseph Stopford and his wife Lydia. In the c. 1915 photograph below, the minister, likely H. W. Brooks, walks past the home of Jeremiah Walker, which was located across the street from the church before burning in 1925. Walker gave part of his land to build the church. (Courtesy of Noyes Lawrence.)

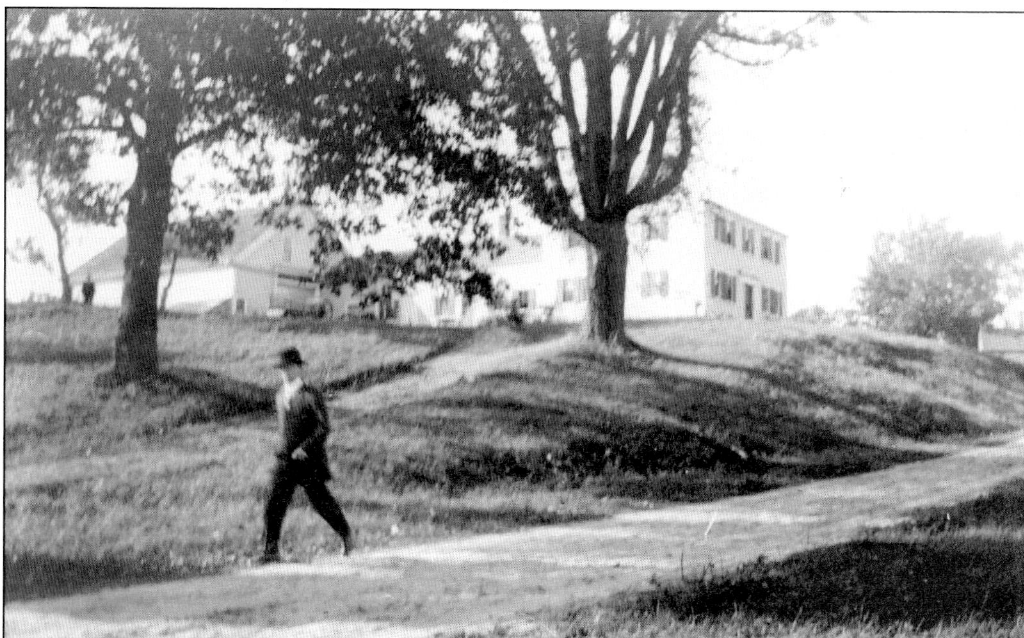

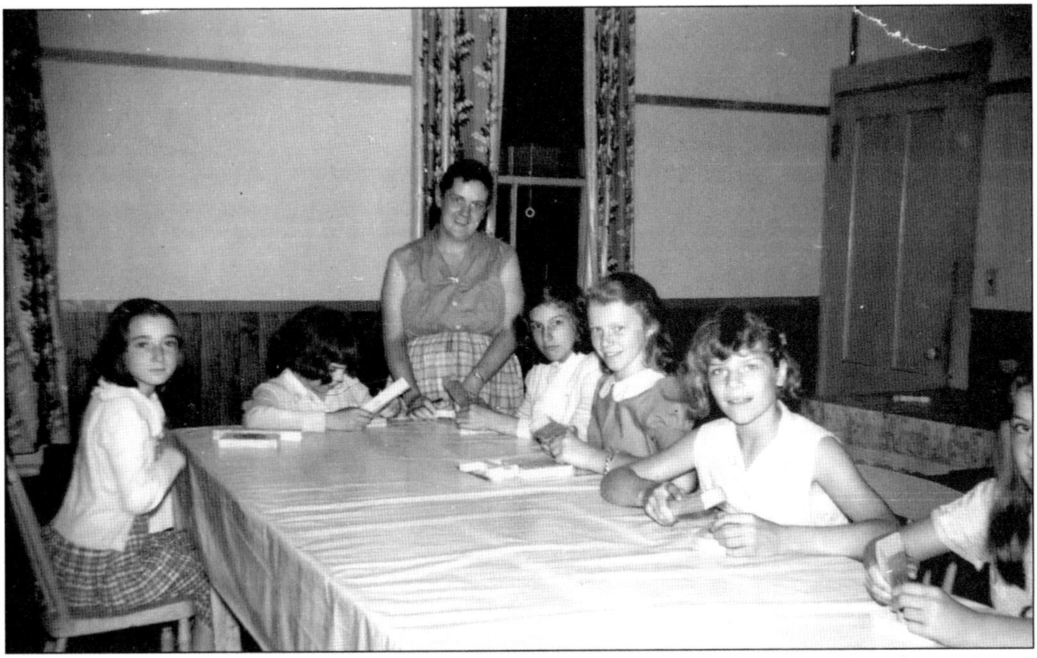

A Sunday school class meets in the vestry of the Methodist Church around 1959. Left to right are Mary Davis, Judy Hilton, Becky Giddinge, Gloria Cote, Judith Bowie, and Beverly Hilton. The vestry was a later addition attached to the church in 1871. It was used for functions including bean suppers, youth group and Camp Fire Girls meetings. The vestry was not torn down with the church and remains in its original location. (Courtesy of Harriet Bowie.)

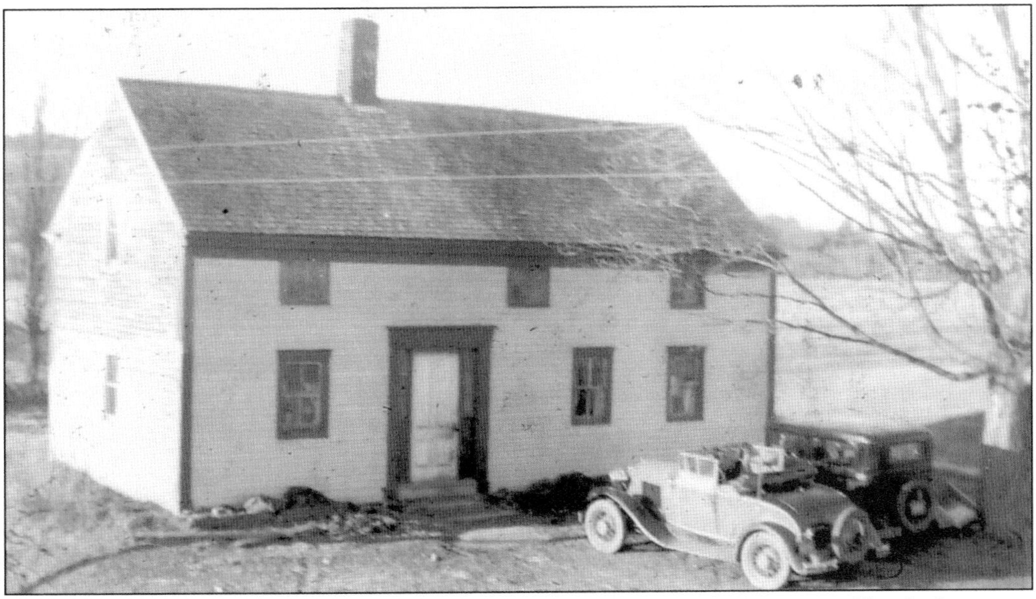

The E. Jordan home, built about 1871 was situated in the "heater," a piece of land where two roads intersect and form a triangle. At the corner of West Pownal and Lawrence Roads, it was directly in front of the Methodist church. Different families including Chadbournes rented the home, depicted in this *c.* 1940 photograph. "Mack" the Jewish peddler spent nights here while selling fresh fruit in the area. The home disappeared after 1955. (Courtesy of Esther Walker.)

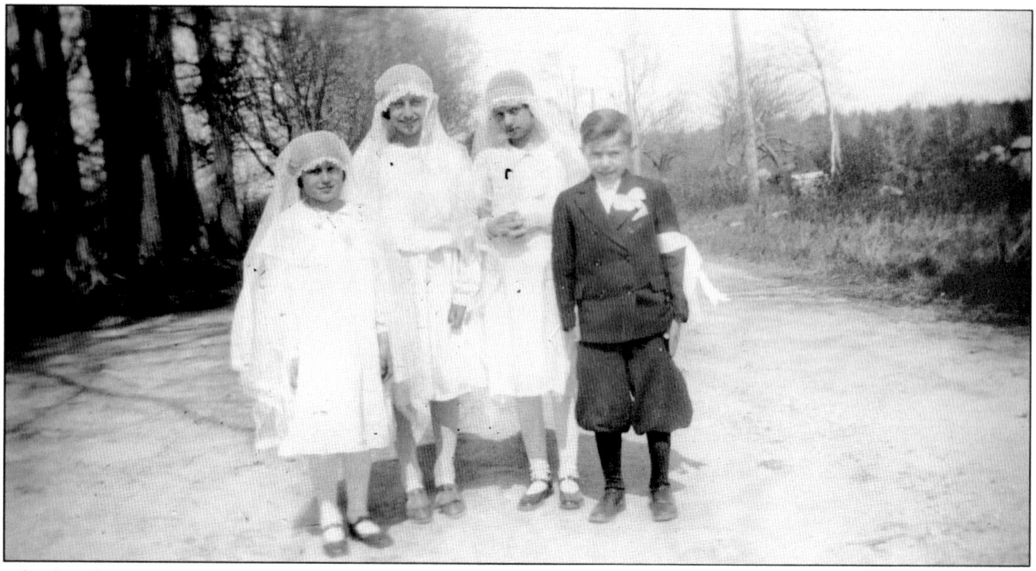

The brickyard owners and workers on Mill Road were French Catholics who traveled to churches in Yarmouth or Lewiston to worship because there was no church in town. Lillian and Irene Liberty and Irene and Roger Blais (left to right) are dressed for their first communion in this c. 1937 photograph. Irene Blais's mother made her dress from remnants an aunt got from her job at the Lewiston textile mills. Roger's white armband was a traditional symbol worn by boys, similar to the white veil worn by girls. (Courtesy of Irene Lavoie.)

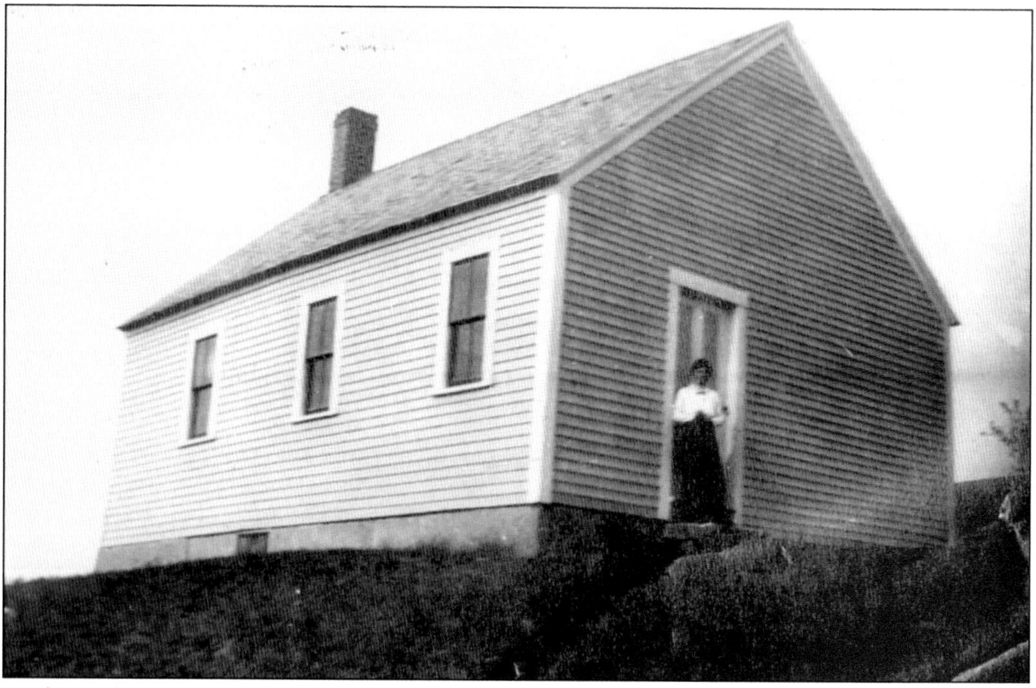

In the early 1900s, the Pratt School was located at the corner of North and Ledge Roads in Yarmouth. Children who lived near schoolhouses in neighboring Yarmouth and Pownal were generally tuitioned to those schools and North Yarmouth paid the cost. Tuition was $57 for children to attend Pratt School in 1906. Edna Marston of North Yarmouth taught here in 1919.

Six

Community We Shared

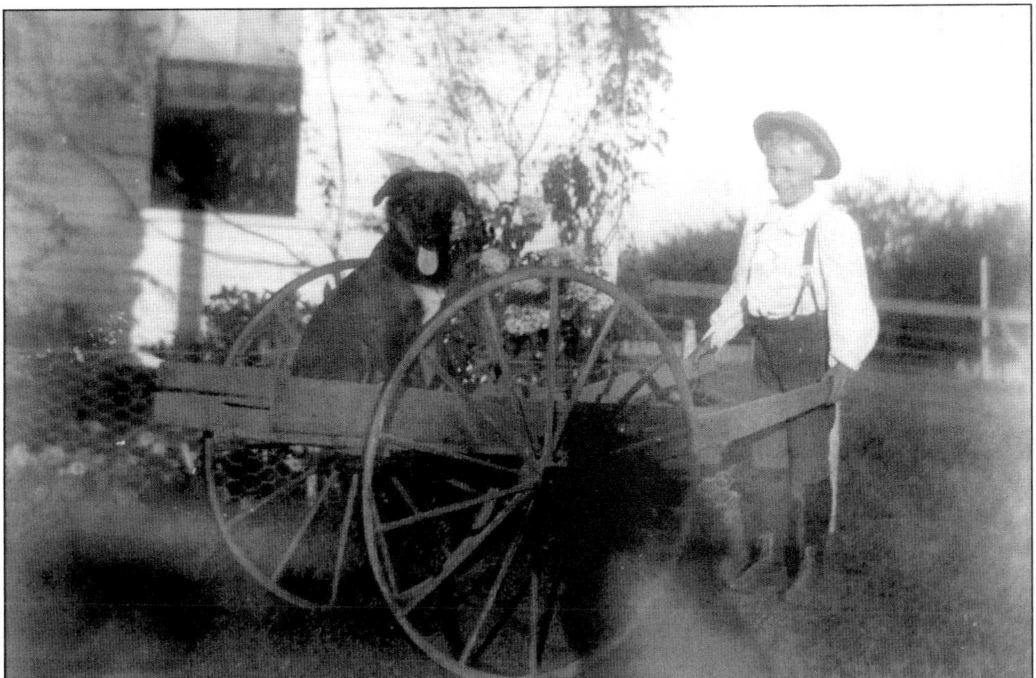

Carroll Brown Skillin (1885–1952) is pictured in front of the family homestead at the end of Lufkin Road around 1895. The home was built in 1817 by his grandfather Isaac Skillin, who had married Susan Gray. Carroll, the son of Edwin Sumner and Elizabeth Anderson Skillin, attended the Walnut Hill School (seen on page 86 with siblings Mabel and Isaac) in District No. 2, North Yarmouth Academy, and the University of Maine. An attorney in Portland, he performed legal work for town residents. He incorporated many of the town's nonprofits, including the Wescustogo Grange Hall Association, the North Yarmouth Fire Department, and the Memorial Park Association, and prepared the transfer of the Congregational church parish property to the church in 1945 when the parish was dissolved. Deerbrook Farm became his North Yarmouth home, inherited by his son Col. Byron Skillin. Carroll's health declined in later years, and he has was confined to a wheelchair and chauffeured to his clients. (Courtesy of Elizabeth Woodward.)

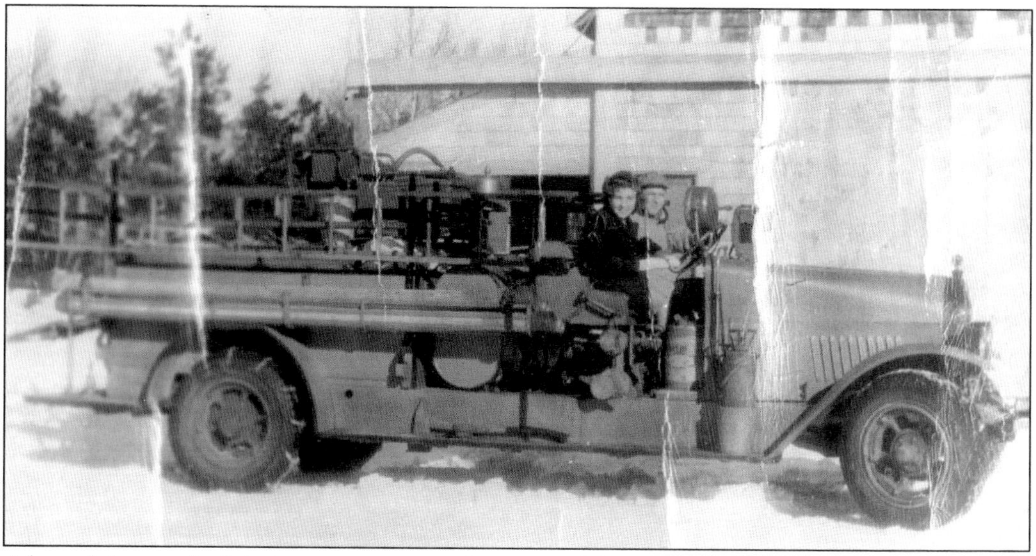

After relying on firefighting equipment and personnel from Cumberland, Gray, and Yarmouth for many years, the North Yarmouth Fire Department was started on March 25, 1945. This used 1928 Larrabee was purchased from Boothbay in 1945 as the first fire truck. Member Sidney Smith, who would later become chief, and his wife, Mabel, sit in the truck in front of the first fire station, formerly the Fred Collins cider mill.

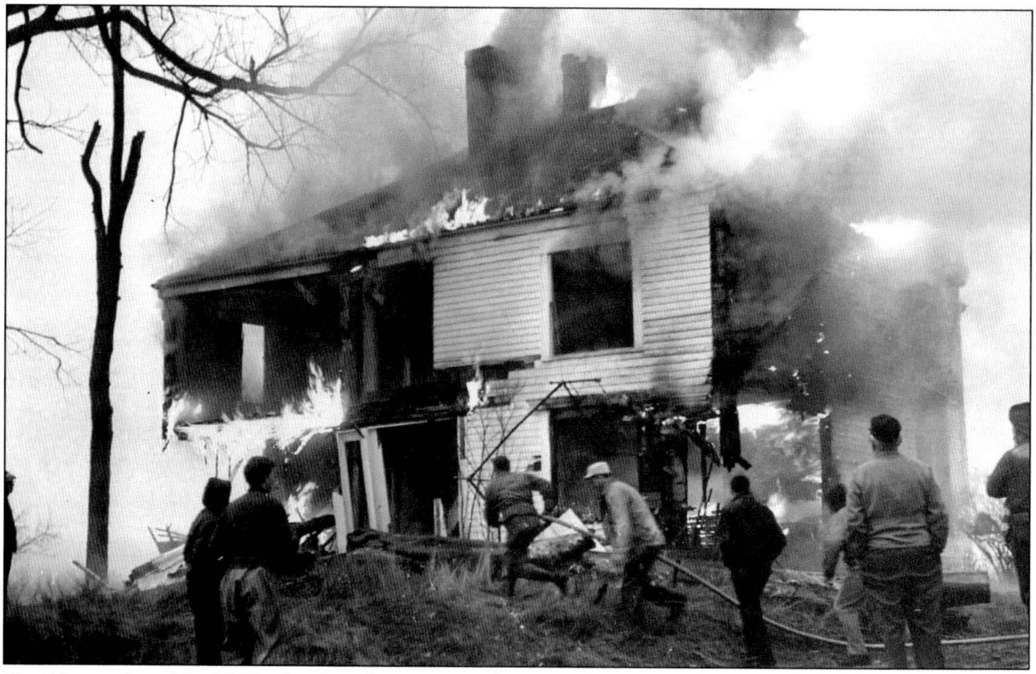

On November 12, 1965, the fire department burned this home at 1203 North Road, formerly owned by Georgie Sawyer, a schoolteacher who worked at the one-room Dunn School. The house had previously burned in a spectacular fire at Christmastime in 1939 but had been remodeled so Georgie could continue to live there with her sister Blanche. Capt. James Sawyer of Walnut Hill was their great-grandfather. They had a hired man who cared for the cows they kept in the barn across the street.

The fire department conducted many fund-raising activities to equip the men and trucks. This photograph shows a 1948 scrap metal drive in which metal was collected and sold. The proceeds were used to purchase materials to build an addition on the right side of the building to store an extra vehicle. When the expanding town required a larger facility for its fire department, residents voted to build the current Fire Barn.

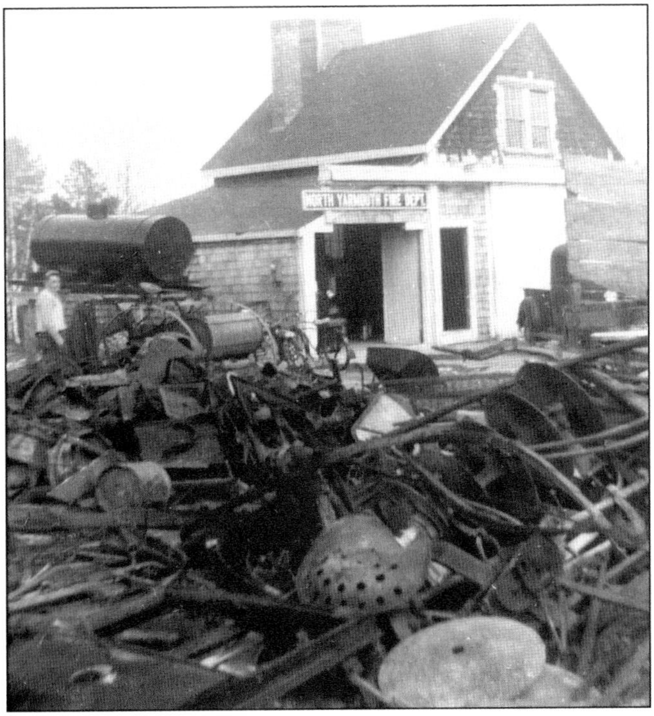

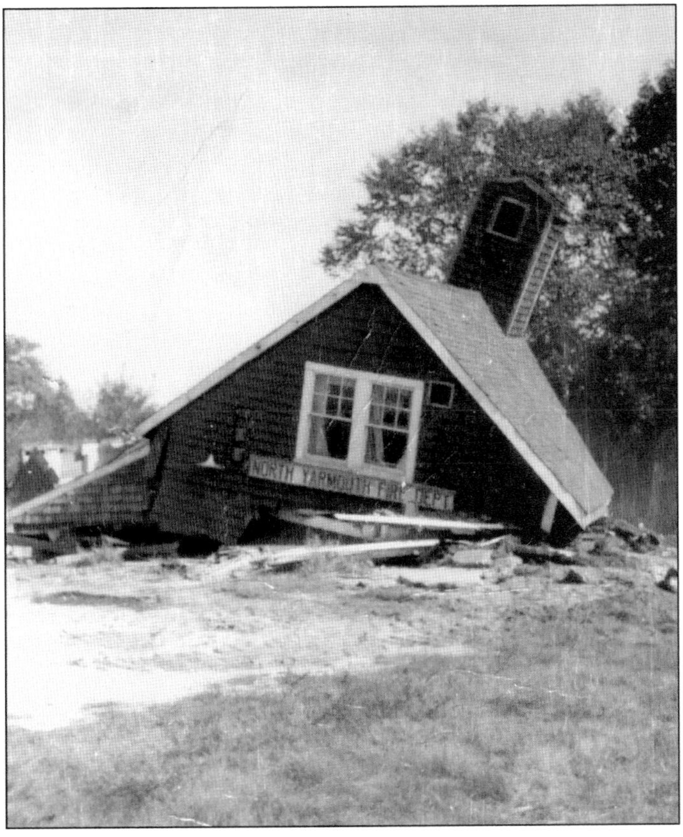

The old fire house was torn down using a bulldozer from local excavation contractor Maynard Robinson. This image, from the spring of 1968, reveals only the second floor remaining during demolition. This is where the members held their meetings and shot pool on the department's pool table. Several bricks were saved from the chimney of this original building and were inlaid into the new brick Fire Barn, built in the fall of 1968. These old bricks are recessed under the words "North Yarmouth Fire Department." (Courtesy of Kenny Allen.)

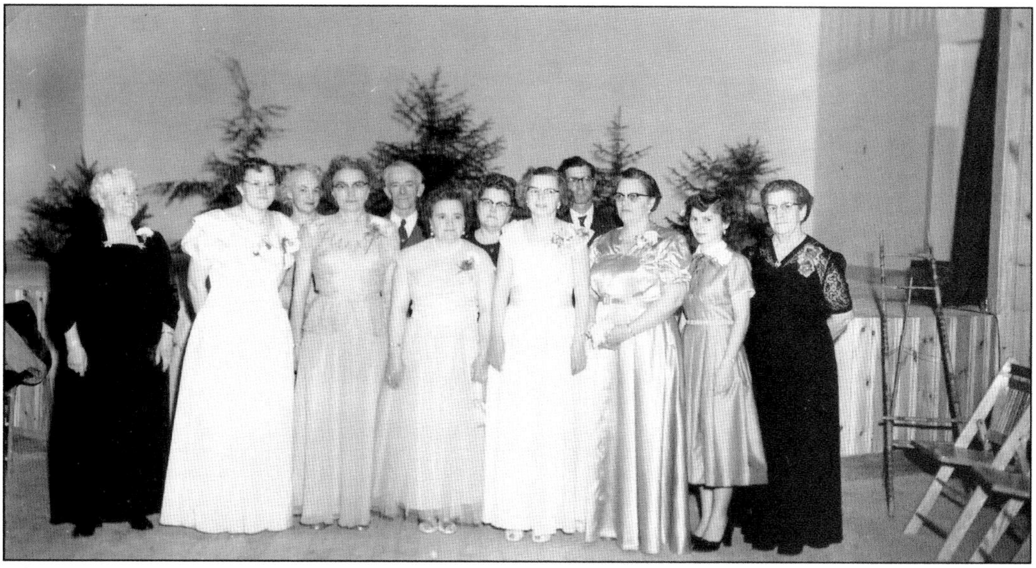

The Patrons of Husbandry, a fraternal organization that began in 1867, was chartered here in 1874 as Wescustogo Grange No. 27. Candidates were initiated for membership through instruction in four degrees, the completion of which made them full voting members. Additional degrees allowed them to join the county (Pomona), state, and national Granges. The degrees, which were lessons taught by members based on agricultural principles, provided a framework for attitudes and behaviors. The first- and second-degree teams of Wescustogo members are shown here around 1957. (Courtesy of the Hayward family.)

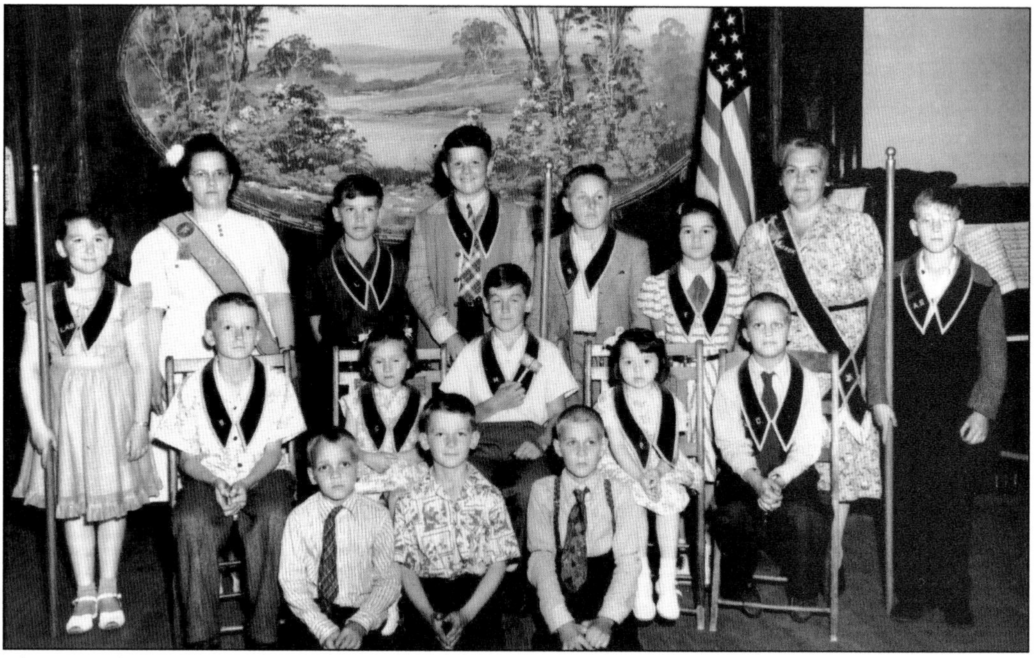

The Juvenile Grange was organized in 1948 for children aged 5 to 14. In the vestry in 1948 are Luella Blanchard (second from left), the juvenile deputy for Cumberland County, and Dot Doughty (second from right), the matron who oversaw the group. Holding the gavel is master Earle Bornheimer. The children come from the Allen, Smith, Semmes, Blanchard, and Knight families.

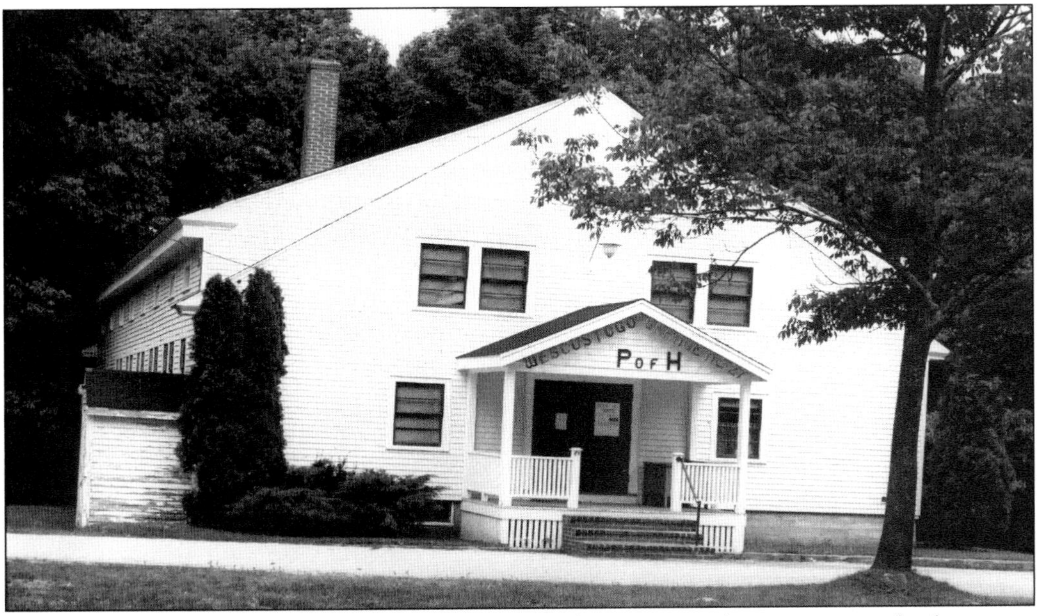

Grange members met in the Congregational church vestry until moving into the basement of their own building in 1952. Volunteers completed the hall over 11 years, and money was raised through fairs and weekly bean suppers. They cut trees by hand in a woodlot off Memorial Highway during the winter and Phil Knight sawed them into boards. In 1959, national Grange master Herschel Newson dedicated the hall, which has since been the site of town meetings and community events. The hall was donated to the town in 1996.

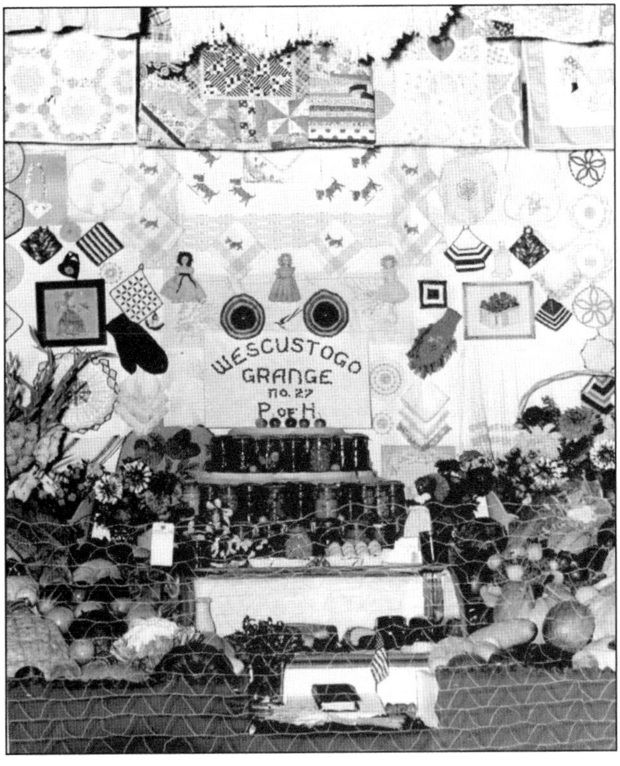

Wescustogo Grange exhibited at Cumberland Fair each September. This display from 1952 shows the variety of products and crafts that members made to meet the contest requirements. Knitted and sewn items, vegetables, flowers, and canned goods are neatly arranged with the Grange's bible and flag prominently displayed. This exhibit earned second place.

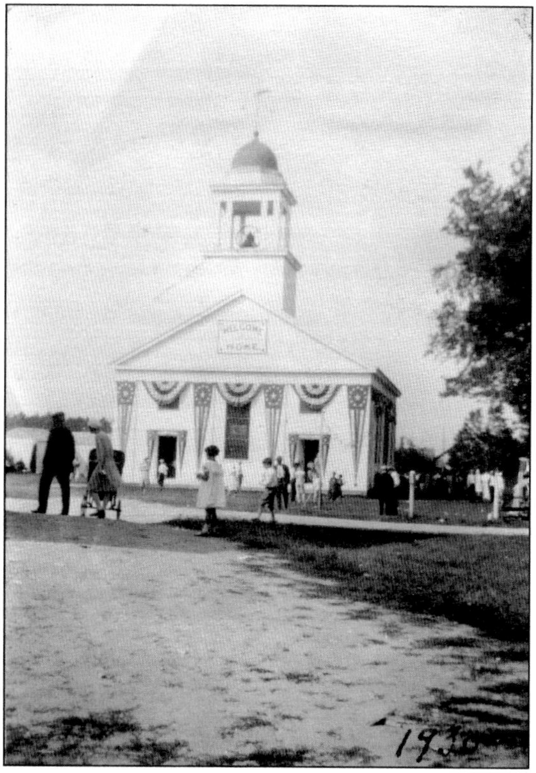

In 1930, the town recognized its 250th anniversary with a major celebration at the Congregational church. The events began with the firing of a 250-gun salute and the ringing of the church bell. A parade of vehicles and floats drove around town passing through Crockett's Corner and Walnut Hill. Entries were judged at the church, which was decorated with red, white, and blue banners. First prize was awarded to the Daughters of Pocahontas for their float depicting a Native American scene.

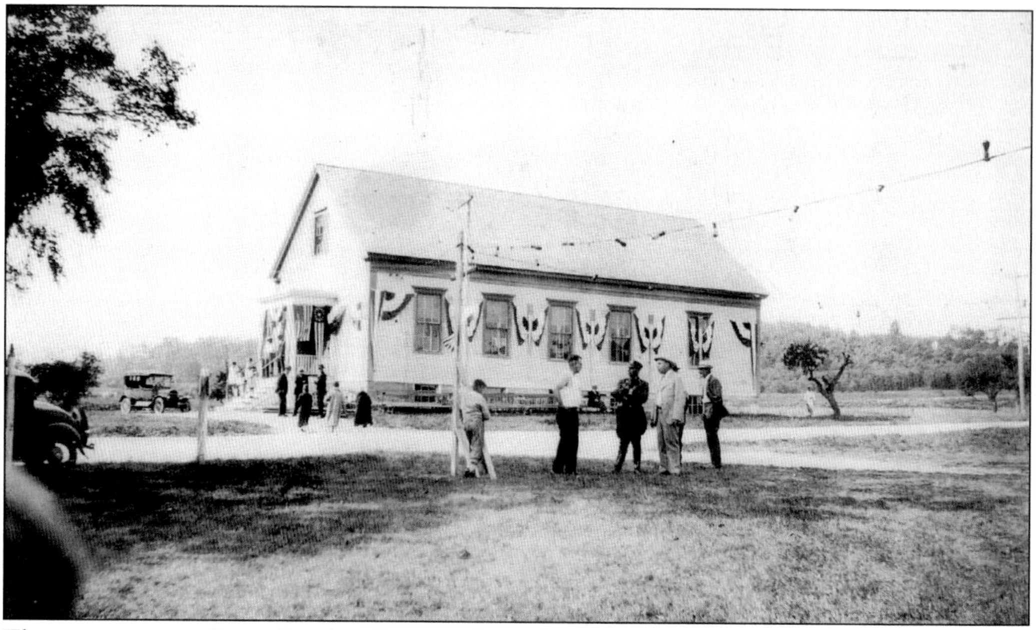

The vestry across from the church was adorned with patriotic colors, as was the home of George Small up the street. Sports events included a "fat man's race," a 50-yard dash, and a rolling pin contest. Other activities were a historical address by Charlotte Lawrence, choral and orchestral performances, a pageant that included scenes of early life, and a grand finale of an evening fireworks show. (Courtesy of Carol Black.)

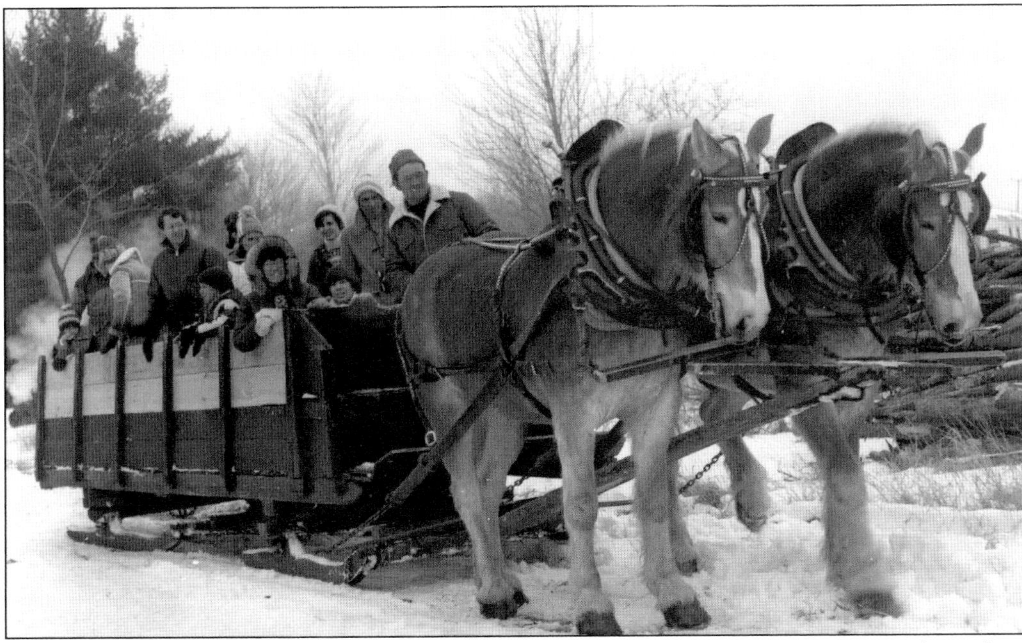

In 1980, North Yarmouth celebrated its 300th anniversary with activities occurring throughout the year. A horse-drawn sleigh ride at the Old Town House was part of the Winter Festival. On September 13, the town celebrated Founder's Day with activities similar to the 250th anniversary celebration. The day began with a cannon salute and ringing of the church bell, followed by a "haymakers" breakfast, races and games, a parade, historical exhibits, concerts, speeches, a cake shaped like the original town, a bean supper, fireworks, and a dance.

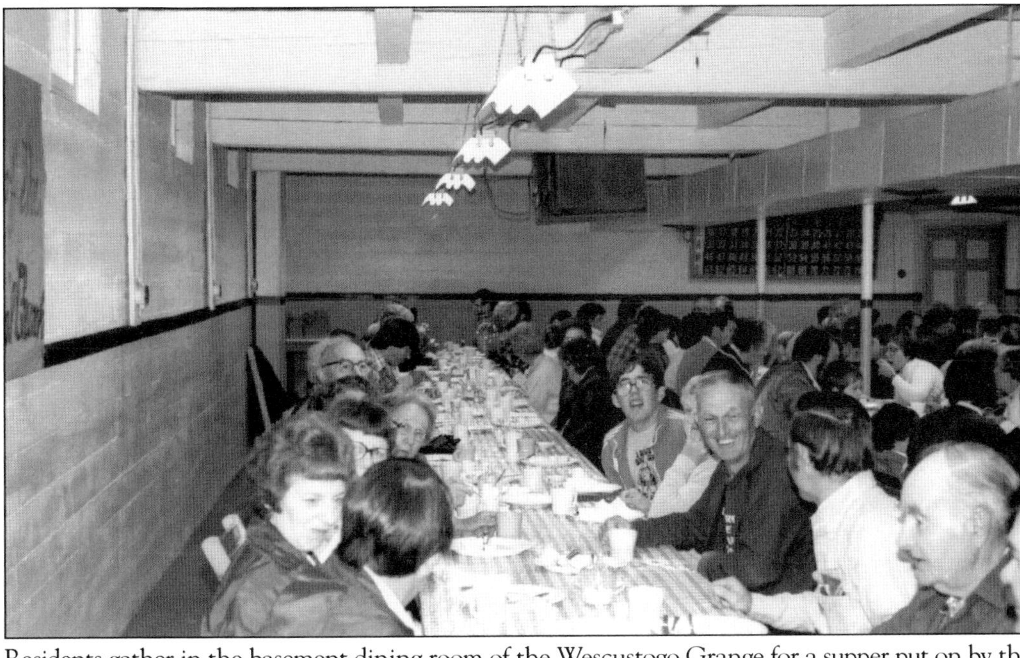

Residents gather in the basement dining room of the Wescustogo Grange for a supper put on by the Congregational church during the tricentennial. On the right side of the table from right to left are Tom, John, and Bill Dexter and Harold Small. Esther Walker is on the left side leaning out.

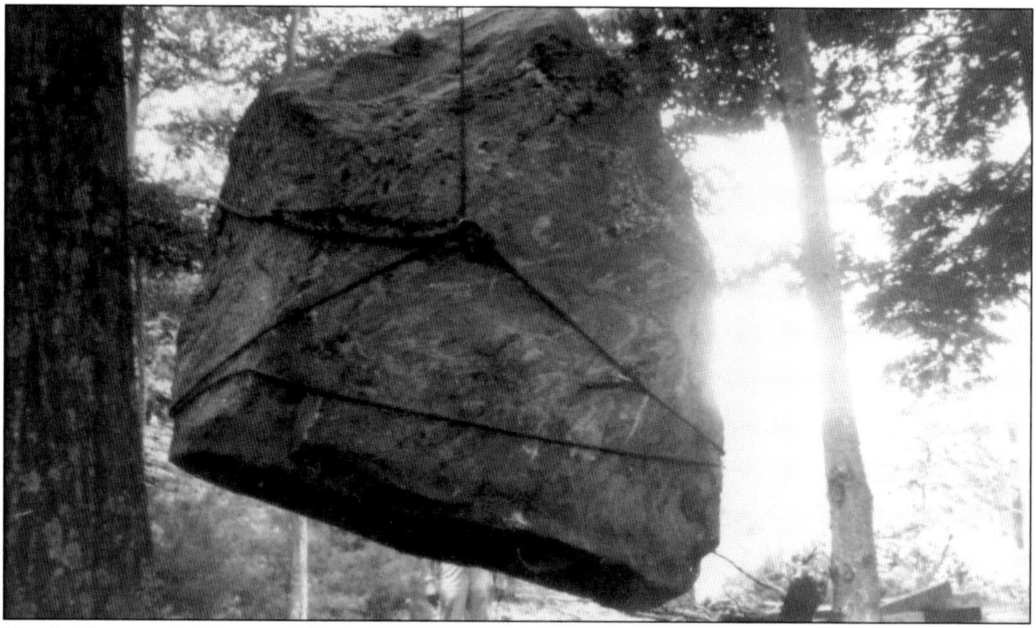

North Yarmouth Memorial Park was formed in 1949 to recognize the sacrifices of local war veterans. Land was acquired for a park, but no progress was made until the Grange took on this community project in 1962. Teenager Kathy Bowie and her father, Philip, identified a boulder that was excavated when the Route 231 railroad overpass was built in 1870. The 15-ton rock was moved to its present location at Parsonage Road and Memorial Highway to serve as the monument. The park was dedicated on August 19, 1963. (Courtesy of Kenny Allen.)

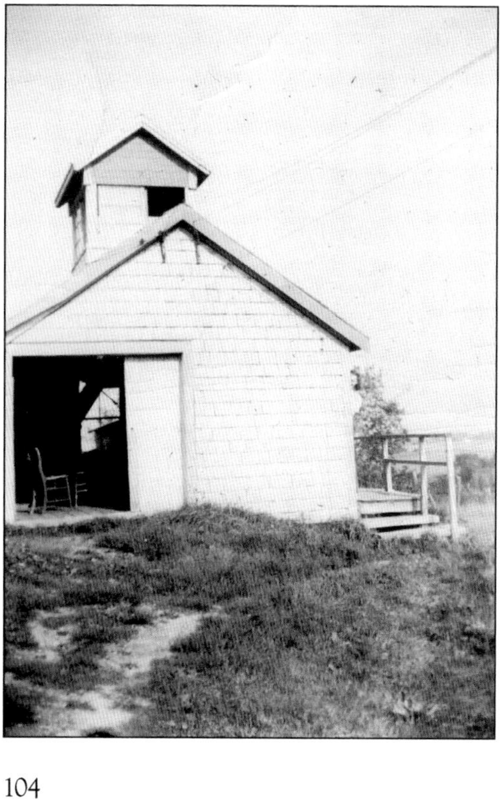

During World War II, from 1942 to 1944, town residents manned this civilian observation post behind Maurice and Isabel Hayes' home at 395 New Gloucester Road. Harold Baston built the cupola on Hayes' work shed for better viewing. Volunteers had watch shifts, four hours each around the clock, in which they reported any sounds or sightings of aircraft by telephone to the army headquarters in Portland. The Hayes family organized the watch schedule and filled-in for volunteers who missed their shifts. (Courtesy of the Jewett family.)

Seven

People We Knew

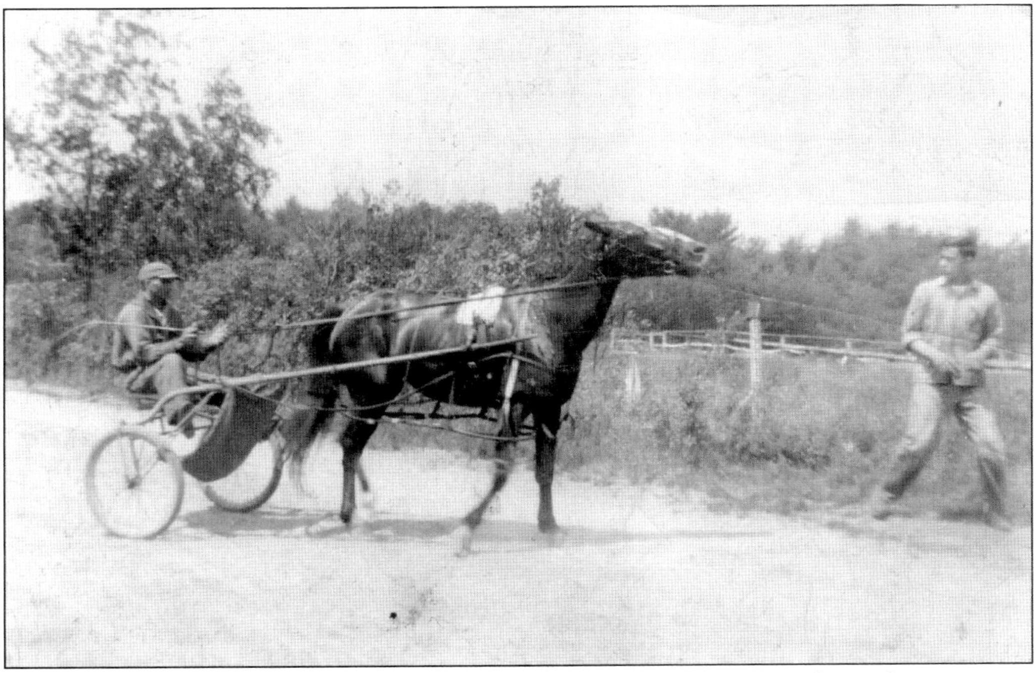

Around the beginning of the 20th century, harness racing was very popular and many towns had their own racetracks. North Yarmouth did not have a track, but local enthusiasts raced at the Cumberland Fairgrounds or at the Royal River Speedway, at 338 Sligo Road in Yarmouth. Patrick Ward, who raised horses and mules during World War I and later owned the Yarmouth stockyards, reportedly developed the Yarmouth track in 1899. Ruth Pullen Ristich recalls watching her uncle William Pullen, who lived on Sligo Road in North Yarmouth, race on this track in the 1920s. Records show race results from 1918, but it is not known how long the track was used. When Clayton Smith bought the property in 1946, local harness racers Don Richards and Charles Reinsborough trained their horses on the old half-mile track. Reinsborough also had a training track behind his barn on Mountfort Road. Richards, age 15, trains on the speedway with his first horse, Gail Climatic. (Courtesy of Don Richards.)

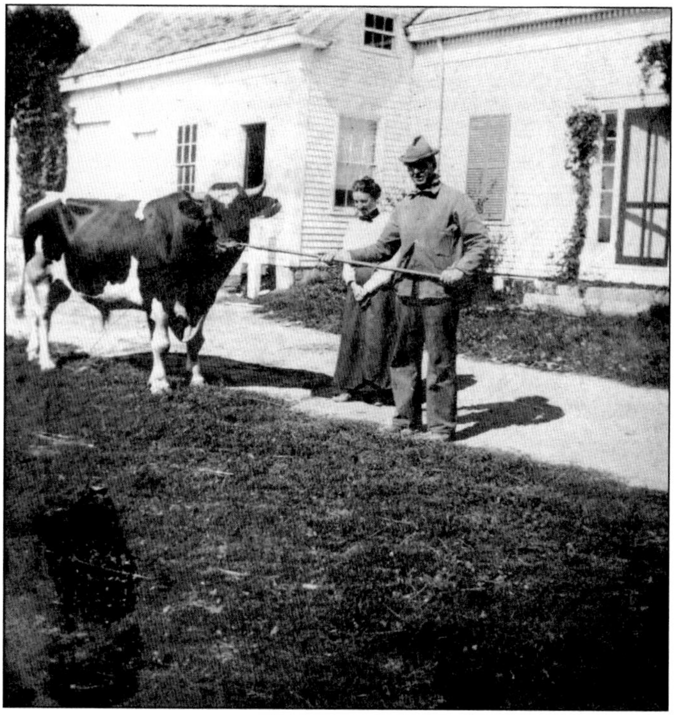

Charles L. and Lucy Lawrence Dunn stand in the yard of their 1264 North Road residence around 1935. Charles was a dairy and crop farmer who lived in the yellow home built by his father, Isaac S. Dunn, in 1858 at the corner of North and Hallowell Roads. This was one of the family's prized Holstein bulls. Charles was a selectman, the superintendent of Dunn School, and an active member of the Methodist church.

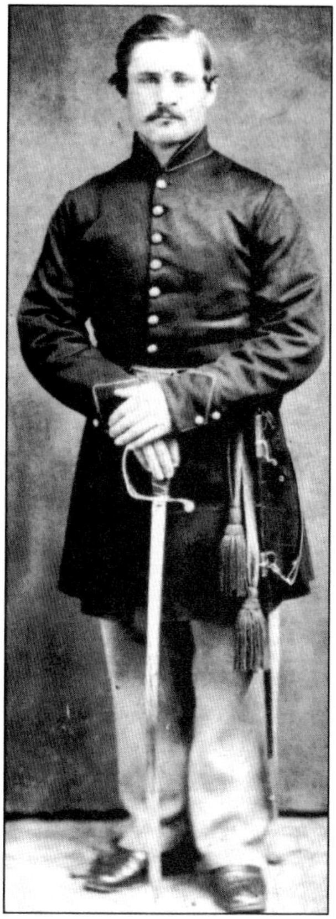

Born in Gray, Capt. Luther Lawrence enlisted in the Civil War with his brother Lt. James Lawrence in 1861. Luther commanded Company H in the 11th Maine Infantry and they fought in battles throughout the South. Luther was killed at Deep Bottom, Virginia, on August 16, 1864, during an assault on Richmond; James was wounded. The historical society owns Civil War letters, papers, and documents from Lawrence family members, including younger brother Charles, who served in a different regiment.

Capt. Levi Marston (1816–1904), shown at right, was the most famous resident of the 1800s. He went to sea at age 14 and eventually commanded his own vessels, traveling around Cape Horn 32 times while trading in the West Indies, China, and on the Pacific and Atlantic coasts. His brig, the *Harriet*, was built in Yarmouth in 1849. On November 9, 1851, Marston and the men of the *Harriet* rescued 325 immigrants from the British ship *Unicorn*, which was floundering in a storm off the Grand Banks. Queen Victoria awarded Marston a medal for his efforts. He moved to Riverside Farm (below), at 1110 North Road, and built the present barn. His daughter Ellen and her husband, James Lawrence, took over the farm when he moved to Yarmouth. An active Methodist, Marston helped begin the Yarmouth church in the 1890s.

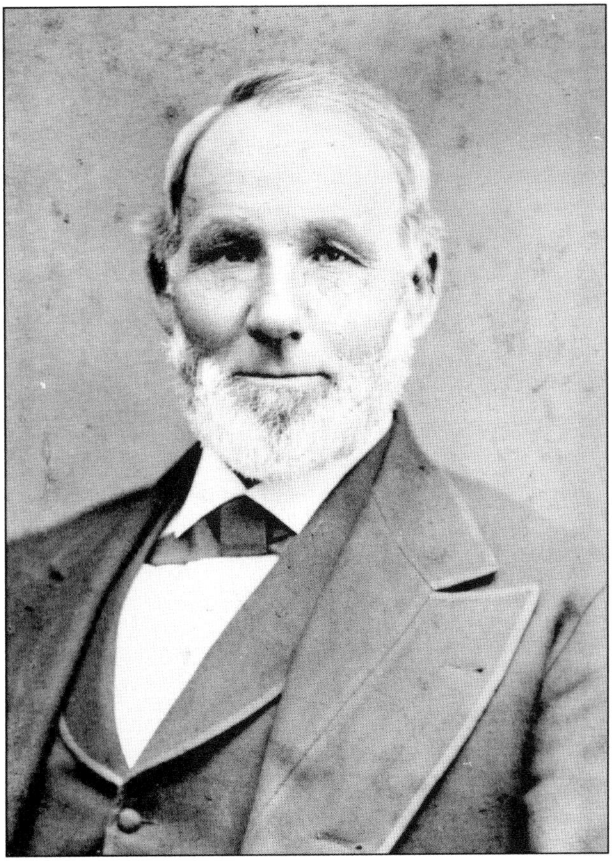

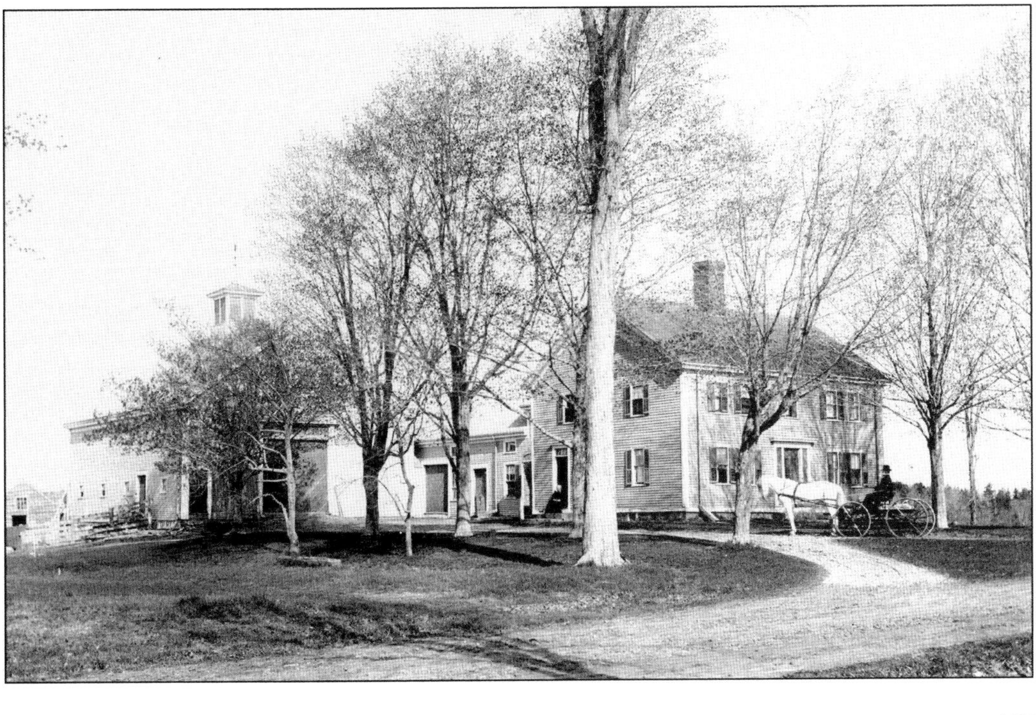

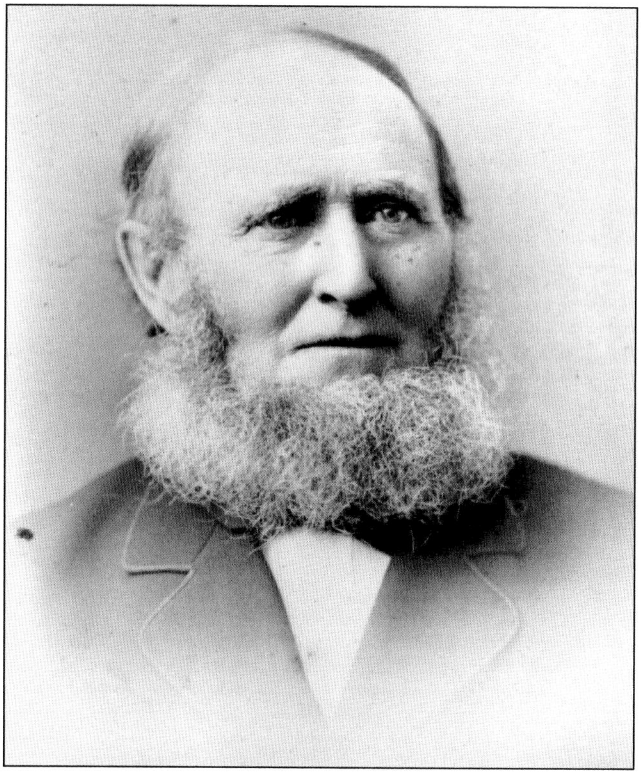

John Mountfort (1828–1904) married Elmira Whitney on April 20, 1848, and moved in 1850 to the house at 263 Mountfort Road, where four of the couple's five children were born. They farmed the property they called Spring Grove Farm (below). Their son James Franklin Mountfort became a sea captain and their son John also followed the sea. Their daughter Emma was a schoolteacher who married Edward G. Hayes and lived at 160 Memorial Highway.

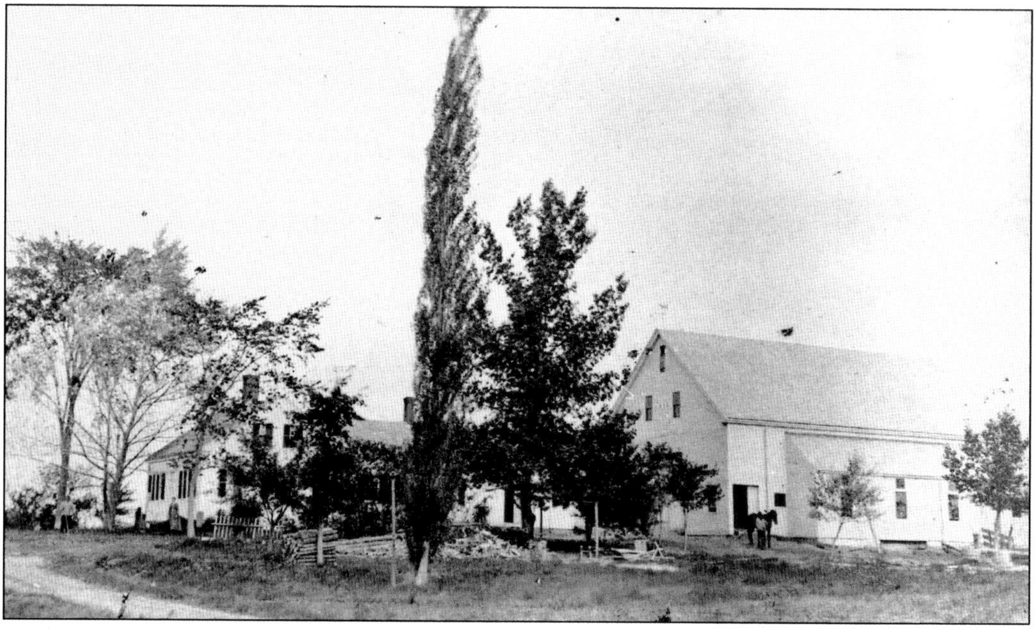

In this *c.* 1885 image of the Mountfort home, family members pose outside with their horse. According to town tax records, the original barn on this homestead was built in 1841, even before the house was built, and was replaced with the modern barn seen here around 1885. The old barn may have become the attached shed on the right side of the new barn. The house was built in 1842 as a center chimney cape for original owner Josiah Lovell. (Courtesy of Dick Baston.)

William B. Skillin, the son of Isaac Skillin of Skillin (later Lufkin) Road, moved to the house at 903 Sligo Road, next to the current Toddy Brook Golf Course, after he married his first cousin. He served as a lieutenant in the 12th Maine Infantry during the Civil War and used his home to enlist Union soldiers. He later became the treasurer of the Congregational church. (Courtesy of the Hathaway family.)

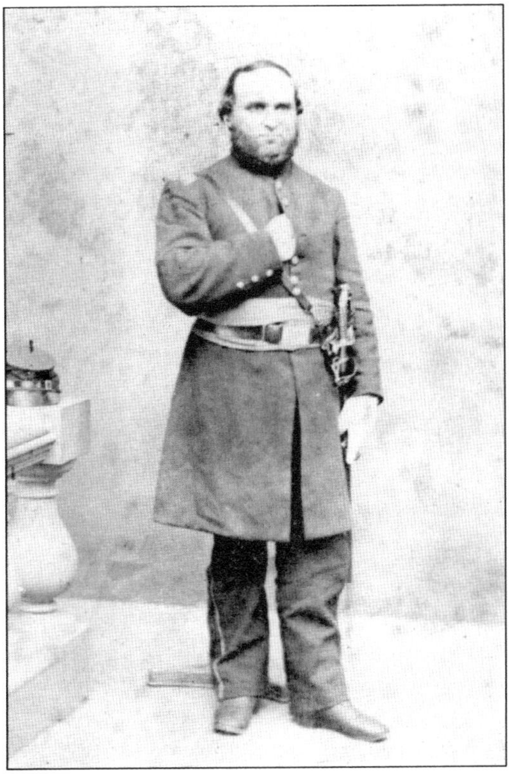

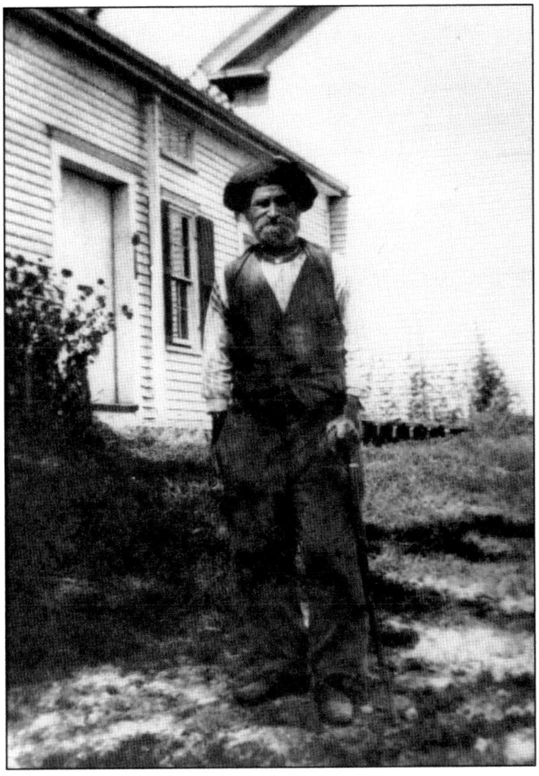

Charles S. Sweetser, a Civil War sergeant in the 25th Maine Regiment, lived at Toddy Brook Farm (Sweetser Road), which he inherited from his grandfather, early settler and deacon William Sweetser. Charles's son Henry cared for foster children here. The apple orchard was set in the 1930s. According to a c. 1880 written legend, Toddy Brook was named by a traveler who, after dropping his liquor bottle in the brook, ran downstream, plunged into the water, and drank, exclaiming, "This here brook makes the charminist [*sic*] toddy I ever tasted on!"

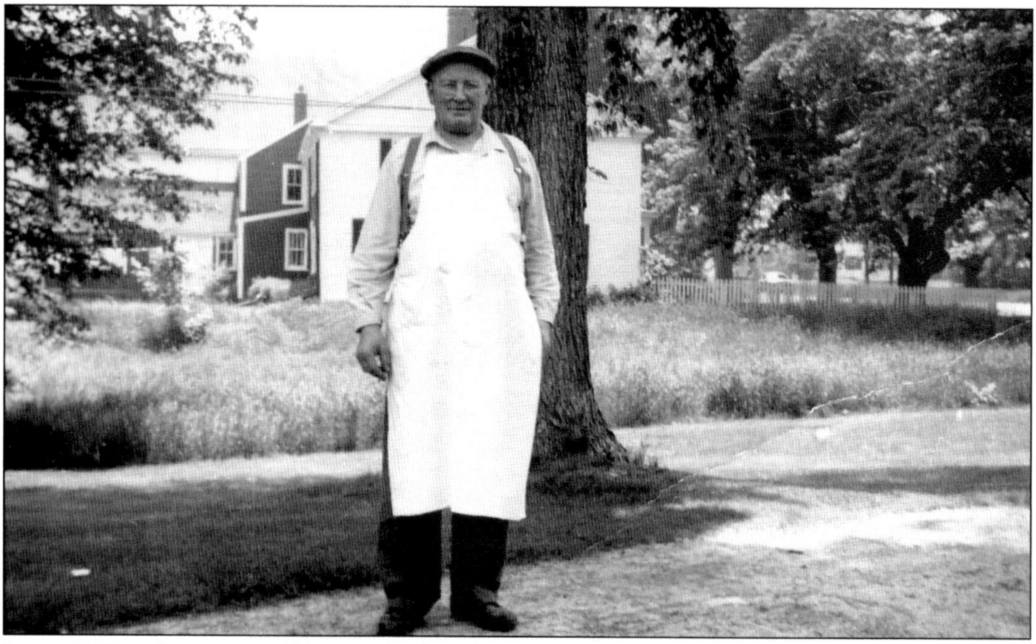

Lewis T. Hamilton was well known both in his own right and as the father of Shirley Hamilton Fountain. He worked for the Forest Paper Company in Yarmouth, but spent many years as the clerk in the general store in Walnut Hill. Many residents remember him working for Lester Smith and later for the Gliddens. Here he poses in his shopkeeper's apron in his yard at the corner of The Lane and Walnut Hill Road. (Courtesy of Norma Grover.)

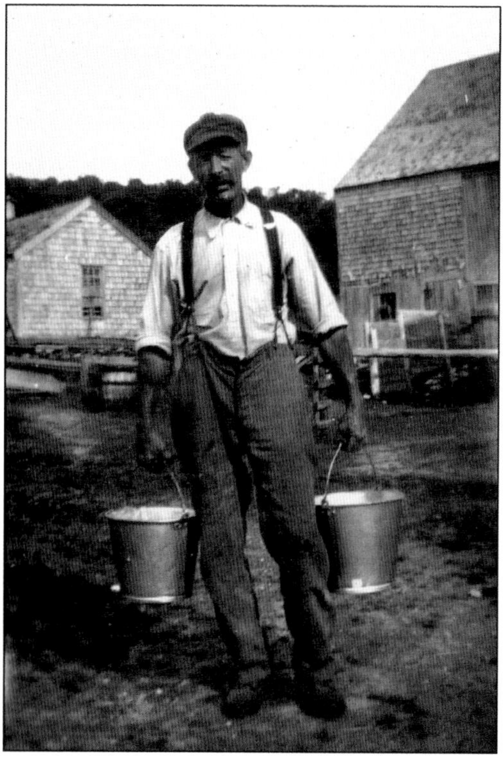

Herbert "Skip" Hamilton (1863–1948) was an accomplished musician who played piano and organ for dance bands and churches in the local area and in San Francisco. After the 1906 San Francisco earthquake, Skip returned to his North Yarmouth home and worked on the family's Walnut Hill farm with his brother Ernest W. Hamilton (1870–1942). Skip, a lifelong bachelor, is shown carrying buckets of milk at the farm. (Courtesy of Dick Baston.)

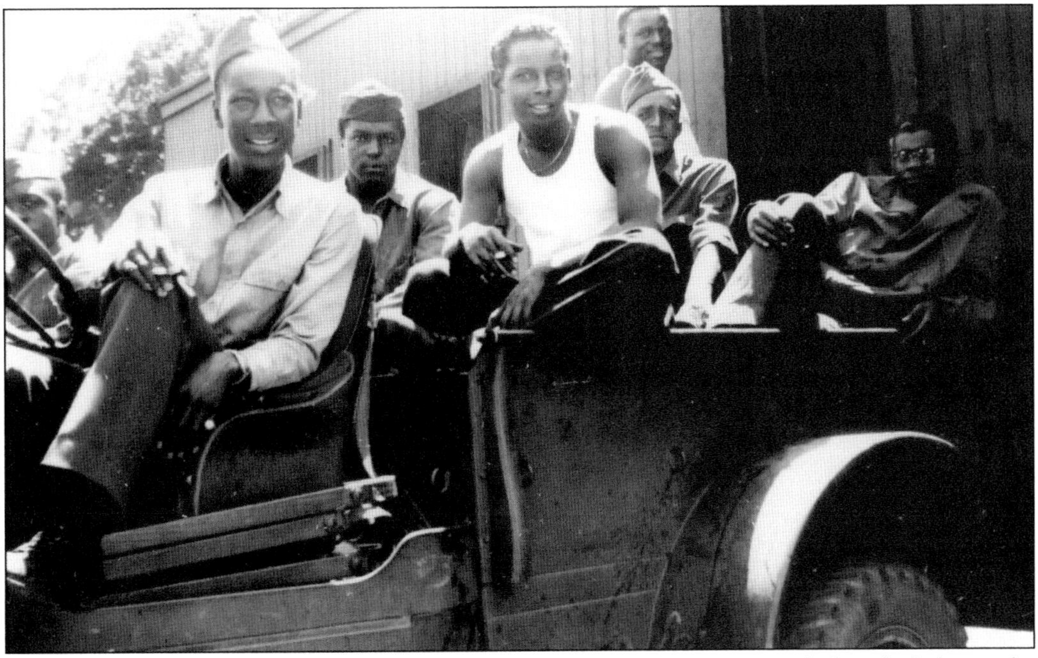

When World War II began, black soldiers in the segregated army struggled to find their role. Many black troops were sent to Maine to guard the Grand Truck Railroad line. They were stationed at bridge crossings from Portland to Montreal to protect this important transportation link from sabotage. If the Germans cut off Atlantic Canada, this railroad would have been Canada's lifeline.

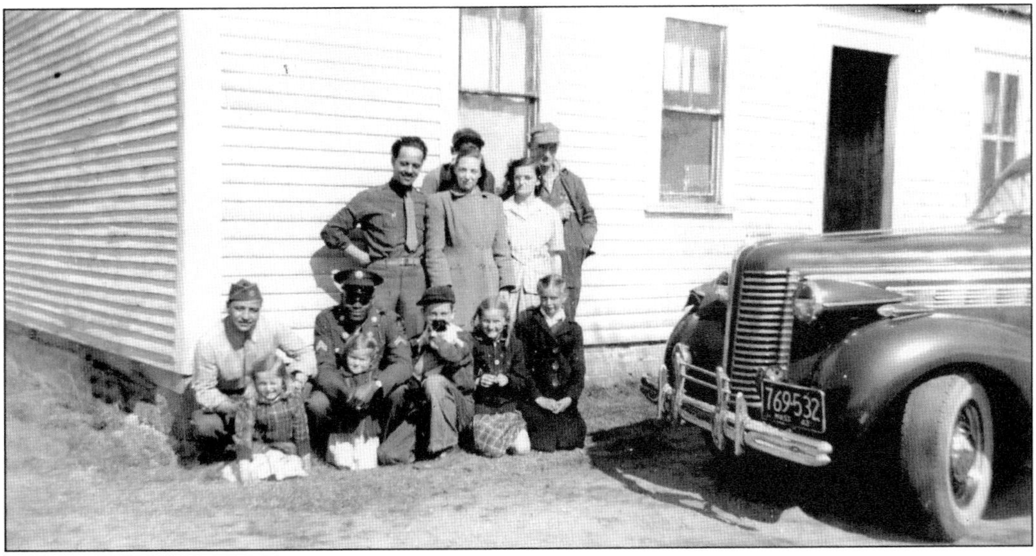

Black soldiers stationed at Dunn's Depot lived in a railroad car converted into a bunkhouse and guarded the North Road bridge over the Royal River. A white officer who occasionally came out from Portland commanded them. The soldiers made friends with local families, who invited them to picnics by the river and brought them coffee on cold nights. They attended bean suppers at the Congregational church. The Arthur Atkins and Bearce families are pictured with the soldiers in 1942 at the Atkins family's 1367 North Road farm.

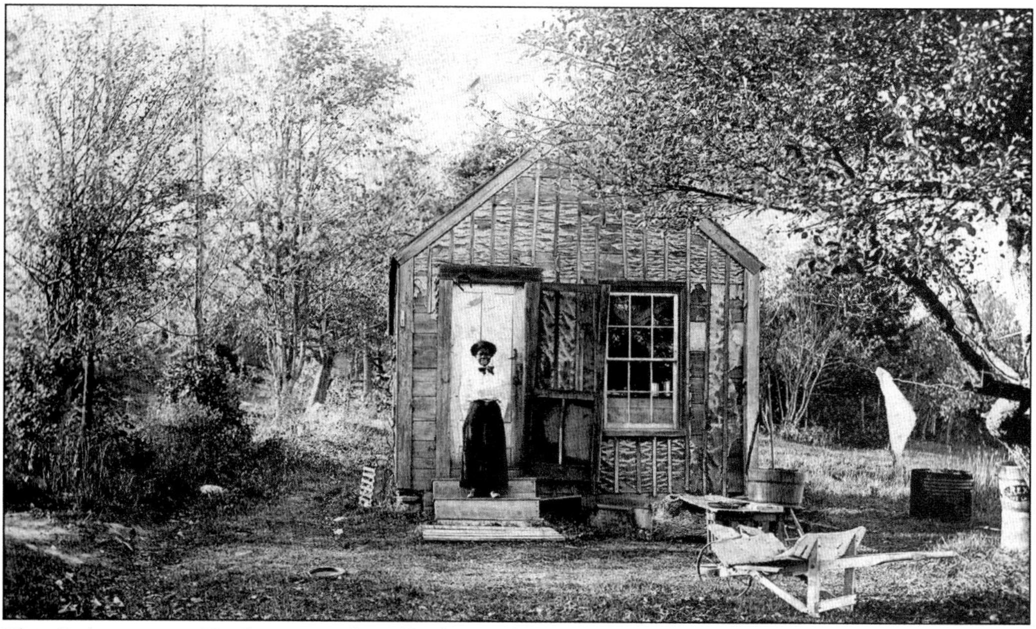

Elsie Bohannon, a black woman from Richmond, Virginia, lived in this small shack near the Old Town House while her husband helped build the new Maine Central Railroad line in 1911. The homemade wheelbarrow in the foreground and the washbasin with clothing on the line suggest a rugged life by modern standards, but Elsie still smiles below a lucky horseshoe. (Courtesy of Ginger Collins.)

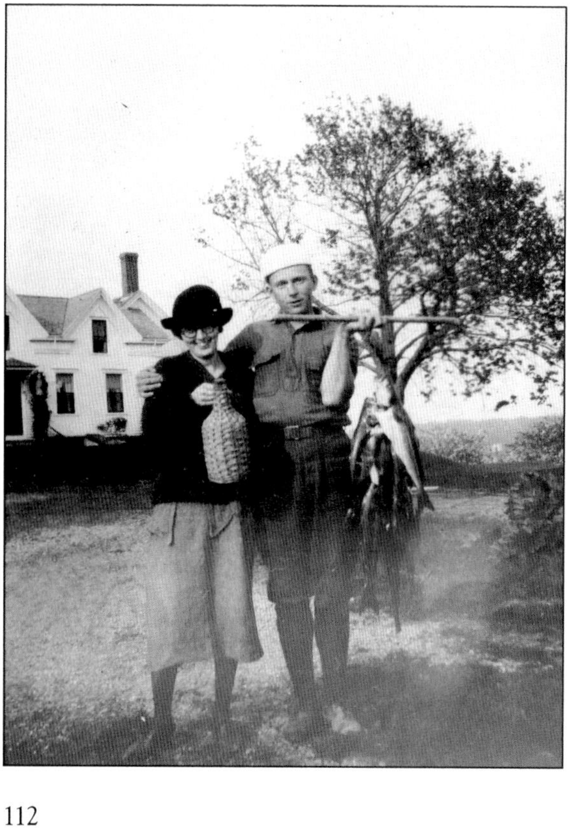

Florence Mountfort and Harold Skillin Baston display the string of fish caught on an outing in Harpswell in 1922 while they were dating. Both descended from early families, they married in 1924. A veteran, Harold was active in the Gray American Legion. He was also a carpenter who taught his son Richard the trade. After Harold died, Florence became a nurse and worked in Boston. (Courtesy of Dick Baston.)

George C. Roberts and his family are pictured outside their home on West Pownal Road around 1918. In the window, a sign reading "FISH" alerts the fish peddler to stop when he comes through, as the family wanted to make a purchase. Peddlers were a common occurrence in rural North Yarmouth and included rag dealers, fruit peddlers, and florists. (Courtesy of Noyes Lawrence.)

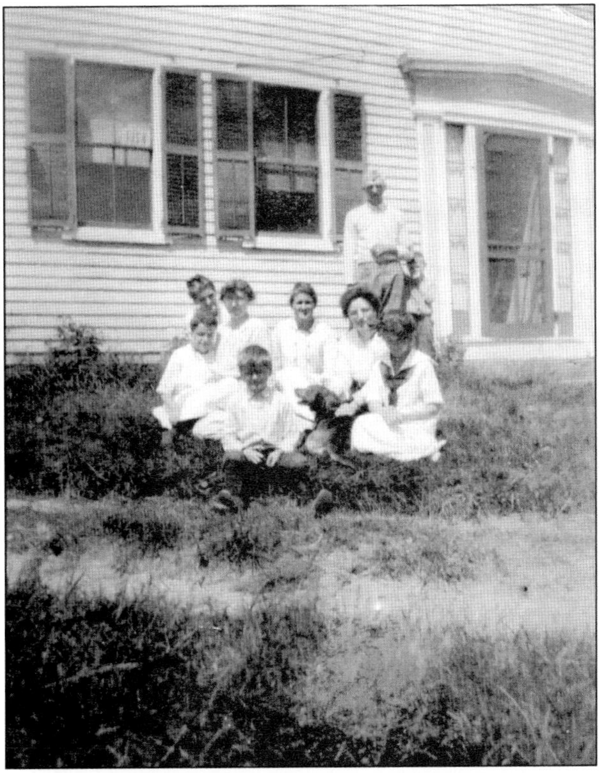

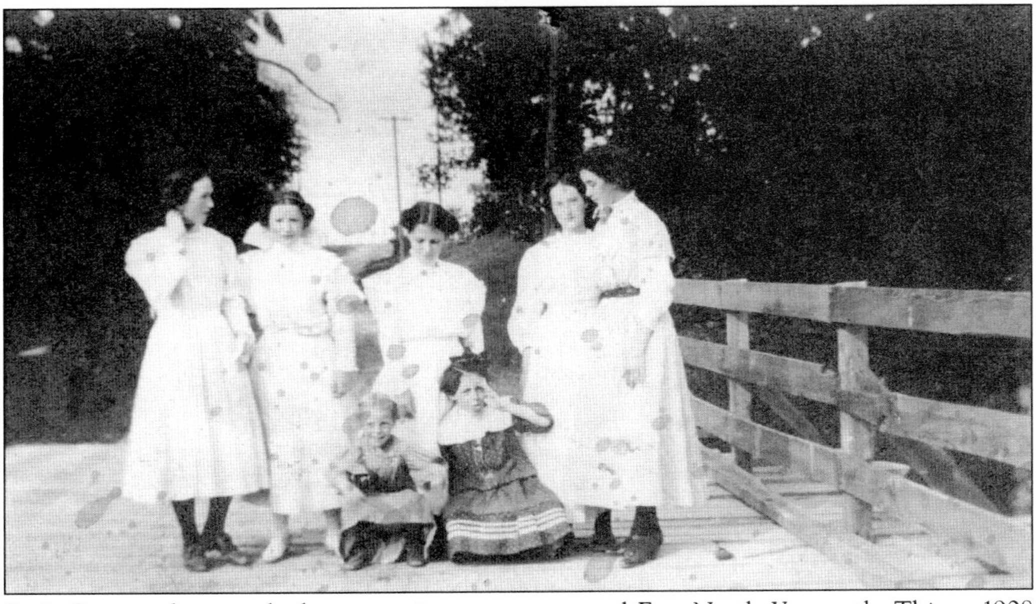

Susie Sawyer photographed many unique scenes around East North Yarmouth. This *c.* 1908 image shows Susie's friends, including Lucy Dunn (lower left), on a wooden bridge over the Royal River. The bridge was replaced in 1911 by a modern one. This view depicts the steep uphill grade from the river toward Dunn's Depot, which made travel difficult before the river was rerouted and the road leveled in 1953. The telephone poles in the distance were set in 1904. (Courtesy of Ginger Collins.)

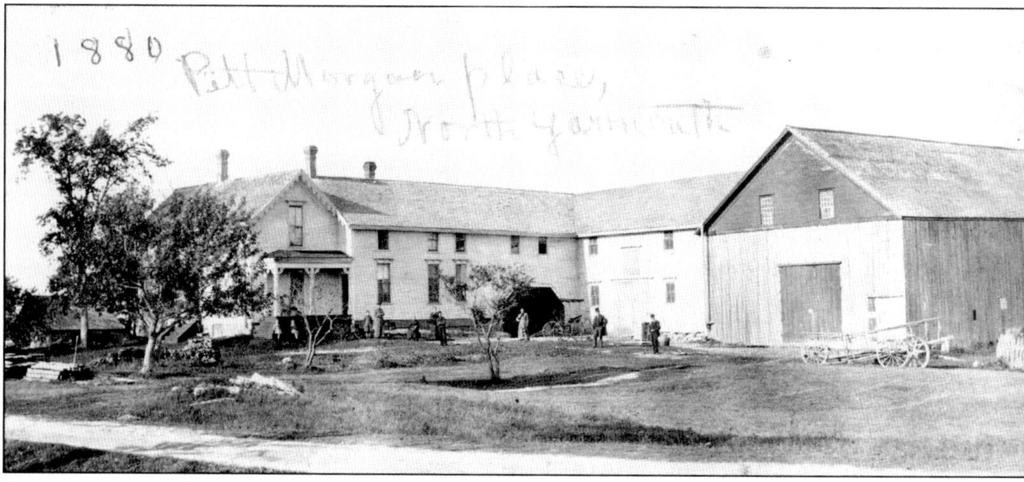

Pitman Morgan (back left in lower photograph) was a very successful farmer who was taxed in 1859 for 147 acres of land and $1,000 in cash. His 1880 family photograph below reveals expensive clothes and toys indicative of wealth. Local lore states that during Prohibition in the 1920s, heavy vehicles would arrive just ahead of the authorities and unload illegal liquor into a secret room under the cattle stanchions in the barn. They were never caught. The house was destroyed by fire in 1937, but the barn and ell remained. The ell was subsequently converted into a house. Vernon and Marion Goff moved there in 1946 and owned a large dairy herd until Bangs Disease destroyed it and the state of Maine had no money to reimburse them. They gave up farming and eventually bought M. L. Barbour's Store in Yarmouth, renaming it Goff's Hardware.

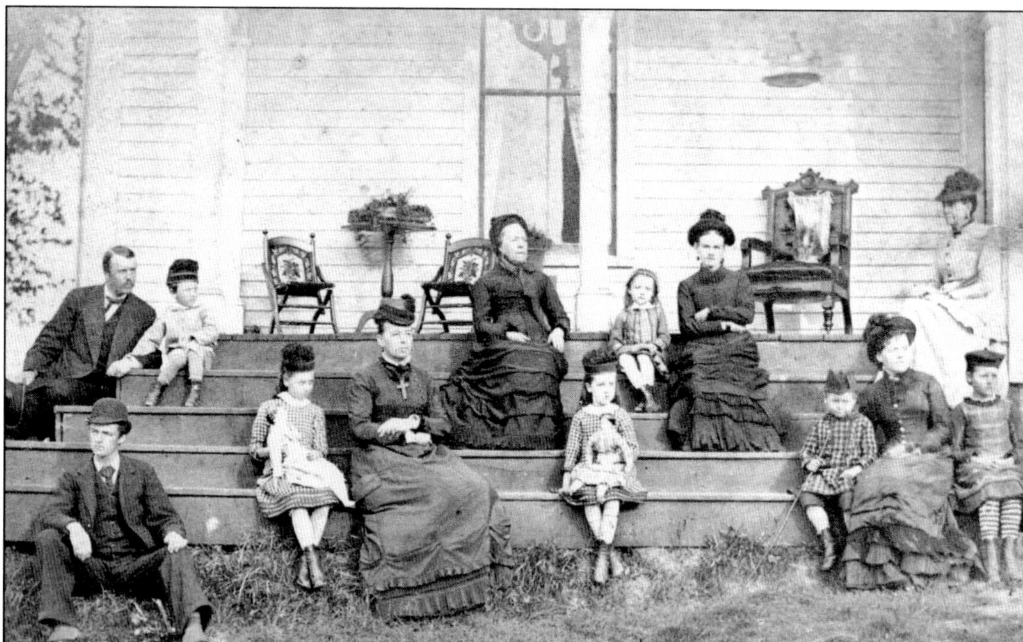

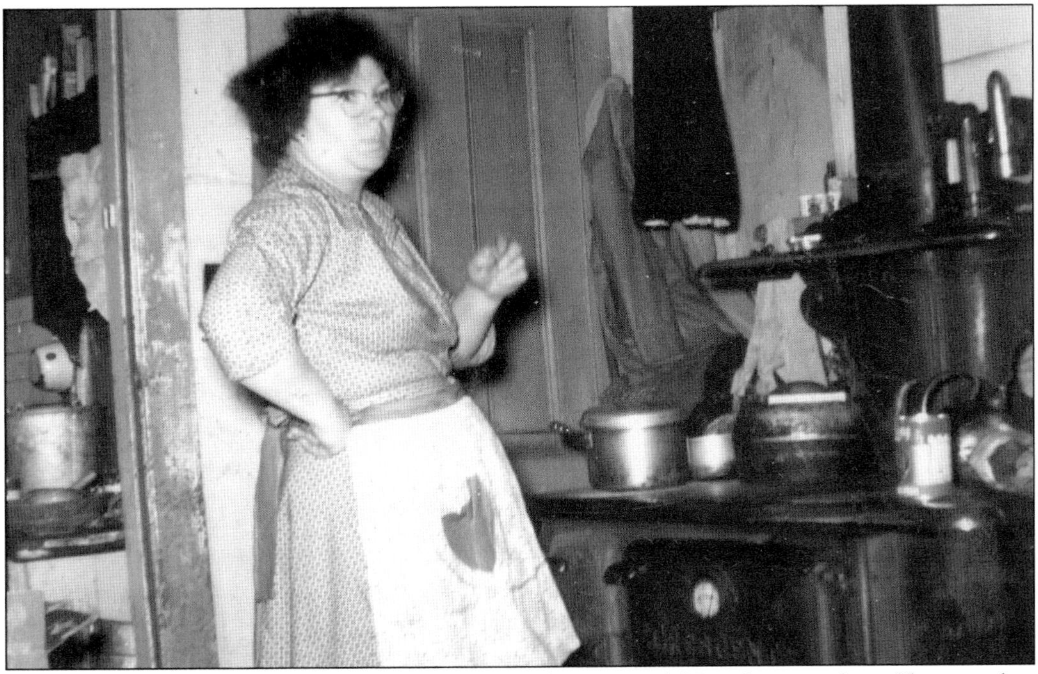

Vyra Hamilton Tompson was descended from the original Hamilton settlers. She met her husband, John Tompson, at a social at the Congregational church vestry. They married in 1932 and raised a large family at 607 Walnut Hill Road. An active member of the church and the Grange, she volunteered in many town organizations. Like her daughter Carol Tompson Black, she was always involved in fund-raising suppers and was known as a good cook. (Courtesy of Carol Black.)

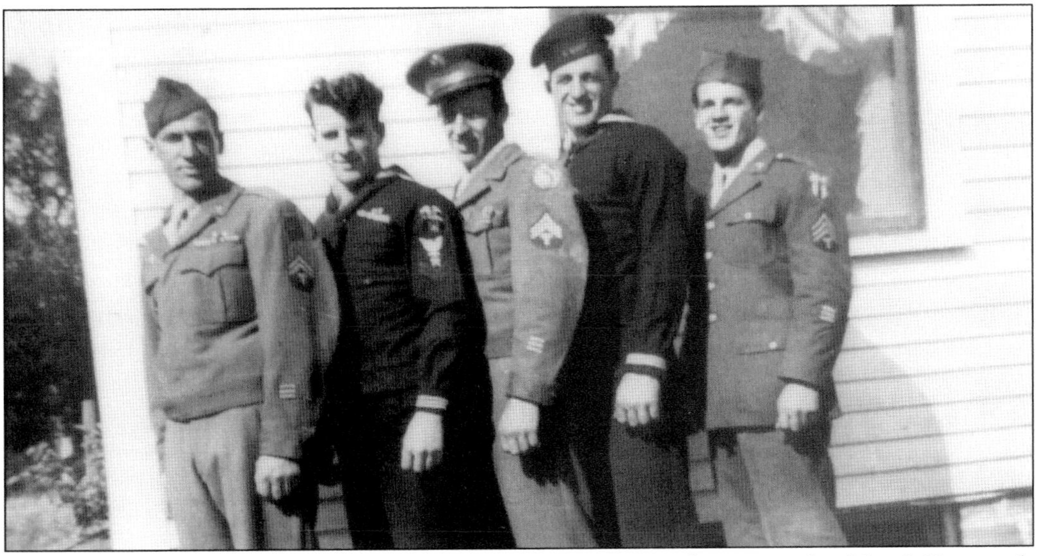

Ralph and Laura Jewett sent six sons to World War II—more than any other North Yarmouth family. Euan was lost off the Cuban coast in June 1942, when the SS *Ruth* was torpedoed. The remaining brothers—from left to right, Ellery, Pleem, Homer, Orville "Babe," and Conan—returned safely. They are pictured in uniform outside their parents' home after the war. (Courtesy of Peter Gagne.)

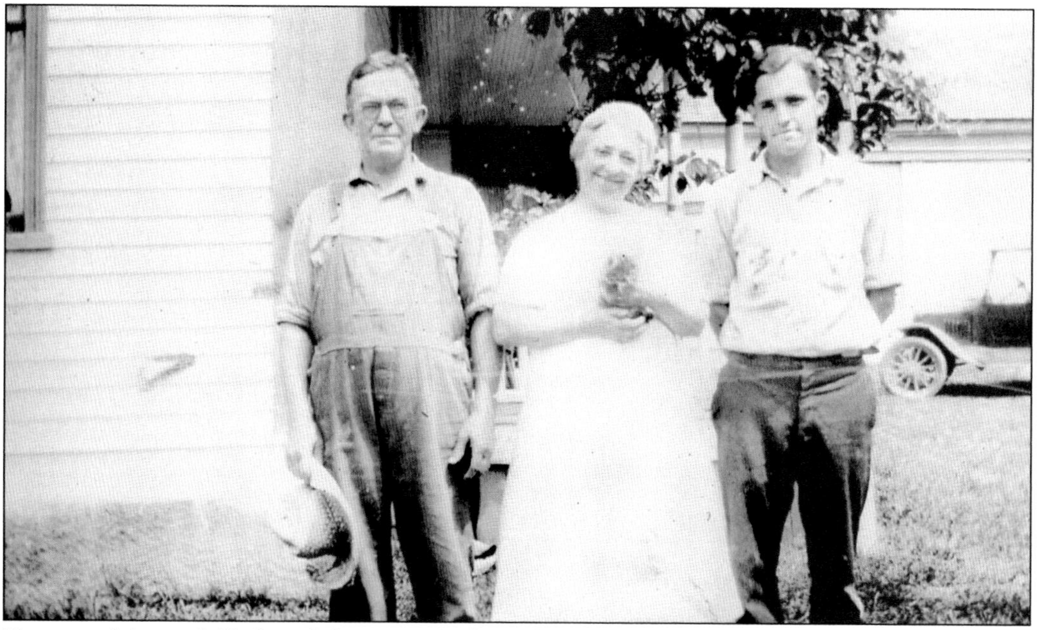

Henry and Asenath York and their son Neal stand in the yard of their home, Walnut Hill Farm, at 83 Gray Road. Asenath became the first woman on the board of selectmen in 1928 and also the first woman town clerk in 1946. Henry worked as a dairy farmer and as the Walnut Hill postmaster. The post office was located in their home for many years after his store at the Maine Central Railroad on Memorial Highway closed. (Courtesy of the York family.)

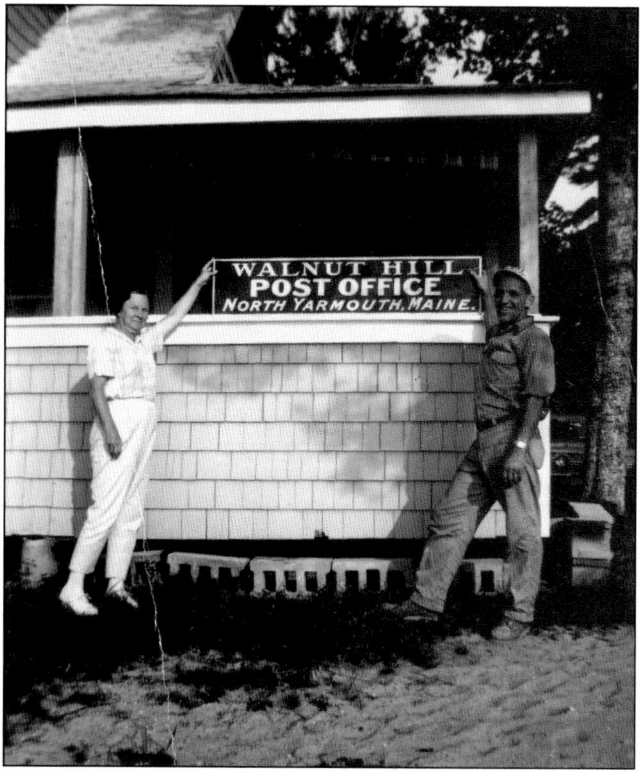

Neal F. York and his wife, Rev. Gladys D. York, are shown with the post office sign that once hung at Walnut Hill Farm. Neal and Gladys married in 1939 after she came to serve as Congregational church pastor, a position she held for 32 years. Neal was a painter, and both held town offices and participated in local organizations such as the Grange. (Courtesy of the York family.)

Dr. Daniel Nash Woodman served as a teacher in North Yarmouth schools and later as a physician. In 1900, he practiced at Crockett's Corner at his mother-in-law's house until constant questioning of his diagnoses caused him to move to Yarmouth. He made his rounds with a horse and buggy or a sleigh in the winter. During the diphtheria epidemic of 1900 and the typhoid fever epidemic of 1911, Dr. Woodman treated patients from the Millard Lovell house, near the Congregational church. (Courtesy of the North Haven Historical Society.)

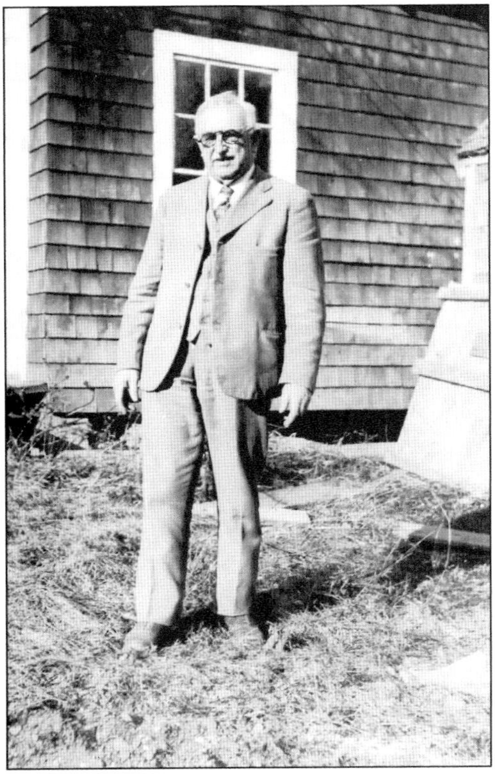

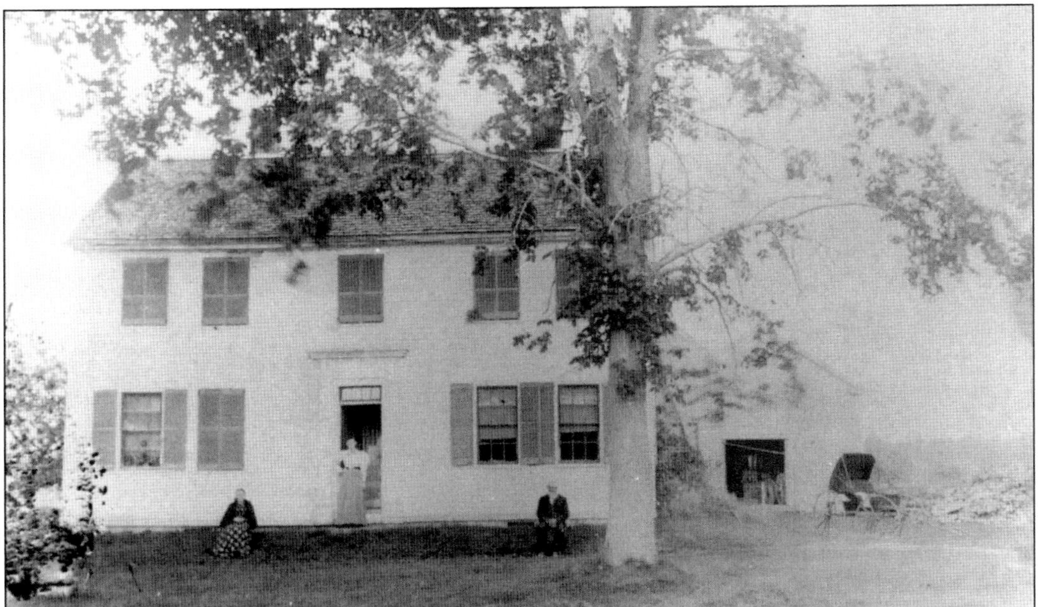

In this c. 1890 photograph, Nathaniel and Eliza Shurtleff family members pose outside their 37 New Gloucester Road home, which was built around 1807 for Maj. John Hayes. The Shurtleffs' nephew Clarence "Cad" Hatch later owned the house and built the barn in 1906. Cad's Quaker wife, Lucy, was known to drain his hard cider barrel, so he hitched it to the hayfork and hid it in the haymow in the barn.

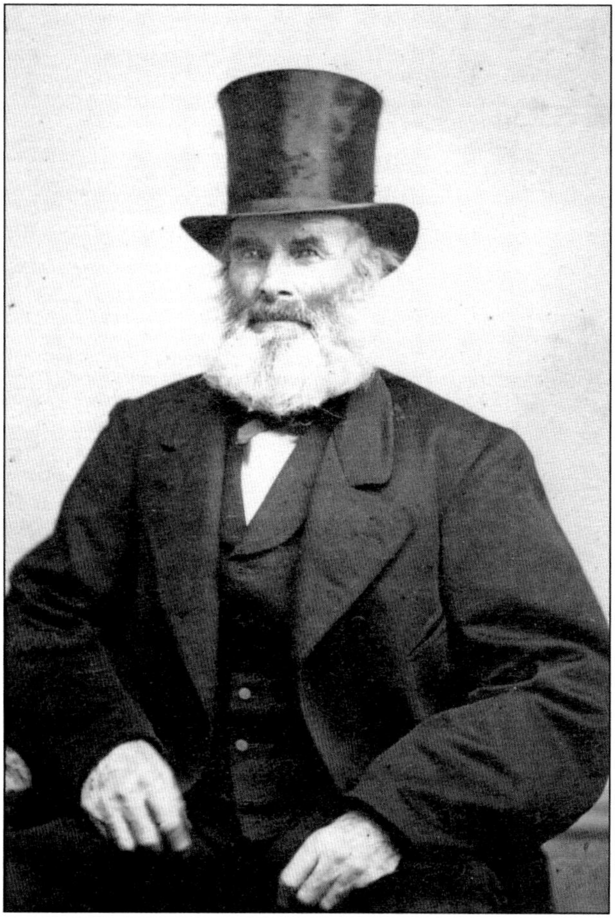

Maj. Charles Earle Hicks (left) inherited the 1775 home of his father, Joseph Hicks, at 534 New Gloucester Road, which eventually burned in 1941. The land became the site of the new District No. 4 Hicks School in 1895. Joseph Hicks, who owned shares in vessels and in the Marston Mill, is known for helping his future son-in-law Samuel Mayall secure a barge to navigate smuggled English mill parts up the Royal River. Mayall found a site on Collyer Brook in Gray and set up the nation's first water-powered woolen mill (below) in 1791 using technology he brought from his British home. Legend says that numerous unsuccessful attempts were made on Mayall's life by the British authorities, who chased him across the Atlantic. He received a gold crown designed to inject poisoned needles into the wearer's head and also a trunk rigged with a gun set to shoot whoever opened it. Joseph's daughter Anna married Mayall, and their children were well educated, cultured, and trained in the arts.

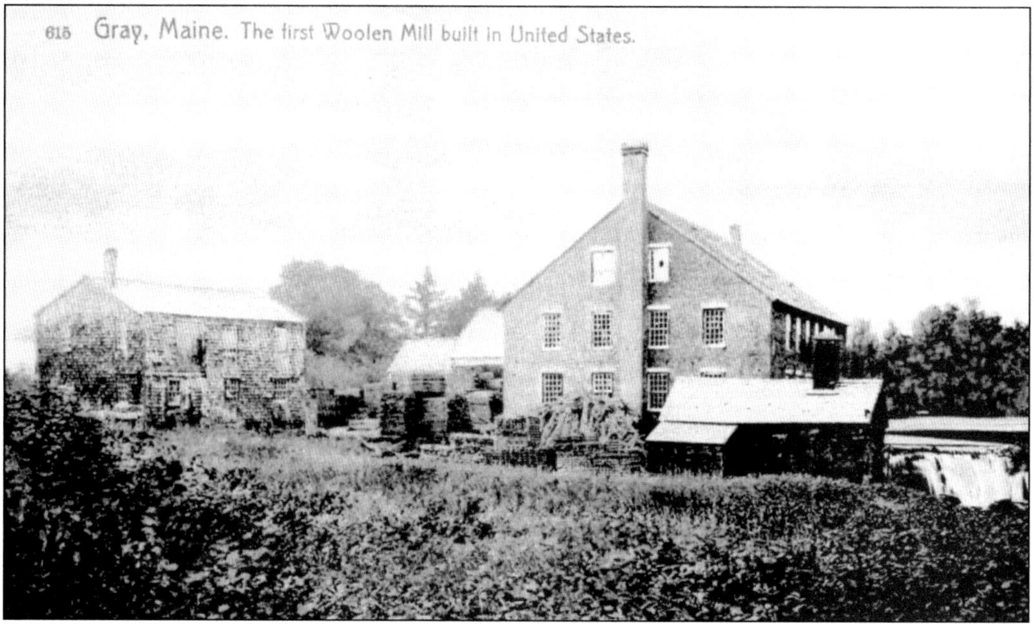

Eight

How We Looked

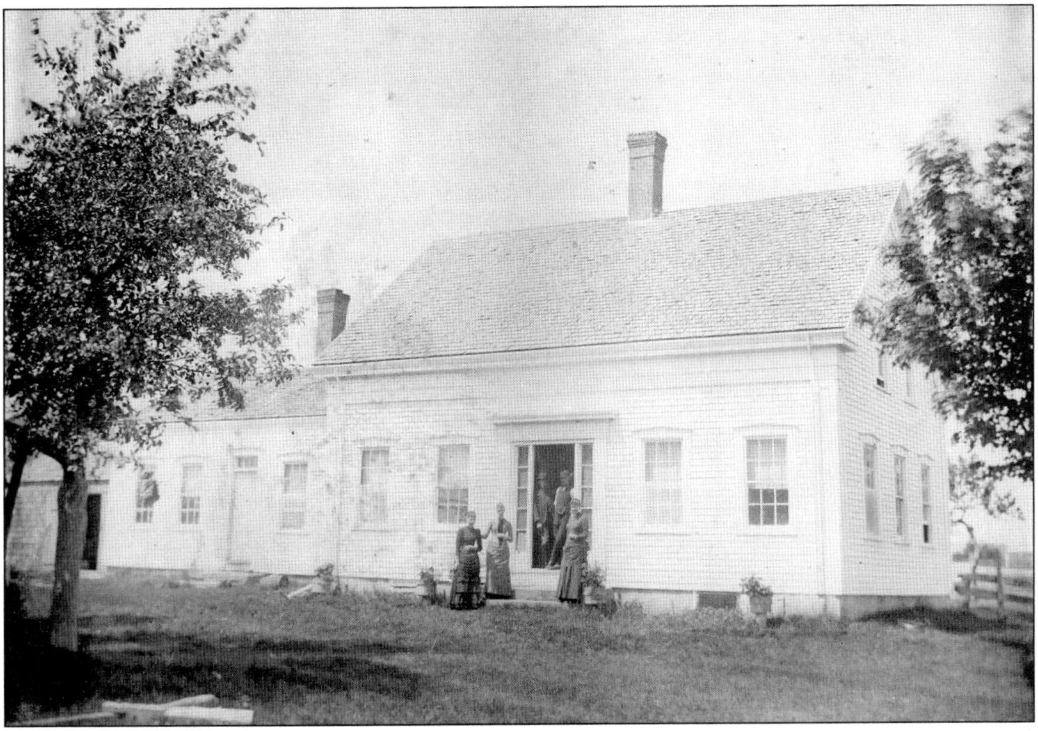

Benaiah Titcomb, who had acquired the land in 1805, built this home at 1424 North Road prior to 1845. There may have been an earlier home on the property, as this house displays the later Greek Revival style. Since this part of North Road was referred to as "the Road to Titcombs" until 1823, this may have been the first or only homestead on the street for a number of years. In 1871, Connecticut-born Charles Huckens Young purchased the property and became a farmer. Here the Young family poses around 1900. Charles died in 1923, although his widow, Mary, continued to live at the house with their son-in-law Jerry Connor. Connor was a Maine Central Railroad employee who was widowed on December 19, 1915, when his wife, Lillian Young Connor, died.

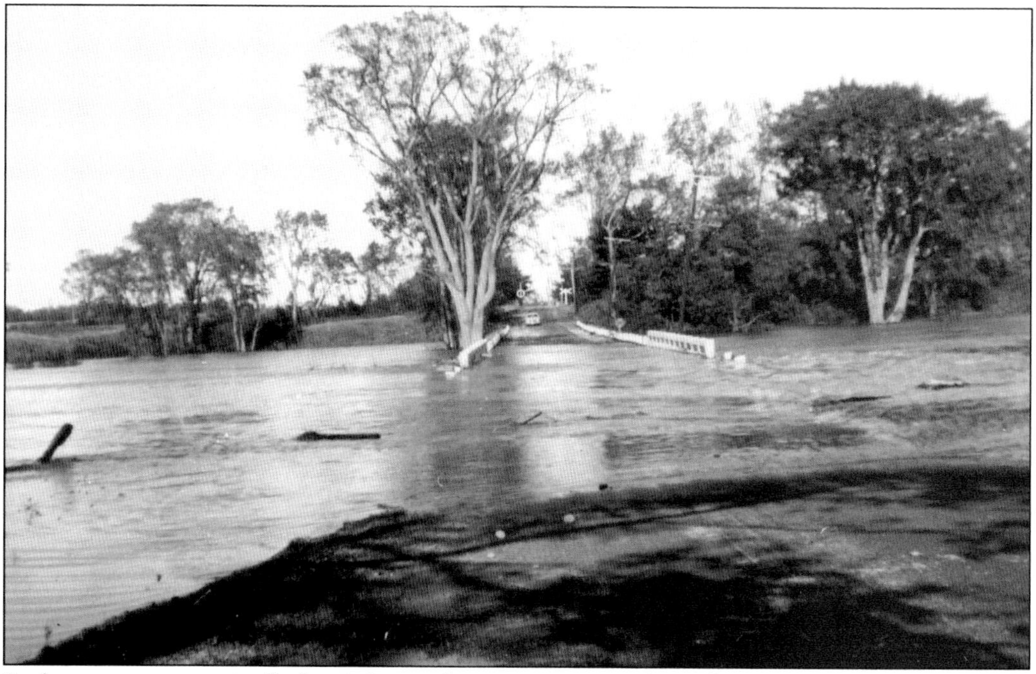

Each year, waters typically flood the roads in many parts of North Yarmouth. This September 1954 photograph of Memorial Highway near Dunn's Corner was taken after Hurricane Edna blew through town. The new bridge that had been built to alleviate this problem by rerouting the river was no match for the storm. (Courtesy of Everett Parker.)

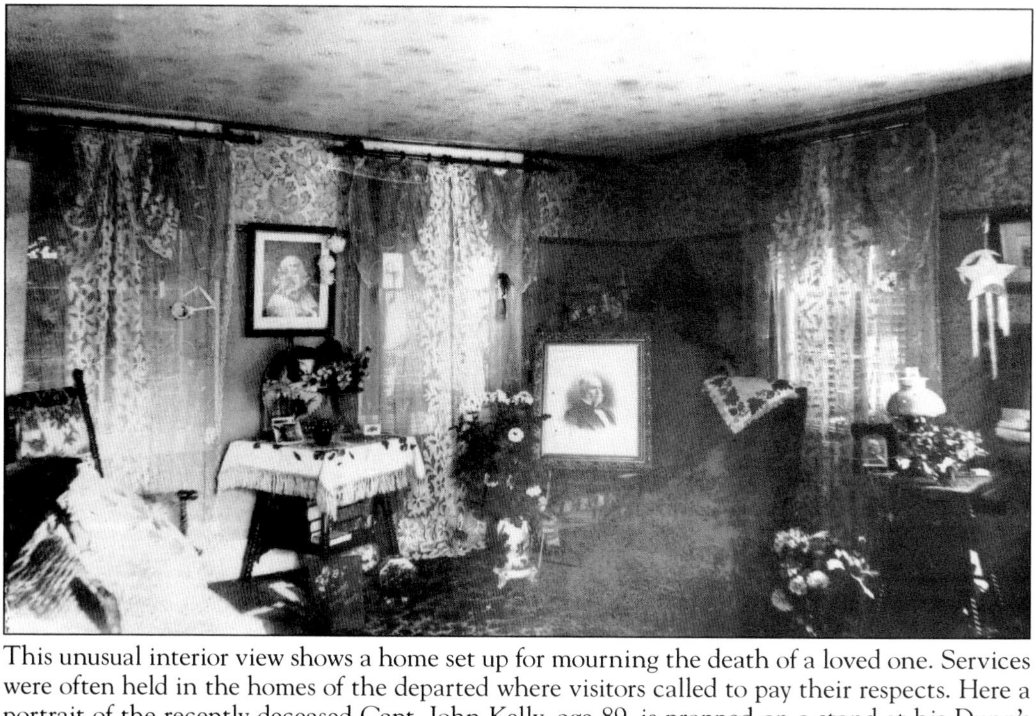

This unusual interior view shows a home set up for mourning the death of a loved one. Services were often held in the homes of the departed where visitors called to pay their respects. Here a portrait of the recently deceased Capt. John Kelly, age 89, is propped on a stand at his Dunn's Corner home in March 1903. Black draping and floral arrangements add to the somber setting.

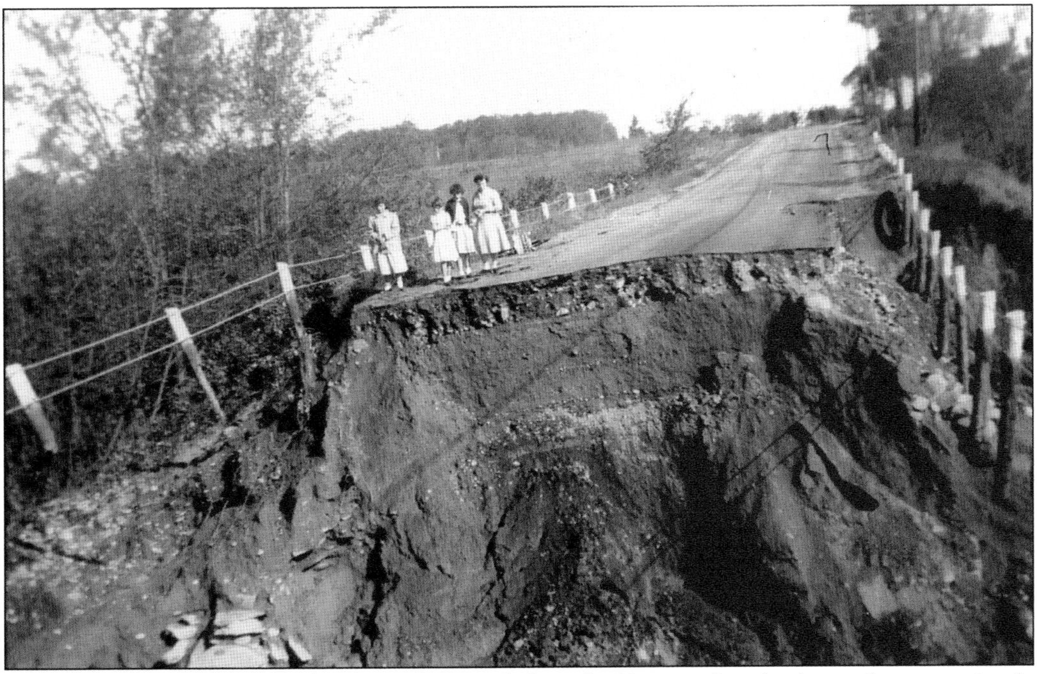

Hurricane Edna also washed out Route 9 just below the Baptist church. A pond was previously located on the upstream side of the road where ice was cut in winter. The hurricane damage and the recently added sidewalks have removed any signs of the pond. The Faith Baptist Church now occupies the vacant field to the left. (Courtesy of Phyllis Smith.)

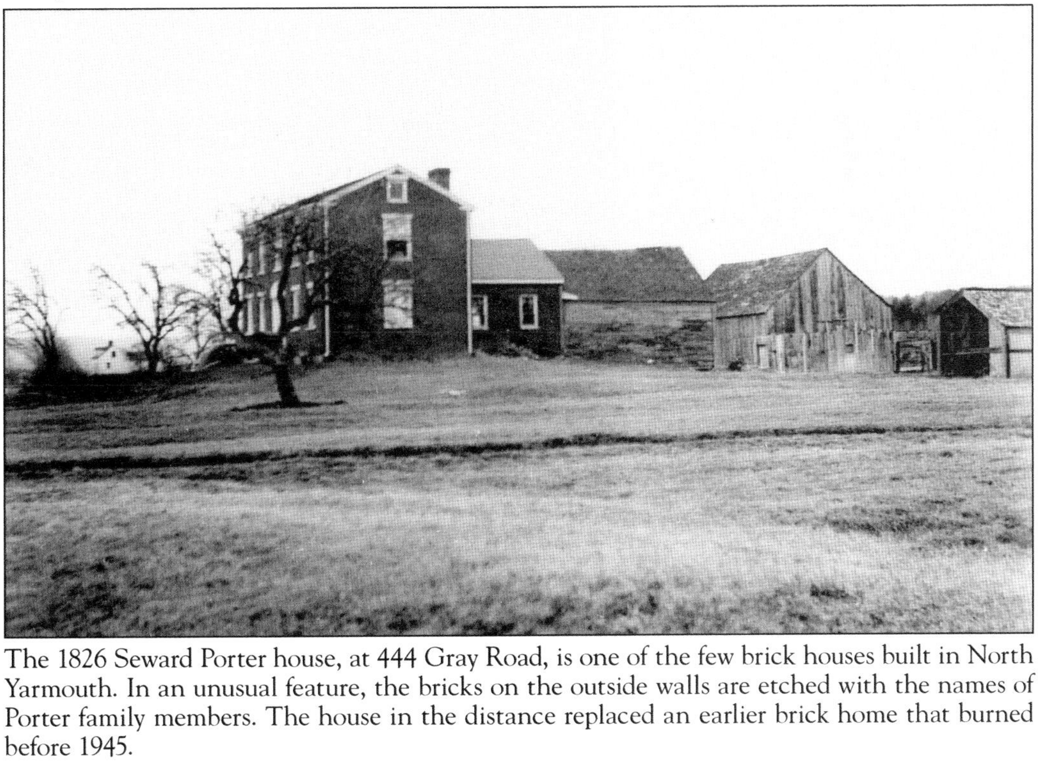

The 1826 Seward Porter house, at 444 Gray Road, is one of the few brick houses built in North Yarmouth. In an unusual feature, the bricks on the outside walls are etched with the names of Porter family members. The house in the distance replaced an earlier brick home that burned before 1945.

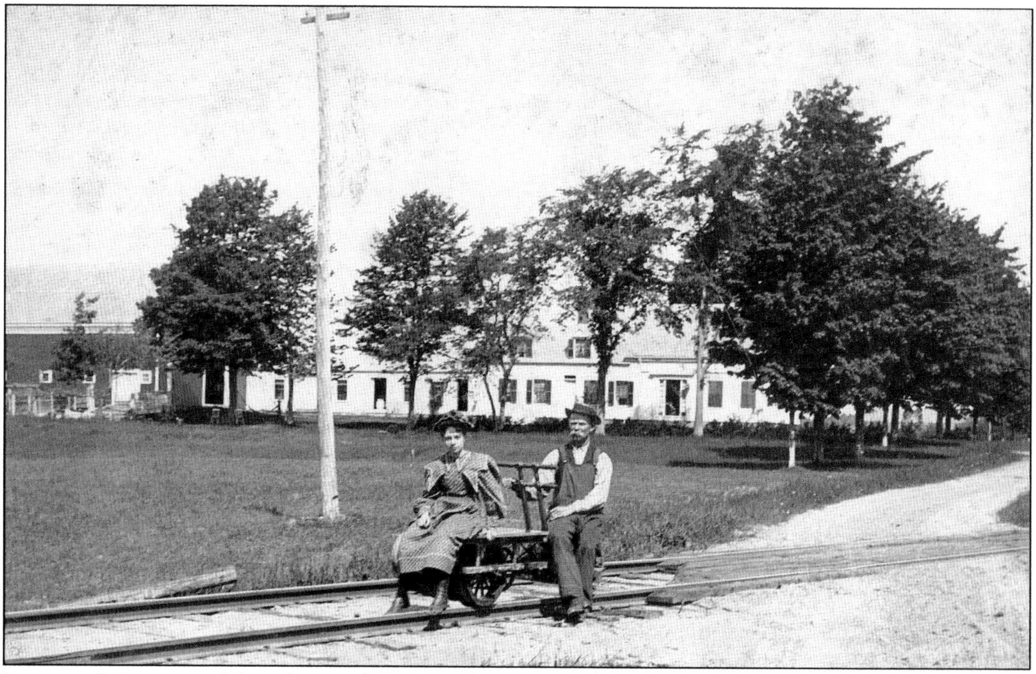

Lucy and Augustus Humphrey of Yarmouth are on a handcar in front of Cedar Spring Farm on North Road on June 4, 1896. The 14-year-old Lucy appears to be enjoying an outing with her father, a baggage master for the Grand Trunk Railroad in Yarmouth. (Collection of the Yarmouth Historical Society.)

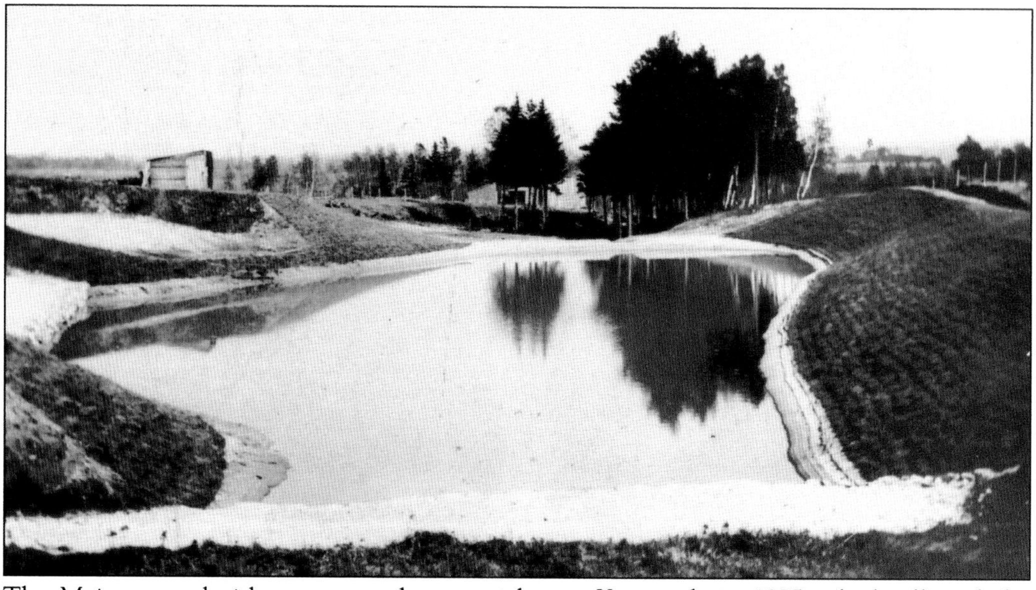

The Maine state legislature granted water rights to Yarmouth in 1895, which allowed the purchase of land from the Hayes family at the corner of Memorial Highway and Sweetser Road. The Yarmouth Water Supply built a dam to contain the Hayes Spring in 1905. The next year, a crew of 40 Italian workers placed the pipeline, which supplied 130,000 gallons of water a day to Yarmouth. It became the Yarmouth Water District in 1923. New wells drilled here continue to provide water to Yarmouth and North Yarmouth residents today.

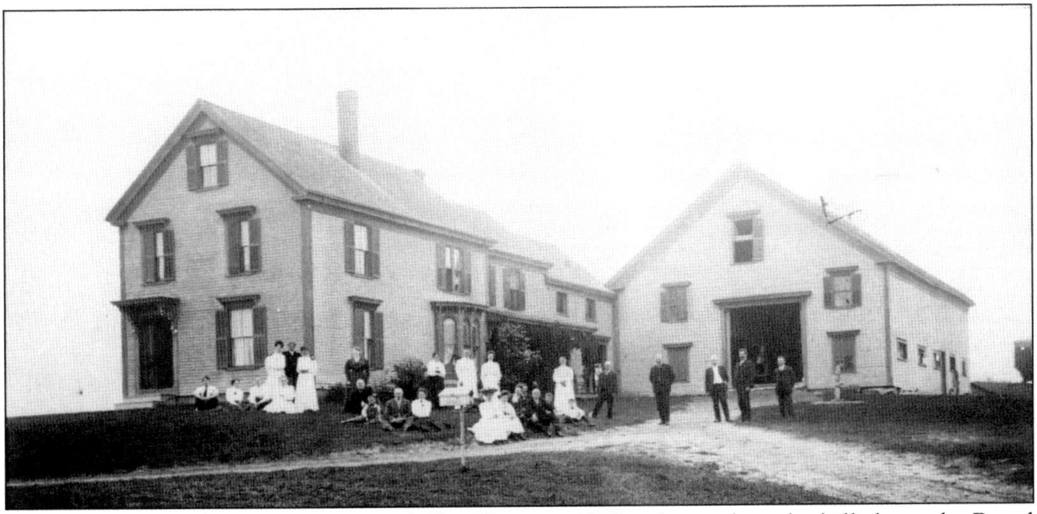

This Italianate house, built by Isaac Skillin Hayes in 1859, is located on the hill above the Royal River at 395 New Gloucester Road. Hayes's extensive family is pictured in this *c.* 1900 image. The family kept the house for over 100 years and expanded its land holdings rapidly. Family members milked cows, custom hayed, and ran a successful sawmill while also remaining active in all aspects of town life.

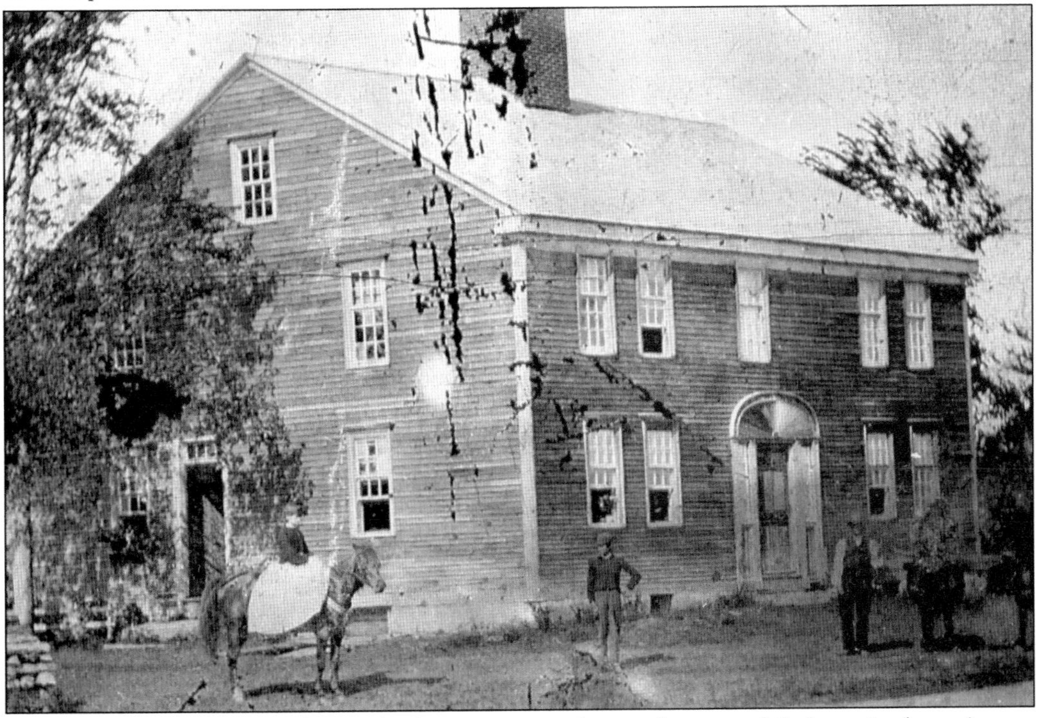

This *c.* 1870 photograph shows the home previously on the site of Robert Anderson's new house at 397 Memorial Highway, near his Toddy Brook Golf Course. It belonged to the Charles Mitchell family when it burned in 1885. Mitchell's daughter Susan married James Prince and moved to the Walnut Hill Farm on Gray Road. Their daughter Asenath married Henry York. North Yarmouth Mutual Fire Insurance Company paid for the loss of the house. (Courtesy of the York family.)

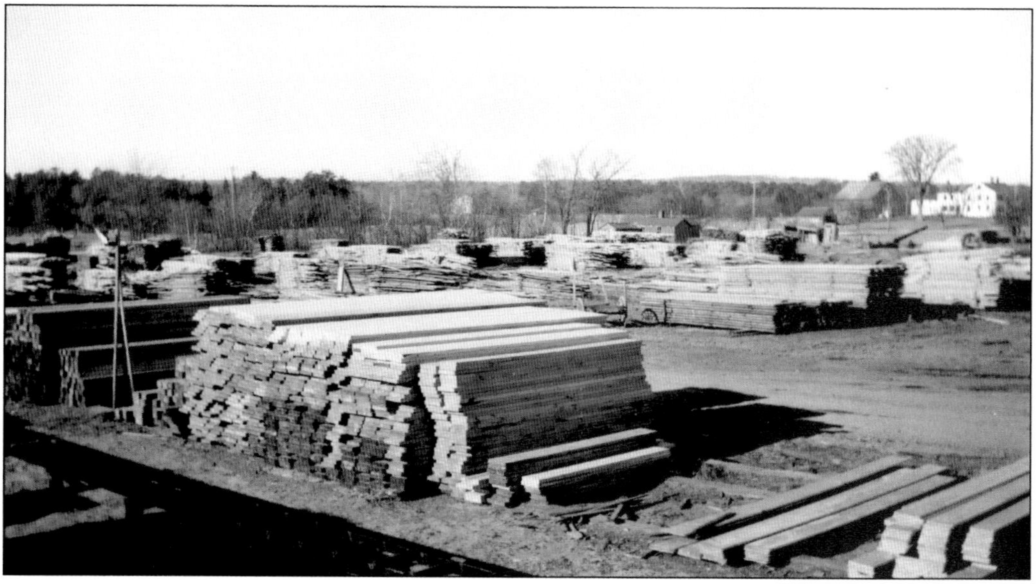

Lumber is stacked in the yard at Knight's Mill around 1953. In the upper right is the Uriel Whitney house, built in 1804 on West Pownal Road, which had been laid out in 1799 at Whitney's request. He was a Revolutionary War veteran and one of the earliest settlers in the area. Also a teacher, Whitney served as the master carpenter for the construction of the Pownal Congregational Church, where he was a member. (Courtesy of Marion Reed.)

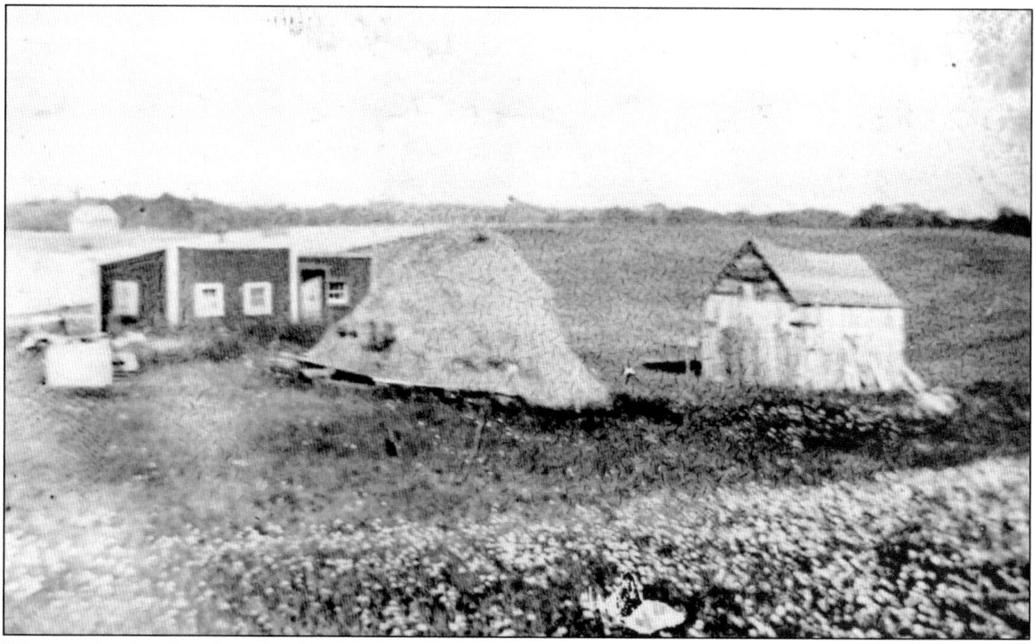

Warren Corliss lived in this home at the site of Toddy Brook Golf Course until his death in 1912. Although few examples of these simple homes remain, they were once more common in town. Although North Yarmouth never had a poor farm after Yarmouth seceded in 1849, the town warrant included an article to provide for one every year from 1852 until 1883. This proposal was always voted down. Instead the town supported the poor by paying individuals to provide necessary goods and services. (Courtesy of Ginger Collins.)

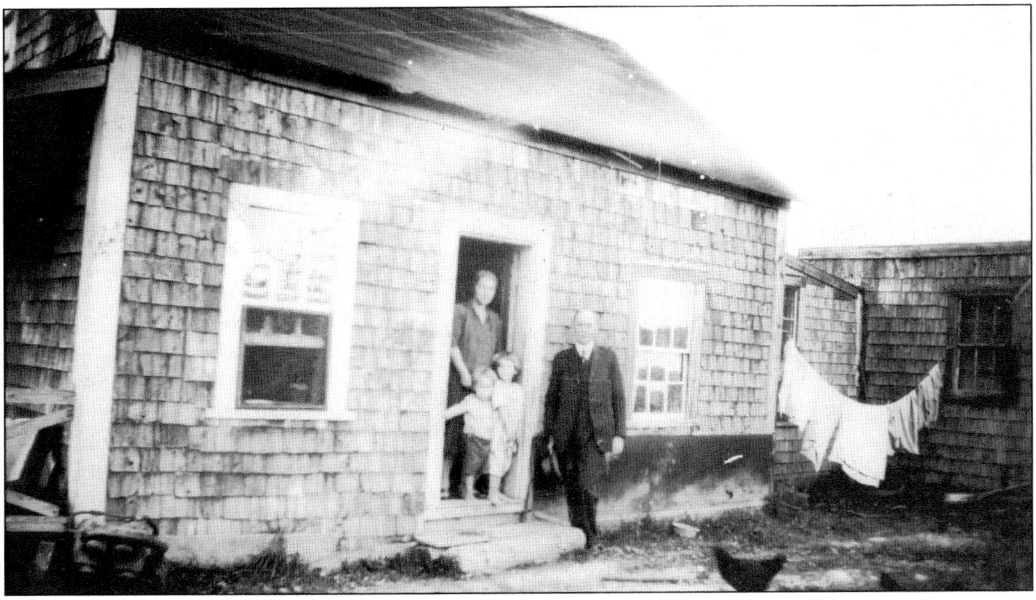

The Arthur and Anna Stowell family moved to a large home across from the present-day Grover farm on Sligo Road in 1918. The house partially burned in a 1924 chimney blaze that left young daughter Beatrice afraid of fire. The family moved into what was left of the property, shown in this 1927 photograph, but in a few years they moved to Yarmouth. Beatrice married Harland Doughty and bought the house at 155 West Pownal Road where she raised horses. (Courtesy of Jeanne Golding.)

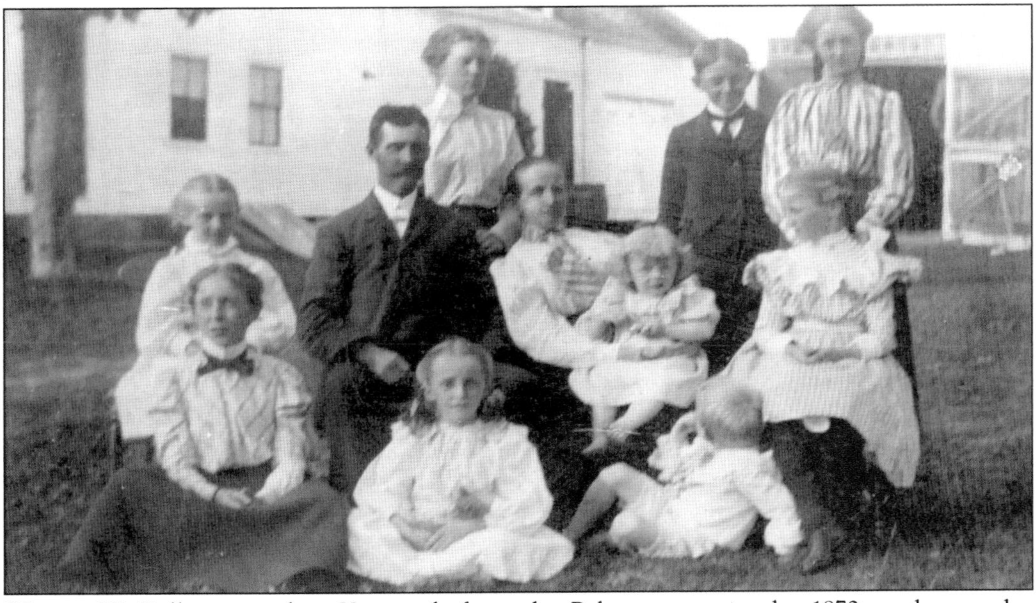

Warren W. Pullen moved to Yarmouth from the Palermo area in the 1870s and opened a successful store. He married Josephine Curtis and purchased a farm at 81 Sligo Road in 1879. Warren's Store closed soon after when his business partner skipped town with the store's goods and money, leaving him destitute. Josephine's mother bought their home so they could care for their 13 children by subsistence farming. Warren's granddaughter Ruth Pullen Ristich currently lives in the home. (Courtesy of Ruth Ristich.)

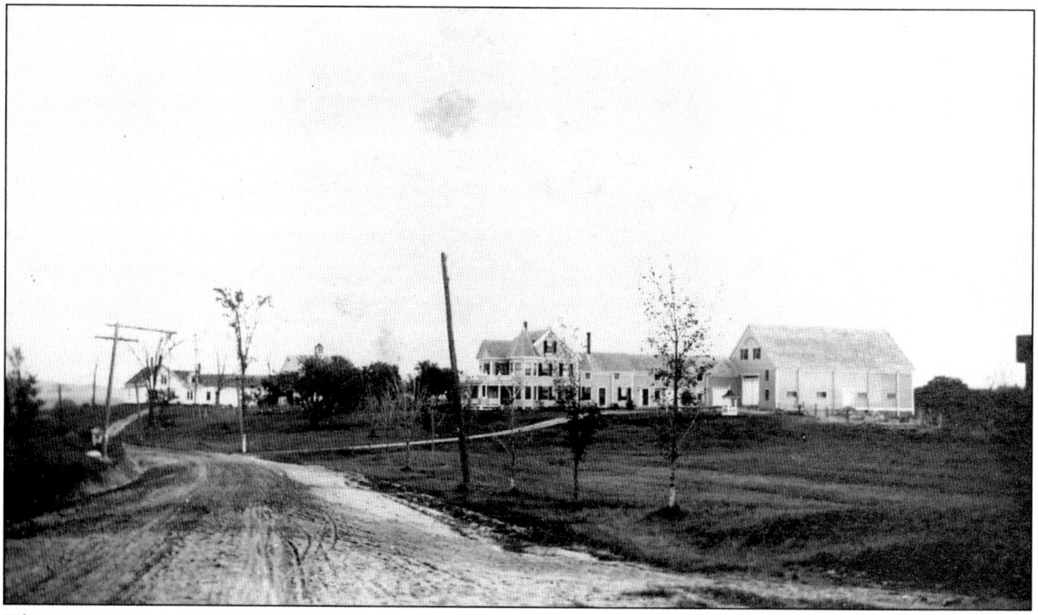

This view, taken around 1900, shows William Johnson's Fairview Farm, at 219 New Gloucester Road, after it was rebuilt following an 1899 fire. Johnson was a prominent farmer who sold pressed hay bales in the city. Charles Allen's farm is located just beyond, and his son Ernest worked as town clerk. The signpost on the right marks where Sligo Road Extension connected New Gloucester Road to Memorial Highway prior to 1950.

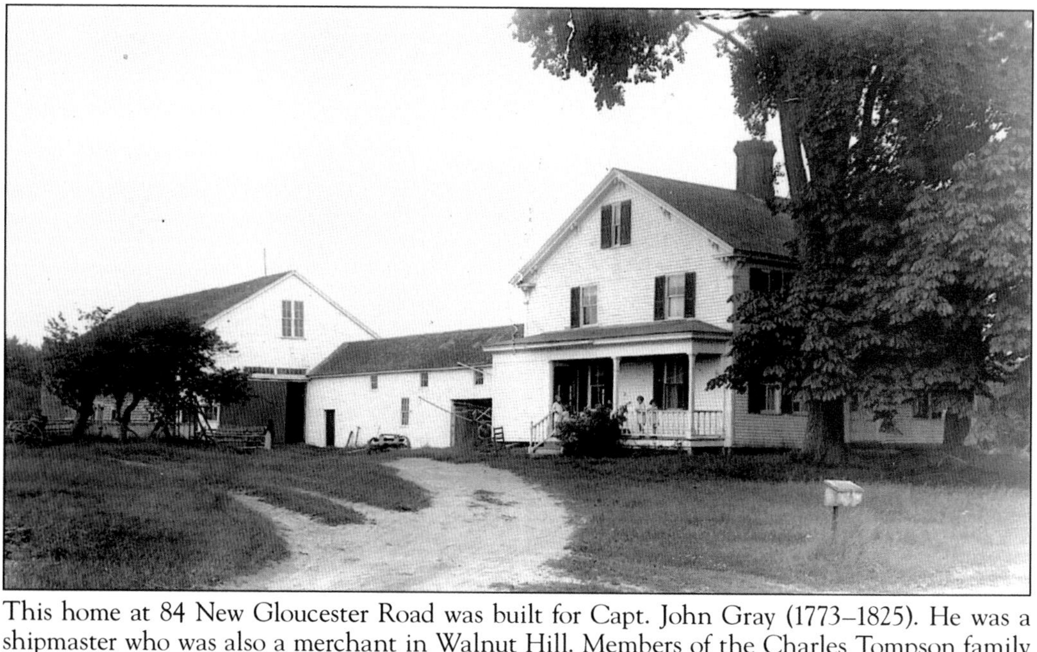

This home at 84 New Gloucester Road was built for Capt. John Gray (1773–1825). He was a shipmaster who was also a merchant in Walnut Hill. Members of the Charles Tompson family are on the porch after they moved there in 1925. Local lore says that there is a cannon stolen in a prank from Yarmouth village buried across the street from the home. The house stood at the entrance to Adams Pit and was taken down in March 1991. (Courtesy of Bertha Kimball.)

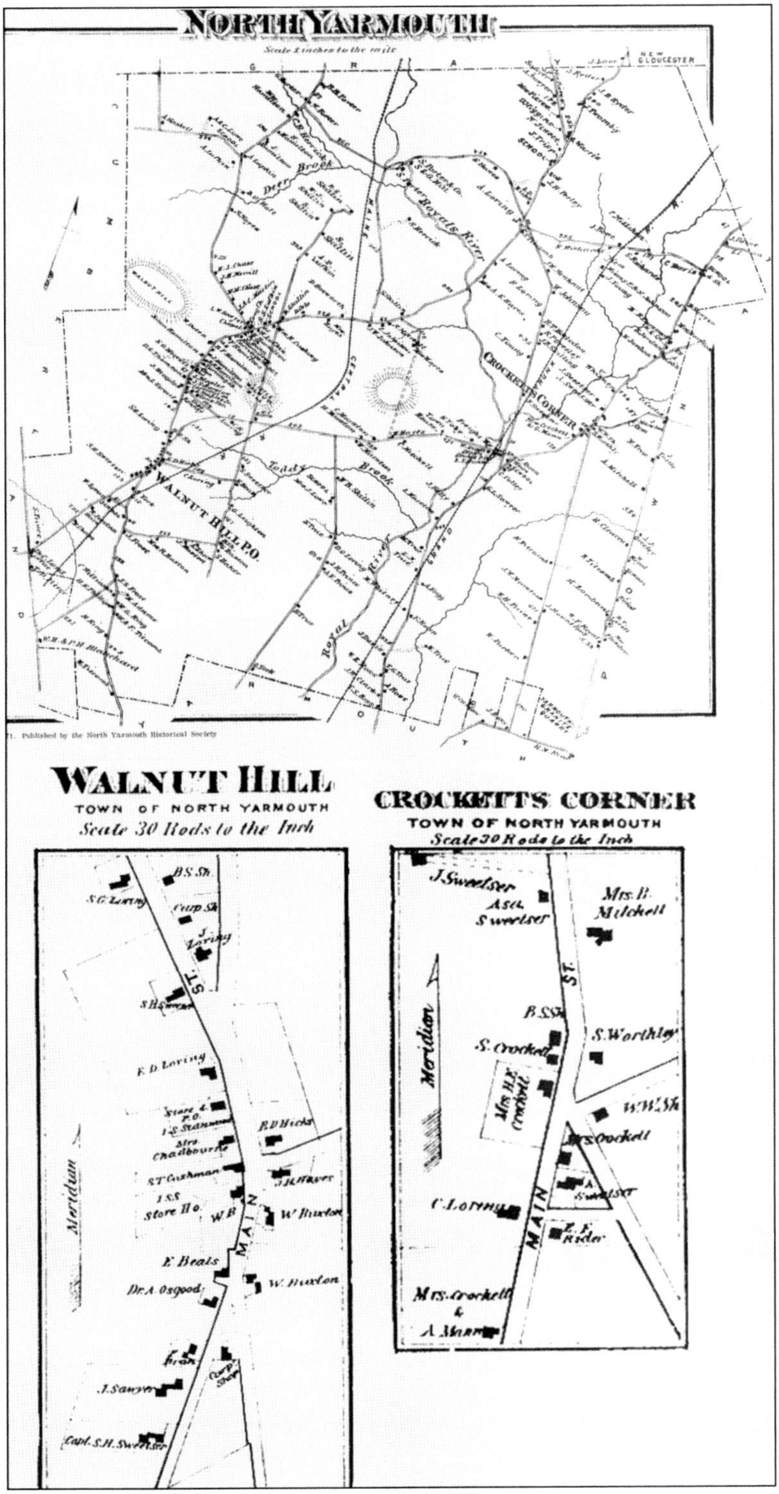

This 1871 map of North Yarmouth shows the town's two villages, the owners of the homes along the roads at that time, and bordering towns.

Consistent with our mission to preserve history on a local level, this book was printed in South Carolina on American-made paper and manufactured entirely in the United States. Products carrying the accredited Forest Stewardship Council (FSC) label are printed on 100 percent FSC-certified paper.

MADE IN THE USA